Date Due

MAR 21 79		
MAY 1 4 1979		
MAY 2 9 1979		
JUN 1 3 1985		

Demco 38-297

3

CHAUCER'S MIND AND ART

CHAUCER'S MIND AND ART

D. S. BREWER   A. C. CAWLEY

R. W. V. ELLIOTT   DOROTHY EVERETT

DONALD R. HOWARD   DOROTHY BETHURUM LOOMIS

JANETTE RICHARDSON   ROGER SHARROCK

JAMES G. SOUTHWORTH   FRANCIS LEE UTLEY

Essays Edited by

A. C. CAWLEY

OLIVER & BOYD

EDINBURGH AND LONDON

1969

OLIVER AND BOYD

Tweeddale Court
Edinburgh 1

First Published 1969

"Chaucer the Man":
© DONALD R. HOWARD 1965

"Chaucer and Patristic Exegesis":
© FRANCIS LEE UTLEY 1965

"Chaucer's Prosody: A Plea for a Reliable Text":
© JAMES G. SOUTHWORTH 1964

"Some Reflexions on Chaucer's 'Art Poetical' ":
© DOROTHY EVERETT 1950

"*Troilus and Criseyde*: Poem of Contingency":
© ROGER SHARROCK 1958

"Hunter and Prey: Functional Imagery in 'The Friar's Tale' ":
© JANETTE RICHARDSON 1961

D. S. Brewer, "The Criticism of Chaucer in the Twentieth Century";
R. W. V. Elliott, "Chaucer's Reading"; A. C. Cawley, "Chaucer's Valentine:
The Parlement of Foules"; and Dorothy Bethurum Loomis, "Chaucer and
Shakespeare"
© OLIVER AND BOYD LTD 1969

05 001779 9

Printed in Great Britain by
Robert Cunningham and Sons Ltd, Longbank Works, Alva

ACKNOWLEDGMENTS

For permission to reprint six of the essays in this collection acknowledgments are due to the following: Donald R. Howard, "Chaucer the Man", reprinted from *P.M.L.A.* (1965), by permission of the author, and the Modern Language Association; Francis Lee Utley, "Chaucer and Patristic Exegesis", reprinted from *Romance Philology* (1965), by permission of the author, and The Regents of the University of California; James G. Southworth, "Chaucer's Prosody: A Plea for a Reliable Text", reprinted from *College English* (1964), by permission of the author, and the National Council of Teachers of English; Dorothy Everett, "Some Reflexions on Chaucer's 'Art Poetical' ", reprinted from the *Proceedings of the British Academy* (1950), by permission of the British Academy; Roger Sharrock, "*Troilus and Criseyde*: Poem of Contingency", reprinted from *Essays in Criticism* (1958), by permission of the author, and the editor of *Essays in Criticism*; Janette Richardson, "Hunter and Prey: Functional Imagery in 'The Friar's Tale' ", reprinted from *English Miscellany* (1961), by permission of the author, and the editor of *English Miscellany*.

INTRODUCTION

This collection is made up of four new and six reprinted essays, to which bibliographies are added. It is intended to serve as a critical introduction to some of those aspects of Chaucer's mind and poetic art which have engaged the interest of Chaucer scholars during recent years.

The essays are, on the whole, fairly sober-sided, although some of them have a fling at the shibboleths and tyrannies of Chaucer scholarship. The authors will be found to disagree not only with the distinguished scholars unrepresented in this collection but, on occasion, with each other. This need not worry the reader; it certainly does not worry the editor, whose hope is that these essays will start, not end, discussion.

If this book has a didactic aim, it is to reinforce the notion that knowledge and insight make a pretty strong combination, and sometimes an irresistible one. In the words of Dorothy Everett: "it is the critic's task to apply the knowledge which has been accumulated, so that Chaucer's poetry may be better understood, and so that as much as possible of its subtleties, its ironies, and its varieties may become clear to us".[1]

A reviewer in *The Times Literary Supplement* (1 Sep. 1966) has distinguished between the scholar, who "subordinates himself to the truth he is helping to establish", and the critic "whose truth is not absolute, but depends on the validity of individual insights". This is an acceptable statement of the extremes of scholarship and criticism. But many of us will continue to make do with a compromise between the two. It is no doubt an uneasy compromise most of the time, but now and then it may produce an interpretation or a judgment which has general validity.

This collection of essays will justify itself if it makes a contribution to the understanding and enjoyment of Chaucer's poetry, and

---

[1] "Chaucer's Love Visions, with particular reference to the *Parlement of Foules*", *Essays on Middle English Literature*, London, 1955, p. 98.

if it adds to the number of Chaucer's "sympathetic readers" (for it is probably still true that such readers are outnumbered by "those who are daunted by his superficial difficulties and those who take too much delight in them").[2]

Anne Elliot (in *Persuasion*) once observed that "it was the misfortune of poetry to be seldom safely enjoyed by those who enjoyed it completely". There is some truth in this, but the risk is worth taking. For those who find the enjoyment of Chaucer becoming dangerous there are always "Melibee" and "The Parson's Tale" "to rouse and fortify the mind by the highest precepts".

A. C. CAWLEY

Leeds
September 1967

[2] Aldous Huxley, "Chaucer", *On the Margin*, London, 1923, p. 204.

CONTENTS

ix

I. CHAUCER AND THE MODERN MIND

D. S. Brewer

THE CRITICISM OF CHAUCER
IN THE TWENTIETH CENTURY

I

Modern criticism of Chaucer (using the term to include the whole range of literary study) has achieved a subtlety and variety unparalleled in the past – sometimes, perhaps, unparalleled in Chaucer's poetry, too. Yet its richness for the most part, even where critics disagree, is genuinely a refraction of Chaucer's own light. His ambiguities, his irony and realism, his cynicism and satire, his projection of himself, his bawdry; all these are in accordance with much that is admired in modern literature and criticism.

The main shift in Chaucer criticism, over the last fifty years, has been due to an appreciation of the qualities revealed by a more sympathetic study of his comic indecent poems, the *fabliaux*. They have been promoted from a lowly position of marginal interest, regarded with amusement and contempt, to the peak of Chaucer's artistic achievement, considered to be of central importance, carrying full burdens of irony, poetic justice, and even morality.[1]

It is not really surprising that along with this, though less marked, has gone a renewed interest in romance, especially in *Troilus and Criseyde* and "The Knights' Tale". Romance and *fabliau* were historically the product of the same courtly environment in the twelfth and thirteenth centuries. The individualism and internalisation of values implied by romance demand as compensation a corresponding emphasis on the physical world,

[1] For details of the change see D. S. Brewer, "The Fabliaux", *Companion to Chaucer Studies*, ed. B. Rowland, Toronto, 1968.

3

and an externalisation of even the most intimate private concerns. It is no coincidence that our own period of unparalleled indecency in literature is also one of unparalleled subjectivism and inner uncertainty.

The correspondence between modern attitudes and what we find, or think we find, in ancient literature, is one of the underlying themes in this essay. It is the function of criticism continually to renew or discover such correspondences. It is equally the function of criticism to do precisely the opposite: to adjust modern thought and sensibility to the historically equally valid though different thought and sensibility of the past. If it fails in this second function criticism betrays itself, for then it merely turns old authors into pale imitations of modern authors. And why bother with imitations when the genuine originals are more easily to hand? Paradoxically an old author appears most new when criticism enables us to recognise the genuine nature of his oldness, his difference from us: when we use him as a window, not a mirror. This dual function has been the success of the best modern criticism. We are now, we may think, moving to a deeper and broader sense of Chaucer's remarkable achievement than ever before. He is a vivid reporter of his contemporary scene, a creator of living characters, a humorist and ironist of the first order. He is a remarkable manipulator of words, a poet whose mind ranged over problems of poetry, of history, science, philosophy, and religion. He was at the forefront of the imaginative and intellectual culture of his times. He is our Goethe, a great artist who put his whole mind into his art. Out of the confusion, gaiety, and pain of his own passing day he created a series of artistic structures of enduring interest.

2

To attempt a brief survey of the modern criticism that has helped to discover and make available this diversity is evidently a rash, if not suicidal, attempt. The reader will hardly need to be reminded of my fallibility, but I ask him to accept my own consciousness of it, and

> To vouchen sauf, ther nede is, to correcte.

My aim is first to discuss a few representative but outstanding books of criticism, which may help to establish the general tone of the twentieth century; then to survey some main literary topics; and then, in more detail, to note how learning has advanced, and where it might still go forward. There has been so much done that I must obviously, if regrettably, omit detailed reference to a lot of useful work.[2]

3

A bridge between nineteenth-century and twentieth-century criticism is made by G. L. Kittredge's still deservedly popular general book, *Chaucer and his Poetry* (1915). He has a brilliant first chapter on "The Man and his Times" which is an excellent appreciative survey, the graceful product of great learning and of a warm and generous mind. Aldous Huxley's essay on Chaucer, recently praised by F. W. Bateson, seems no more than a simplification of this chapter, with an undue emphasis on Chaucer's "paganism". Nevertheless, Huxley's essay and Kittredge's book are of the same kind: humane, appreciative, non-technical, and, as one might say, non-scientific. Kittredge had published many articles and books of precise scholarship in medieval and later literature which supported his general criticism, and which his general critical concepts in turn guided. These general critical concepts in part derived from the dominant literary interest of his day, which was in the novel and in the general appearances of the visible world. He rejects hidden meanings, symbol and allegory. Above all, in a way that recalls Bradley's work on Shakespeare, he emphasises the dramatic and psychological autonomy of the characters. After Shakespeare, he says, Chaucer is the greatest delineator of character in our literature. The separate tales in the *Canterbury Tales* are seen essentially as dramatic soliloquies of the characters. This rather simple notion reinforces a rather simple notion of the relationship between morality and literature, and he does not much care for the *fabliaux*, describing "The

---

[2] Since this is a broad survey and not a full bibliographical exercise I omit or barely mention many good books and, with rare exceptions, all articles, essays, and lectures. I also omit almost all ancillary studies and literary histories; such works are of course noted in the Select General Bibliography. Regrettably I have had to forgo a consideration of foreign "images of Chaucer".

Summoner's Tale", for example, as "sordid". *Troilus and Criseyde*
is "inevitably ethical", and because it is a great work of art it
represents, though in historical terms, "eternal truth". It is the
first novel, an elaborate psychological novel, a tragedy of character, though he does not seem to rate it so highly as the *Canterbury
Tales*. He emphasises Chaucer's realism.

Some of these judgments continue still in Chaucer criticism,
as will be seen. Kittredge also introduces some new – or at that
time new – concepts. Irony, then only recently discovered in
Chaucer,[3] is given honourable mention. He praises Chaucer's art,
his rhetoric, perhaps because the notion of rhetoric seems never
quite to have been lost in the American intellectual tradition,
as it has been in the English. He sorts out the confusion between
man and poet that was a Romantic inheritance, and in his admirable discussion of the *Book of the Duchess* he even foreshadows
the concept of the Dual Narrator.

An interesting contrast and comparison with Kittredge's book
is offered by Chesterton's of 1932. It is not a work of scholarship,
and does not claim to be. Many of its purely literary notions are
fairly conventional – Chaucer the novelist, ironist, realist,
humorist; he considers that a poet deals with "eternal things".
Yet the book is comparable with Kittredge's in that it is addressed
to a general educated public, and witnesses to a warm and generous personal response. It does not aim at objective, "scientific"
analysis, but deals with literature in a literary way, a man meditating
with his whole mind and feelings on the values of imaginative
experience. Chesterton perceives certain values in Chaucer
through a direct intuitive sympathy. He is still within the same
general tradition of thought and feeling, the same European and
English tradition. He no doubt exaggerates the similarity in
some ways, for twentieth-century Roman Catholicism is more
different from medieval Christianity than Chesterton might have
admitted. But Chesterton still says many things about Chaucer's
greatness, his historical position, his capacious mind, and the
richness of medieval culture – to mention only the most general –
which are the product of a natural sympathy that enables him to

[3] For nineteenth-century and earlier general critical notions of Chaucer
see "Images of Chaucer", in *Chaucer and Chaucerians*, ed. D. S. Brewer,
London and Edinburgh, 1966.

create a living sense of Chaucer's work. Chestertonian spriteliness and paradox can at times be a little tiresome, and some of his contemporariness dates, but it is a most intelligent and refreshing book, which extends one's feeling for Chaucer. One feels the better for reading it; and if the more one knows the less one believes it, it is also true that the more one knows the more one enjoys it.

Only a couple of years later than Chesterton, J. L. Lowes, the pupil of Kittredge, continued Kittredge's line of scholarly criticism and appreciation with another book that is also pleasing to read. Lowes emphasises further Chaucer's realism, attributing to him an instinct for "the concrete" and an ability to be immersed in "life". ("Concrete" and "life", with their roots in such Romantic critics as Ruskin, have become magic modern words throughout Europe and America, though Lowes can hardly have foreseen truly "concrete" poetry, or that potent formula "making for life".)

For Lowes, Chaucer's ultimate glory is his creation of "living characters", and in his enthusiasm for the Wife of Bath he goes so far as to say that she is close kin to Chaucer. The interest in character had clearly inspired the valuable research by J. M. Manly into historical records to seek real-life originals for the portraits in the "General Prologue". Lowes makes good use of Manly's fascinating account of his findings, *New Light on Chaucer*. There is no doubt that some of Manly's identifications are as certain as these things can be (Harry Bailly, the Host, for example) and others (such as the Sergeant-of-Law) very likely. Manly thus helped to introduce a new dimension into the understanding of Chaucer which makes a pretty example of how a critical concept (that of the nineteenth-century autonomous character in a novel) can lead to the discovery of new facts. At the same time, while recognising the sense of living people that Chaucer can convey, and the value of this criticism in the hands of Kittredge, Lowes, Manly, and more recently Lumiansky, we cannot but be sceptical of the *kind* of characterisation it seeks to establish, and of the over-simple relation between life and literature it sometimes implies.

Lowes represents some new developments. He sets Chaucer's comic tales, including the *fabliaux*, as his highest achievement, and

particularly praises parts of "The Summoner's Tale". He discusses
the importance of an oral tradition in medieval literature, for
"literature" that is meant to be heard may be very different from
literature that is meant to be read, as the nowadays very fashionable
work of Marshall McLuhan,[4] important for medievalists, has
recently emphasised. The relation between the spoken and the
written word, and the unusual position of Chaucer's work,
poised between the two, are certainly worth more investigation.

Perhaps the most valuable part of Lowes's book is its investigation – based on much detailed work by him and others published
in learned journals – of the conditioning ideas and feelings of
Chaucer's time, which were "nature" to Chaucer though "convention" to us. Lowes had deep knowledge of the literary and
scientific knowledge available to Chaucer, and his learned and
imaginative presentation of this material is an excellent example of
creative scholarship and criticism, leading our minds into those of
other men.

There are a number of books published from the 'thirties to the
early 'fifties which continue this empirical, historical, appreciative
type of criticism, such as those of Patch, Shelly, H. S. Bennett,
Coghill, Sister Madeleva, Kemp Malone, Preston, Brewer, on
which space (and, in the last case, propriety) forbids much or any
comment. Patch discusses Chaucer's humour (a subject still
worth more examination), Preston the way he anticipates many
later poetic effects. Some of these authors include accounts of
Chaucer's life which, provided it is not confused with his poetry,
is surely of some interest in relation to it. All contribute in
varying ways, with varying historical material, to the work of
sympathetic re-creation and interpretation. A contribution
notable in sympathetic insight has been made by B. H. Bronson
over many years. His conception of Chaucer's poetry is essentially
late-Romantic, but his extra-Chaucerian concern with oral
"literature" has led to interesting comment on Chaucer's audience;
and he writes gracefully.

A more characteristically modern note begins to be sounded,
however, more intellectual and *a prioristic*. An early forerunner
that deserves note is Germaine Dempster's *Dramatic Irony in*

[4] M. McLuhan, *The Gutenberg Galaxy: The Making of Typographic Man*,
Toronto, 1962.

Chaucer (1932). More of a monograph than general criticism, it is convenient to notice it here because of the perception with which the author singles out *fabliau* and romance as the most important developments in Chaucer's later work. Her emphasis on realism and irony continues the late nineteenth-century tradition with a more modern emphasis. John Speirs's *Chaucer the Maker* is a valiant and contentious attempt, unmatched before and since, to draw Chaucer within the somewhat restricted pantheon of Dr Leavis's school of criticism by emphasising Chaucer's supposed roots in an idealised agricultural community. Speirs's book is of real value and stimulus in its emphasis on Chaucer's modern literary value, on verbal texture, and on the possibilities of symbolic interpretation, such as his suggestion that the tale of the cock and the fox is an allegory of the Fall of Man.

Exposition of Chaucer's contemporary relevance has been furthered by the work of E. T. Donaldson, much of it in witty and perceptive essays and lectures still uncollected, but some of the main points of which have been gathered together in the commentary included in *Chaucer's Poetry: An Anthology for the Modern Reader* (the word *modern* is significant). First, it should be said that Donaldson is firmly rooted in the empirical, historical, tradition that demanded a close philological grasp of the historical language, its phonology, grammar, and vocabulary, and which, being laborious to acquire (and in some hands abused by pedantry), has unfortunately become unpopular. Donaldson is that rare bird, a critic with a strong editorial grasp, as well as being that equally rare bird, a textual editor with a sensitive critical insight. Traditional learning and skills have united with a sharp modern sensibility and with a concentration on the diction of the poem itself reminiscent of the New Criticism. The result has been improved texts, some illuminating studies of diction, and – for all his apparent empiricism – some potent general notions about Chaucer's conduct of the poems. Donaldson was the first to make real critical use of the notion (foreshadowed by Lüdeke's study) of the Narrator as an actor within the poem, which has been taken up, sometimes too crudely, by many critics since. The notion of the stupid but amiable Narrator as a lay-figure, so to say, held in front of the poet himself, in the *Canterbury Tales*, has enabled Donaldson to make a delicate analysis of the ironic ambivalences of tone and of the various levels of narration. It is a valuable concept for analysing the other poems in which Chaucer presents himself; it is a more dubious notion as applied to *Troilus and Criseyde*, though not without its uses. In general the notion of the Narrator emphasises the action of the whole poem as a conscious work of art, and prevents a simple-minded response to the characters alone as if they were real people. Donaldson has at least two other valuable concepts, one of meaning, one of principle. One is the concept of the significance in Chaucer's thought of *trouthe* and *freedom* (integrity, loyalty; and generosity); the other is the concept, vital to truly literary understanding, that logical contradictions in a poem do not cancel each other out. The austere moralist can exist cheek-by-jowl with the jester, can indeed be the same man.

Donaldson, however, always begins with the words, and the totality of the poem as an effect of style is further developed in what seems to me at the present moment the most valuable general book of criticism of Chaucer, Muscatine's *Chaucer and the French Tradition*. The tradition Muscatine seeks to establish is the relationship, which he finds in earlier French writing, between a "realistic" or "bourgeois" style, on the one hand, and an "idealistic" or "conventional" or "courtly" style against which the realistic style makes its way. Muscatine sees Chaucer following a path from "realism" to "naturalism" very similar to that followed by the nineteenth-century novel, especially in France. Chaucer's naturalism culminates in the *fabliaux* and also in "The Canon's Yeoman's Tale" (the latter a sort of poetry of technology, and the subject of a brilliant and original chapter). Muscatine's essential concept, however, is of the interplay between the two styles; and although it seems likely that the notion of a bourgeois realism is more modern than medieval, the concept of a dualistic relationship of styles – pressed into service by Muscatine's strong, unsentimental, but sympathetic mind – enables him to unravel and expound the Gothic inclusiveness and tensions of Chaucer's poetry with remarkable success. His work on "The Clerk's Tale" is as sympathetic and illuminating as that on the *fabliaux*. He also invokes other valuable general concepts, borrowing from the art-historians the notion of "Gothic form" as process and symbol, and from twentieth-century thought in general the concern with "order". Both concepts allow him to present the symmetry of "The Knight's Tale", especially, with great originality. Muscatine's book is armed at all points with modern scholarship. There are few relevant articles in the professional journals that he does not refer to. By its powerful intellectuality, literary insight, and severely professional, indeed technical manner, focussed so sharply on the poems themselves, his book removes the subject to another plane of discourse.

Another valuable contribution along somewhat similar lines has been made by R. O. Payne in the book he describes as "A Study of Chaucer's Poetics". Payne's starting-point is the rhetorical tradition as it developed from classical to medieval times, and he makes a particularly useful, because sympathetic, attempt to grasp the essential quality of the medieval rhetorical art of poetry, without getting tangled up in a discussion of the complicated but superficial stylistic devices which the twelfth- and thirteenth-century rhetoricians recommended. Payne's central thesis is that the aim of the rhetoricians, and of Chaucer's own theory of poetry, was to make available the wisdom of the past in terms viable in the present; to make knowledge emotionally convincing. This enables him to show convincingly the unity of feeling and intellect in Chaucer's poetry, and to show how, for example, the lyric element in *Troilus and Criseyde* joins with the rational commentary which accompanies the telling of the story. Payne's analysis also enables him to undercut fairly convincingly any unduly simple concepts of autonomous psychological drama, and of "naturalism". The poet is always in charge, and it is not his purpose merely to present an illusionist "picture of life" like a nineteenth-century anecdotal genre painting.

A somewhat similar purpose is to be found in an impressive and controversial book both very similar to, and different from, Muscatine's and Payne's. This is D. W. Robertson's remarkable *Preface to Chaucer*, a very big book to which a few lines of summary and comment must be even more unjust than they have been to the books already mentioned. Robertson has two basic themes of great weight: one is that the "reality" to which all literature attempts to point was, in the case of medieval literature from St Augustine in the fifth century onwards, a non-materialistic, conceptual reality; specifically, the concept that the love of God (*caritas*) is all-important, and that any other love or interest or obsession or desire (*cupiditas*) is evil. He sees all medieval literature, whether written in Latin or in the vernacular, as recommending *caritas* and reproving *cupiditas*. Clearly, much of Chaucer, including *Troilus and Criseyde*, fits this general pattern very nicely. (Just as clearly, much literature does not.) Robertson's other main thesis, deduced from St Augustine's theory of Biblical criticism, is that the superficial action and description of all medieval poetry is governed, not by cause and effect, or any other interest belonging to the world of physical reality, but by the underlying concepts which refer to a non-physical reality. (This may be compared with the similar thesis, now generally accepted, of the French scholar Emile Mâle, concerning much medieval religious art.) Robertson is able to demonstrate a moral, but non-naturalistic, structure of character, for example, in *Troilus and Criseyde*. For Robertson believes that all medieval literature, Latin and vernacular, religious and secular, fifth-century or fifteenth-century, is an allegory commending *caritas* and discommending *cupiditas*. Robertson is thus making an important attempt to recreate intellectually and imaginatively a genuinely different feeling about the world and about reality that characterised medieval life, and was fruitful of great literature. To support this attempt he has brought back into modern consciousness much almost forgotten medieval literary exegesis, and employs illustrations of many medieval works of visual art. He shows that there are different kinds of reality, and that literature has an important claim to represent reality. He makes a bold defence, in accord with modern science, though not with modern literature or literary theory, of abstract against concrete, of intellectuality against mere sensation, of morality and purposiveness against random sensation.

All this is admirable. If Muscatine perhaps sums up the best modern criticism so far, Robertson has perhaps a prophetic touch. Yet his book is controversial, for several reasons. In some ways he is even excessively medieval: he sometimes seems to share the distrust of thirteenth-century schoolmen for literature as literature, that is, as not philosophy or ethics, but an essentially equivocal, elusive, protean, ambivalent phenomenon, for which the concept of meaning, even disputed meaning, is important, and concepts of right or wrong, true or false, are not. One may question the application of Augustinian Biblical exegesis to fourteenth-century courtly and secular entertainments. After all, why did Chaucer, in the Retraction to the *Canterbury Tales*, condemn all his secular works, if they were really allegories recommending *caritas*? One can often question Robertson's reading of specific words of the texts, and his sense of the actual empirical circumstances of life in the Middle Ages.

Yet Robertson's work seems to me important in that it is intensely stimulating, and really does try to get away from an automatic modern response to ancient literature, though it does so in a very modern way – "tenderminded", in William James's original sense of that term, *i.e.* systematic and *a prioristic* (as all conceptual, intellectual, analytical criticism tends to be, even Muscatine's). There is no doubt that Robertson, like Muscatine, has written an outstanding work of creative criticism, for in a sense all criticism is a work of fiction, recommending old wisdom in modern forms, attempting to unite knowledge and feeling. Some of Robertson's own work may need re-interpreting. If we abandon his concept of *intentional* allegory in favour of non-intentional *potential* symbolism, for example, we can see a different facet of Chaucer's genius, since symbolic understanding, un-trammelled by any Intentionalist Fallacy, is the quality of all literature, and gives contemporary criticism much of its excitement.

In a brief retrospective glance at these few samples of criticism we might make two main points. First, the "image" of Chaucer has been more or less successfully assimilated to modern interests, even while, as will be shown more fully in the following sections, our knowledge of his historical quality has been extended. A naturalistic, almost Zolaesque Chaucer has been seized upon, who has effectively rid us of the childlike, sentimental, naïve, and inartistic Chaucer of the nineteenth century (even though there are a few late protagonists of this view occasionally still to be heard, like P. F. Baum). But just as modern thought, in science and literature, is going beyond naturalism, so we are beginning to be shown a less naturalistic Chaucer.

The other point is also connected with science. Typical modern criticism of Chaucer is much tinged with modern scientific professionalism and apparent objectivity. Payne, for example, refers to his own critical activity as that of "the modern investigator". With the older critics of the empirical, historical, tradition (of whom Chesterton is the extreme example), an attitude, it is not too much to say, of love and admiration was the mainspring of criticism, and the critic tried by his appreciation to get "inside" the author. Such literary study has the quality of being part of what it studies. A scientist's activity, however, is greatly different from the raw material of his study, even if the pure objectivity once attributed to science is no longer thought to exist. Typical modern professional criticism is detached, analytical, and conceptual. Doubtless the New Criticism, with its isolation of the poem as an artefact of the present moment, and its powerful verbal tools for analysing poetical anatomies, has had a pervasive influence. Modern critics, like modern scientists, are usually "tenderminded", systematic, interested in demonstrating theories, in discovering general patterns. They have a natural interest in symbolism and in irony (that most intellectual of poetic effects, which some New Critics identify with poetry itself). They are less content with that description of the uniqueness and arbitrariness of historical fact and context which characterises what William James called "toughmindedness".

Scientific method has begun to bring a much-needed intellectual force to English studies. It corresponds to much that was scientific, intellectual, conceptual, and abstract in Chaucer himself, and will be fruitful of discoveries. Nevertheless, when one contemplates, not the books I have mentioned, but the vast mass of scholarly articles in learned journals that lies behind them, one hopes that scientific rigour will not degenerate into mere pedantry, and that the sense of the modern will not destroy the sense of the past. There have been relatively few attempts to see Chaucer as part of the culture of his time, to unite general historical and literary interests; when Speirs attacks even the attempt to understand the poet in his historical actuality he expresses with characteristic boldness a widespread modern attitude. This attitude arises from the necessary scientific belief that past views and beliefs are wrong, for if they were right they would be held now, and so be views not merely of the past, which is dead, but of the living present. Historical and literary knowledge works otherwise. Nothing human is alien to it. Literary criticism, words about words, is necessarily part of what it studies, and is therefore concerned with the specific, the unique, and so the historical, as science, concerned with generalities, can never be. Much of Chaucer's own interest seems to have been in historical, specific, even arbitrary detail. The vitality of his presentation of living people, as revealed, say, in the portraits in the "General Pro- logue", partly derives from the way he broke up the orderly pattern of the rhetorical *descriptio* and included much detail that is frankly arbitrary. Recent critical discoveries of Chaucer's acceptance of logical inconsistencies, of his realism, of his sense of the past, point to the conclusion that his was a very tough mind.

4

Some topics of the modern criticism of Chaucer need to be discussed in terms of subject-matter. Chief among them are love, allegory, and rhetoric.

Love is always interesting. Chaucer is notable for his interest in the purely personal life (of which the dominant concerns are personal relationships and abstract thought) rather than in the public, social, institutional, matters which so concerned his contemporary Langland, and even Gower.

Since love, like all other forms of life, takes on a specific historic form that differs in different periods in its expression of permanent human desires, medieval love in literature is different from modern. It has been called, since the late nineteenth century, "courtly love", though the men of the Middle Ages called it *fine amour*, "refined love". A vast secondary literature has grown up around this subject. The pioneering modern study in relation to Chaucer is W. G. Dodd's *Courtly Love in Chaucer and Gower* (1913). Dodd steered into the full current of Chaucer criticism the now celebrated *De Arte Honeste Amandi* by Andrew the Chaplain, which has recently been the subject of much scholarly argument. Most of the assumptions by Dodd and others that Andrew was the chaplain of the gay and luxurious court of Marie de Champagne have recently been shown by J. F. Benton to be unfounded. Whoever he was, Andrew wrote a fascinating book about the goings-on in high places. He expounds and analyses *fine amour* according to scholastic rules which can be understood, on the literal level, by anyone, while he illustrates the precepts by witty anecdotes and judgments drawn, he says, from the great ladies who presided over the "Courts of Love". The most famous judgment is that a lady cannot possibly love her own husband. Andrew complicates matters by repudiating, in his third section, what he seemed to be advocating in his first two. He has written a textbook of love (not without sex) that seems to save one reading literature, though it is perhaps likely that we have here an early example of the well-recognised fact that a work of "criticism" can easily be a fiction. Dodd shows that "courtly love" is (as we might have guessed) Sensual, Illicit (usually adulterous), Secret, Hard to Get. Dodd does not claim that all sexual love in Chaucer and Gower conforms to this pattern, but he works carefully through the poems to see where it does.

Dodd's system was taken up in one of the most influential, brilliant, and probably misleading, critical books of this century, C. S. Lewis's *Allegory of Love* (1935), so perceptive, learned, lively and generous-spirited. It is a creative and imaginative work that will live long in its own right. Lewis emphasises, and over-emphasises, the novelty of "Courtly Love" as something entirely new in the human race, beginning in Provence in the twelfth century, and distinguished by four characteristics, Courtesy, Adultery, Humility (of the lover), and Secrecy. He ranges over many texts with sympathy and insight, not least over Chaucer. But where, one may ask, is the secrecy of love in the *Parlement of Foules* or even in "The Knight's Tale"? Where is the adultery in "The Knight's Tale" or, for that matter, in *Troilus and Criseyde*, where Troilus is a bachelor and Criseyde a widow? Hardly any medieval English love literature treats adultery as anything but a comic immorality (as in Chaucer's *fabliaux*): the exception is Malory, for whom it is tragedy. Yet so persuasive is Lewis's book that the majority of critics in the last twenty years or so have asserted that all courtly love is adulterous, and all love in Chaucer is courtly. One must assume that adultery is more of a modern than a medieval interest. Yet there is some truth in the mistaken modern emphasis on adultery and secrecy in medieval romantic love. It expresses the realisation that such love is personal and private, not social like marriage, and that though it normally leads to marriage, with marriage and the easing of sexual restrictions (which are essential to romantic love) it naturally changes character. E. E. Slaughter has recently examined the relation of love to virtue in Chaucer, and the presence in Chaucer of two contradictory conceptions of love. No doubt we have still not measured the full complexity of Chaucer's presentation of *fine amour*, let alone other forms of love, familial and brotherly.

Lewis's treatment of his other topic, allegory, was not so influential. Although Lewis shows characteristic insight and verve in his discussion, the topic needs a much stronger substructure of scholarship and intellectual history than was available when he wrote. Allegory lies deep in the intellectual and literary tradition of Europe, beginning with the Greeks and with the Rabbinical exegesis of what is now the Old Testament. In the Middle Ages there was an elaborate scheme of allegorical interpretation of the Bible and of certain secular Latin texts, notably Virgil's *Aeneid*, of which the allegorical interpretation had been begun early by pagan scholars. In addition, much medieval visual art was created to communicate a literary programme which could then be read back in terms of allegory from the work of art itself. Such levels of meaning represent a dimension of artistic experience which became unfamiliar and was therefore often rejected with disgust by later readers; but modern art and science in their own movement towards symbolism and away from "common sense" surface realism, are making us much more tolerant of the complexities of medieval art and literature. Lewis's discussion remains of value as a contribution to the criticism of individual texts, but the subject as a whole has been transformed by such general works as those by Smalley, Lubac, Seznec, and Spicq, by Robertson's work (as noted above), and by the arguments against Robertson of scholars like Bloomfield and Donaldson. The nature and degree of allegory (or symbolism) in Chaucer remain a fruitful subject for debate.

Allegory is associated historically with rhetoric, another complicated and controversial subject, more difficult to define than at first appears. "Rhetoric" may be thought of as equivalent either to "the art of writing" or to "the adornment of writing" (the rules for which are sometimes known as "stylistic rhetoric"). The two are connected, but the latter concept gave rhetoric its bad name in the Romantic and post-Romantic period, when it was thought that all good poetry had to be "sincere". The influential Latin rhetoricians of the twelfth and early thirteenth centuries wrote "stylistic rhetorics", and J. M. Manly, who discovered their influence on Chaucer in his seminal British Academy lecture, took a sternly Romantic view (backed up by somewhat doubtful statistics) of rhetorical tricks which he believed Chaucer progressively rid himself of. Manly's lecture inspired Naunin's study on similar lines, and many articles, some disputing rhetorical influences, which are discussed by Payne in *The Key of Remembrance*. Payne's book has advanced our understanding of the different expectation from literature and of the different literary effects created by a consciously rhetorical tradition. Concepts such as characterisation, realism, *organic* unity, were not known, but harmony, integrity, beauty were. There is still work to be done through the examination of rhetoric, making use of such continental scholars as de Bruyne and Zumthor, towards an understanding of medieval literary aesthetics, and consequently of individual literary works. A Romantic attitude to rhetoric is hopelessly outdated; yet in the end one also remembers that in England there has always, at least since the Norman Conquest, been an empirical suspicion of rhetoric; both Chaucer and Shakespeare were moulded by rhetoric, and both mocked it. Manly was not utterly mistaken.

5

The discussion of such topics needs knowledge, and surely it is in the handling of knowledge that the true critic exercises his judgment. I turn now to that organisation and extension of learning without which modern criticism becomes narcissistic, but which modern criticism must also inspire. In the nineteenth century such learning was largely promoted by the Chaucer Society started by Furnivall in London. The Society continued into the early twentieth century but the bulk of scholarship, now so much greater, has appeared in learned journals and separate books. The story of Chaucer scholarship in the twentieth century, as with the criticism, is largely that of the devotion, diligence, and genius of United States scholars.

The first need was of Bibliographies. Miss Hammond's splendid analytical and evaluative work of 1907 must still be consulted, and the later bibliographies and bibliographical articles make any superficial critical ignorance inexcusable. (The latest, by W. R. Crawford, also has a valuable introductory essay.) Brusendorff's close scrutiny of the manuscript tradition is a highly technical work for scholars only. By contrast the bibliographical guide by F. W. Bateson is a shrewd, impish, lively, and biased book for general readers. He denies that any first-rate criticism of Chaucer exists.

Chaucer's relation, as man and poet, to the general culture of his time, and the interpretation of his work in the light of this relation, have been somewhat patchily carried out. But much valuable detailed work has been done. The most considerable achievement, consummating the work of several scholars over fifty years, is the publication of the new *Life-Records* by M. M. Crow and C. C. Olson, in which all the documents relating to Chaucer in his own lifetime are gathered together with a learned commentary. Our general knowledge of Chaucer's life, as represented by the old *Life-Records* completed in 1900 and repeated in biographies such as Marchette Chute's lively book, or Brewer's, is unchanged, except for a hitherto unknown Spanish journey in 1366. The new *Life-Records* is a foundation stone for specialists, and we may hope that its learned editors will now produce the "Life and Times" which we need. A notable collection of illustrations and modernised or translated extracts from contemporary documents was made by Edith Rickert in *Chaucer's World*, edited by Crow and Olson. Though intellectual life is neglected, physical and social circumstances become vivid to us in this book. A somewhat similar book, composed only of illustrations, though these are annotated, and are often unfamiliar, is R. S. Loomis's *Mirror of Chaucer's World*. And at a much lower price and scholarly level has just appeared M. Hussey's *Chaucer's World*. Coulton's *Chaucer and his England* of 1908 is still useful and delightful, though somewhat dated, with the critical section of little use. Sylvia Thrupp's *Merchant Class in Medieval London* is illuminating for the social and economic environment, though Chaucer is not discussed. Brewer's *Chaucer in his Time* appeared in 1963.

Detailed study of Chaucer's intellectual environment and heritage has been the subject of a few excellent books, but more are needed, and there is no twentieth-century equivalent of Lounsbury's splendid essay on the learning of Chaucer. Curry, in a valuable if critically old-fashioned book, shows how Chaucer makes use of science in character-description; Plimpton discusses education pleasingly if a little amateurishly; Jefferson makes a valuable survey of Chaucer's use of Boethius. Shannon discusses Chaucer's knowledge of classical Latin literature in a work needing much revision, and as this essay goes to press a welcome book on Chaucer's use of Ovid by R. L. Hoffman is announced. Fansler has discussed Chaucer's relation to the *Roman de la Rose*, Braddy to the French poet Graunson, and Cummings to Boccaccio. Schaar has made an impressive if over-schematic analysis in *The Golden Mirror* of the European tradition of describing people and emotions. There have in addition been many detailed articles, but all these topics are far from exhausted and there are many similar ones little explored – fertile, and truly literary, fields for research.

This brings us to the question of specific sources, and here the excellent work of nineteenth- and early twentieth-century scholarship has been consolidated by the admirable *Sources and Analogues* edited by Bryan and Dempster. One would have thought that the work of discovering actual sources was now complete, but R. A. Pratt has discovered that Chaucer used a French crib when working on *Il Filostrato*, his main source for *Troilus and Criseyde*. We still lack a collected *Sources and Analogues* for the poems apart from the *Canterbury Tales*, but clearly the next general stage must be a fuller critical understanding of how Chaucer used his sources, and more critical comparisons with the analogues.

We also need to follow him to his English origins, so far more neglected than his European borrowings. This leads us back not only to the English romances, as I have shown elsewhere, but to the English language. Poetry must arise out of the common language; yet it also defines itself by contrast with the common language. The common language is general: poetry unique. We need to see one in terms of the other. Both the older historical philology and the modern descriptive or structural linguistics could be usefully employed here, and a few scholars have begun to show the way: but we have no twentieth-century equivalent of Ten Brink's old, if still useful, study of language and metre. Editors have given summary accounts (Baugh's in his edition is excellent), and Kökeritz's pamphlet with recording is helpful. Foreign scholars lead the way here. Wild's study of the language of the manuscripts is a pioneering work, unfortunately very difficult to obtain. Recent books by Masui and Kerkhof help to make possible an ever closer analysis of text. Without such guidance nuances of syntax and subtle patterns of rhyme are easily overlooked by the modern critic, with consequent distortion of meaning. Work on vocabulary and semantic structure whets one's appetite for more. Mersand's analysis of Chaucer's romance vocabulary, though to be used with caution, shows how fresh and perhaps *avant-garde*, certainly neologistic, Chaucer's vocabulary was.

Critical studies based on careful analyses of Chaucer's specific verbal uses are a fundamental literary activity. Much of Donaldson's and Muscatine's criticism is based on a careful attention to diction. In another direction, Héraucourt's examination of moral values in Chaucer's poetry, as revealed in word-associations, shows Chaucer's progressive interest in more inward, less worldly, values. Héraucourt's method deserves more attention. Within this same general field might come more study of Chaucer's imagery, only recently attracting attention after Klaeber's painstaking classification of 1893. Schaar has made a technical analysis of some of Chaucer's narrative techniques. Studies of rhetorical usages may also be mentioned here, the fullest being perhaps Naunin's, which has been noted above. The nature of much detailed work of this kind (including what the late D. D. Griffith called, and classified in his Bibliography, as Word Study) demands that it be swallowed up in editions and larger studies. Twentieth-century criticism has been notable for close study of the text and for its refusal to evade literary study by recourse to backgrounds and biography, but such criticism has often been more subjective than it appears at first sight and there is still plenty to be done. Burrow indeed comments that critics (with some exceptions) seem often to have "given up the words" – proverbs, poetic diction, technical jargon, staple idiom. An invaluable tool, however, has been provided by that fine product of both nineteenth- and twentieth-century American scholarship, the *Concordance* to Chaucer's *Works*, edited by J. S. P. Tatlock and others. Much smaller in scope, but also useful and interesting helps to study, are Magoun's *Gazetteer* and Whiting's book on proverbs. Such books support the memory, as well as helping analysis.

We still are not quite sure about Chaucer's metre, and there has been interesting controversy recently. The great (though still incomplete) achievements of nineteenth-century philology showed what intervening centuries had not realised, that Chaucer's language had been inflected and that his final -*e*, in particular, was often the survival of an earlier fuller inflexion. It became possible and usual to claim that his metre, at least apart from the so-called "octosyllabic" poems, is "regular"; that like most English poetry from the sixteenth century onwards, the verse has a basic "regular" structure of alternating light and heavy stresses, varying between nine and eleven in total number, against which the speech-rhythm, as determined by the sense, plays its varying counterpoint. The verse as actually spoken is the product of the interaction of natural speech-rhythm with the basic pattern of stresses. Such is the view of Skeat and of all modern editors; it has recently been reasserted in Baum's extensive though rather informal discussion of Chaucer's verse. Earlier critics of the sixteenth and seventeenth centuries, ignorant of the development of the English language and of the decay of inflexions, thought Chaucer had a rough, or "riding", rhythm, which they deduced from their pronunciation of his verse without inflexions. This view has recently been revived in an energetic way by J. G. Southworth, who has promoted a useful discussion about the actual sound of Chaucer's verse. We still lack a full scholarly treatment of the subject, written from the commanding heights of both the old philology and modern structural linguistics.

Such a study depends on sound texts (though sound texts depend also to some extent on one's view of metre), and again, in the provision of good texts one can report much progress and much more to do in the twentieth century. In 1933 Robinson's one-volume annotated edition appeared – a remarkable achievement. The texts were sound, if not final, and the annotations then provided a most useful index to current Chaucer scholarship, as well as offering some help to the reader. The only serious weakness was the Glossary. A second edition appeared in 1957, to some extent brought up to date, though it could not be relatively so complete as in 1933, and it had more misprints. It remains our nearest approach to a full standard edition, though a team of American and English scholars with Donaldson as general editor are now at work on a major edition in several volumes. An important step forward was made by Manly and Rickert, who published in 1940 *The Text of the Canterbury Tales*. This is very much for a small inner circle of scholars. A critical text is given with a vast selection of variants from some ninety manuscripts, which are minutely analysed. Although the Manly-Rickert textual theory is somewhat mistaken,[5] the edition remains a foundation stone on which others can build. A similarly fine if not so huge an achievement was Root's edition of *Troilus and Criseyde* in 1926, with textual and explanatory notes. There have been no other radical re-editions of Chaucer's poems except for the *Parlement of Foulys* by Brewer and the *Romaunt* by Sutherland: but Manly's edition of selections from the *Canterbury Tales* and the copious selections from all of Chaucer's poetry by Donaldson and Baugh are scholarly works designed for the non-specialist reader, with excellent apparatus and some important new readings, while Cawley's glossed edition of Robinson's text of the *Canterbury Tales* is very helpful.

The canon of Chaucer's work, except for one or two very minor problems, was effectively settled in the nineteenth century by Skeat, and apart from Ethel Seaton's learned but eccentric book, has not been questioned since. It has been added to, in all probability (though not yet certainly), by D. J. Price's discovery of an astronomical work, *The Equatorie of the Planetis*, in a manuscript which may even be in Chaucer's own hand. This may be of considerable help to editors, and of course has great sentimental interest to those of antiquarian tastes. Tatlock made a useful contribution to our knowledge of the development and chronology of Chaucer's work, and though many of his arguments are now questionable the general chronology of Chaucer's work as represented by Robinson in his edition is not now a matter of debate. But there are still some problems among the shorter poems and we still have no detailed chronological account of the composition of many of the *Canterbury Tales*; nor is there so far any sign that a satisfactory method for distinguishing chronological order over a relatively brief period of time can be devised.

[5] *Cf.* G. Kane, *Piers Plowman: The A Version*, London, 1960, p. 53 ff.

Interest in *fabliau* and romance has characterised much discussion of the *Canterbury Tales* on the one hand, while on the other
hand there has been a strong attempt to establish overall thematic
unity. The robust and sensible survey of scholarly and critical
problems by W. W. Lawrence is an example of the first. Besides
praising the *fabliaux* he defends the order of tales as devised by
Skeat but rejected by Robinson and Manly-Rickert. The other
type of interest is represented at its extreme by Ralph Baldwin's
The Unity of the Canterbury Tales (1955), which finds a unity
by referring the variety of tales on the road to Canterbury
to the organising principle of a pilgrimage to Heaven. The
nature of artistic unity is one of the most interesting problems
of Gothic works of art and literature, and probably Baldwin
oversimplifies, but at the same time he creates new possibilities of
understanding.

In a recent important book on *The Art of the Canterbury Tales*
P. G. Ruggiers further emphasises "thematic unity". In this
thoughtful and scholarly work he examines problems of the
relationship between art and moral vision, and sees the *Canterbury
Tales* as a complex, integrated structure in which Chaucer reconciles "the multiformity of human experience" in an ultimate
spirituality. The emphasis on "thematic" rather than dramatic or
narrative form enables Ruggiers to avoid old-fashioned notions
of characterisation, and to make good use of concepts of rhetoric.
His concentration on *fabliau* and romance is modern enough, and
he ingeniously interprets them as "infernal" and "purgatorial"
forms of rendering human experience, though he finds the
fabliaux fully moral – perhaps more moral than they are. If his
general approach is "tenderminded", his critical insight, sympathy,
and good sense save him from crushing the poetry into a dis-
torting mould. An older view is represented by R. M. Lumiansky,
who makes a vigorous argument for the dramatic principle of the
Canterbury Tales, according to which every tale is suitable to the
character of the teller and depends on inner psychological
motivation. Lumiansky's work illustrates a general thesis, but
it also helps us to remember and do justice to the extraordinarily
vivid sense of living men and women that Chaucer presents to our
imagination. A somewhat similar sense of individual variety is
given by Craik's acute commentary in *The Comic Tales of Chaucer*,

though he eschews general principle. He comments on the comic tales as Granville-Barker comments on Shakespeare's plays, step by step, in a manner humane, appreciative, empirical, refusing all generalisations. Many individual articles on parts or aspects of the *Canterbury Tales* are also found in the collections of essays edited by Wagenknecht, Schoeck and Taylor, Brewer, and Rowland.

These collections also include work on *Troilus and Criseyde*, which has been extensively discussed by Sanford B. Meech, who gathers up most previous criticism. His book is immensely detailed, highly specialised, very long, and written in a somewhat extreme version of the American learned style. It is also penetrative and judicious. Meech concludes by emphasising Chaucer's ironies and the way in which Chaucer, while praising love, shows the illusoriness of transitory sublunary things. The basis of Meech's method is an empirical comparison of *Troilus and Criseyde* with Boccaccio's *Il Filostrato*, but he hugely covers many other topics. The comparison with Boccaccio has indeed been fruitful for many critics since Karl Young first set out the origins and development of the story of Troilus. Such a study illustrates the technique of rehandling a known story – a technique in which medieval literature is so different from modern. Comparison provides, besides an historical control, a useful critical entry into some of Chaucer's uniqueness. The historical approach is also that of T. A. Kirby's valuable reading of the poem as a study in "courtly love". There have been some interesting refinements on the notion of psychological character in *Troilus and Criseyde*, though we are beginning to escape from the simpler notions of the "psychological novel" of the nineteenth century. At one time the sense of destiny in the poem attracted discussion, but most controversy has centred on the propriety of the ending, and the question of whether Chaucer at the end betrays the love he seems to some to portray so fondly in the middle of the poem. On this hangs a variety of laws and prophets – is it a poem in praise or blame of love?

Chaucer's shorter poems have not received the attention they deserve until quite recently. The best general survey is Clemen's revision of his already excellent earlier book *Der junge Chaucer*. An empirical and judicious critic of great sensibility, he demonstrates the careful modern scrutiny of the verbal texture of the poems, yet on the basis of such "practical criticism" can lead out to illuminating comparisons and generalisations.

Most discussion of the shorter poems has centred on the *Parlement of Foules*. The older interest in discovering what occasion it might have been written for has lapsed in favour of considering its poetic merit, philosophical implications, and literary relationships, culminating in J. A. W. Bennett's fine commentary, where great learning is linked with literary insight to reveal the poem's infinite riches in little room. A similar book by Bennett on the *House of Fame* is about to be published as I write, but up to now the most useful general account of that poem has been Sypherd's early study, though scholars have wrestled with its problems of unity and meaning, and many have referred to its apparently autobiographical elements. With the *Book of the Duchess* these two poems are indeed notable, among much else, for Chaucer's tantalising self-projection in his poetry, abandoned (as some think) in *Troilus and Criseyde*, and resumed in the *Canterbury Tales*.

Chaucer's lyrics, and, what is not quite the same thing, the lyrical element subsumed in his narrative work, have received little specific attention. His prose, however, has begun to appear a good deal better and more sophisticated than it used to be thought, thanks to the pioneering work of Margaret Schlauch. Miss Schlauch relates Chaucer's prose to the mannered artificial and sophisticated prose of European chancelleries, and has helped to recover a new rhythmical dimension for modern ears in the sound of medieval prose. In this respect as in others Chaucer continues to grow for us in stature as a literary artist and man of letters.

Thus critical estimates fluctuate: knowledge makes perception and judgment possible; judgment reflects back on knowledge and calls for more. Nothing illustrates more vividly the interrelation of knowledge and judgment than the fate of the Chaucerian apocrypha. To take one example that we can examine in a good modern edition by D. A. Pearsall, *The Floure and the Leafe* was universally regarded as one of Chaucer's most charming poems, frequently commented on and modernised, until Skeat quite rightly ejected it from the canon. Since then it has been universally neglected by critics till Pearsall. As with other artistic works of doubtful attribution, if it is felt to be part of the larger structure of a great poet's work, it is valued. If it is isolated it is despised. There is something of fashion, the scholar's enemy, in such changes, but they also illustrate very vividly the importance of context, of historical connexions and continuities, to our understanding. No linguistic phenomenon, even a poem, can be fully comprehended in isolation, any more than it can be understood if the words are not read with appropriate attention to their uniqueness.

Part of the context of Chaucer's work is its influence and after-life in the cultures that have accepted it. The collection of comment on and allusion to Chaucer's work was begun in the late nineteenth century and three large volumes of comment and allusion from Chaucer's own day onward have been published in the twentieth century by Caroline Spurgeon. They enable modern critics to see how severely conditioned by contemporary circumstance earlier critics have been, so that perhaps we moderns can rise a little above ourselves – though it can hardly be said that Miss Spurgeon's late-Romantic view of Chaucer, delightful as it is, achieves such historical detachment.

Another form of allusion and comment is offered by modernisation and translation, but nobody has yet compared the various versions of different ages and in the many languages into which parts of Chaucer's work have been translated. The twentieth century has seen a great increase of modernisation and translation, very properly undertaken by scholars and critics. Representative are the complete works translated by Tatlock and Mackaye, the versions of the *Canterbury Tales* by Coghill (in verse) and Wright (in prose), and of *Troilus and Criseyde* by Krapp, Lumiansky, and Margaret Stanley-Wrench. Translations and modernisations lose or distort much of Chaucer's quality, but half a loaf is better than no bread, and such versions are also another way of assimilating Chaucer to the contemporary culture of any given period. Each period needs its own translations, and when they are honestly done they bring something fresh (because genuinely old or genuinely foreign) to contemporary sensibility. They are only to be deplored when students of English rest content with them, rather than going on to read Chaucer.

Paradoxically, it is easier to understand Chaucer now than it has ever been in any other period later than his own because of the tremendous growth of modern scholarship. We can even hear more accurately what he sounded like from gramophone recordings. Of several recordings made one of the best is the Argo readings, where a fairly close approximation to philological accuracy is combined with literary expressiveness. A modern English speaker needs only a little practice to adjust to the accent of the fourteenth century. The poems come to life in a special way with oral delivery. In imagination Chaucer himself may stand before us. How delightful for the critic; yet how modest the imagined presence of the poet must make him feel! Of the critic it is true enough to say that he mostly gives what he receives. Yet there is something that he, like any other good reader, can bring – his own knowledge and imagination. It takes two to make a poem: the poet and his reader or hearer. The modern image of Chaucer must depend on an honest twentieth-century re-creation of the fourteenth century. Then there can be a meeting of minds, made possible by Chaucer's art.

II. CHAUCER AND THE MEDIEVAL MIND

Donald R. Howard

CHAUCER THE MAN[1]

I

So much study has gone into the rhetorical workings of Chaucer's
satire that almost anyone who reads Chaucer is now acutely aware
of the persona or narrator in each poem. The fact of a disparity
between the narrator and Chaucer himself has become a kind of
premise or dogma of Chaucer criticism; we have become accustomed to phrases like "the fictional Chaucer", "the postures of
the narrator", or "the finiteness of the narrator-role". And yet
because his major poems confer upon him the status of a major
figure, we continue to be interested in Chaucer the man despite
the prevailing formalism of Chaucer criticism. We read minor
works by him for which, were they anonymous, we should not
take the trouble to turn a page. We talk about his education,
thought, "development", "mind". And in his best poems we
feel him as a "man speaking to men". As for the man himself, we
have a few records, though none of these really proves that civil
servant and poet were the same person. Mostly, we believe in
him. Of course it is entirely possible that someone will come
along and argue that the *Canterbury Tales* were an instance of
group authorship, or were really written by John of Gaunt: but
if someone did, we should all question his sanity.

My theme is that this man, whom we feel that we know, is a
real and living presence in his works, and that his presence in
them is what makes them interesting and good. I present this not
as a corollary of any humanistic or existential principles, but as a
fact. I say that we are interested in the fictional narrator, the
rhetorical workings of the irony, the method of creating illusion

[1] [Reprinted from *P.M.L.A.*, LXXX (1965), pp. 337-43.]

and reality – all the "devices" of his high art – not because they are devices, but because everywhere *in* and *behind* them lies Chaucer the man. I will even go a step further: I say that this is the point which various analyses of "narrator" and "persona" have really proved.

It was, to begin with, the point of Professor Donaldson's famous article: he was attempting to show how Chaucer the poet masks himself behind the comic figure of Chaucer the pilgrim in order more effectively to say what he has to say.[2] Professor Bronson's objection was that this is not a matter of the rhetoric of fiction, but a result of oral delivery – that it is a perfectly natural manner of ironic conversation.[3] The disagreement, it seems to me, is a kind of pseudo-problem.[4] Any such device, conversational or literary, is rhetorical and can be analysed by distinguishing between the author and his projected persona. That the persona is wholly a fictional character – a "puppet" – with no element of the author's own character in it, I think few would maintain. Is it not, after all, a matter of degree? Does not the writer project some element of himself into any character? Do we not all present ourselves in various roles to various people – even to ourselves? And can anyone know his "real" self well enough to present *or* conceal it? To borrow a phrase from Patrick Cruttwell,[5] the writer is by necessity an exhibitionist, and so presents something of himself in everything he writes. He may choose to do so by fragmenting himself behind various masks, but he does not, and cannot, make himself disappear. However we analyse his presence in his works, we are therefore all of us "in search of Chaucer".

2

This search for an author on the part of his readers is a cultural phenomenon of some interest. We could say that the reader's

[2] E. T. Donaldson, "Chaucer the Pilgrim", *P.M.L.A.*, LXIX (1954), pp. 928-36.

[3] B. H. Bronson, *In Search of Chaucer*, Toronto, 1960, pp. 25-32.

[4] *Cf.* R. M. Jordan, "Chaucer's Sense of Illusion: Roadside Drama econsidered", *E.L.H.*, XXIX (1962), pp. 19-33.

[5] P. Cruttwell, "Makers and Persons", *Hudson Review*, XII (1959-60), pp. 487-507. The idea is developed by W. C. Booth, *The Rhetoric of Fiction*, Chicago, 1961, esp. pp. 16-20, 67-77, 396-8.

curiosity is piqued by the self-projection of the author, and the more so if the author attempts a masked presentation of himself. But this is not quite the whole story, since authors would perhaps avoid more than a very elementary, or naïve, self-presentation if they were not able to anticipate curiosity on the part of readers. Readers have, that is, a "sense of the author". Authors may encourage it, but they did not necessarily invent it. Simple and natural as it seems, it has not always been so important as it is in modern times. Indeed, our curiosity about the *private* life of the author – our desire to read his letters and know hidden facts about him – does not appear to have come into being until the eighteenth century; it begins, probably, with Boswell.[6] Before the eighteenth century, except perhaps in vituperative public controversies, the reader's curiosity was satisfied by what the writer *said* about himself. No one seems to have wondered, until quite recent times, whether or not (for example) Sir Philip Sidney really did look into his heart and write, just as no one tried to shed any light on the Dark Lady.

In the earlier Middle Ages, the sense of the author, the mention of his name, and the expression of his pride in his achievement were not entirely absent. But they were counterbalanced by frequent anonymity and by warnings against pride and worldly vanity. Moreover, the poet's name was sometimes mentioned only to ask forgiveness for shortcomings and request the prayers of readers;[7] Chaucer's Retraction would be an instance of the latter convention. It is not until the twelfth century that we begin to find open pride in authorship. Poets begin then to argue that true nobility springs from the individual intellect, and that letters are equal to arms as a means of conferring nobility.[8] By the time

[6] Cruttwell, pp. 497-500.

[7] See E. R. Curtius, *European Literature and the Latin Middle Ages*, tr. W. R. Trask, Bollingen Series 36, New York, 1953, pp. 515-18. L. Spitzer, "Note on the Poetic and the Empirical 'I' in Medieval Authors", *Traditio*, IV (1946), pp. 414-22, argues that medieval readers had little interest in the empirical person behind the "I", and tended to regard him as representative, though the autobiographical touch might add poignancy. R. W. Chambers, on the other hand, argues against the idea of "personas" in medieval poetry, showing with many examples that the dreamer or narrator in a medieval poem *is* the author; see "Robert or William Longland?", *London Mediaeval Studies*, I (1948 for 1939), pp. 442-51.   [8] Curtius, pp. 476-7, 485-6.

of the Italian Renaissance, the argument is carried further: poets begin to claim not merely a kind of nobility from what they write, but the power to confer fame upon others and the expectation of an earthly immortality through reputation.[9] In Chaucer we can find something like this Renaissance interest in fame, but it is much more sparing that the extravagant claims of the humanists. The *House of Fame* shows Chaucer, quite early in his career, thinking about the problem of fame. Still, what does the *House of Fame* teach but the old medieval lesson that good or bad fame is often conferred unjustly in this transitory world? The envoy of *Troilus* is a better place to look for Chaucer's hope of an earthly immortality:

> Go, litel bok, go, litel myn tragedye,
> Ther God thi makere yet, er that he dye,
> So sende myght to make in som comedye!
> But litel book, no makyng thow n'envie,
> But subgit be to alle poesye;
> And kis the steppes, where as thow seest pace
> Virgile, Ovide, Omer, Lucan, and Stace.[10]

Still, while the poet puts himself in very noble company, the passage is, in form at least, a conventional protestation of humility:[11] the poet's book is to be "subgit to alle poesye" and to kiss the steps where it sees these great poets go. One might quote the sentiment of "The Knight's Tale", "Thanne is it best, as for a worthy fame, To dyen whan that he is best of name",[12] as evidence of Chaucer's interest in a just reputation as a reward for good

[9] J. Burckhardt, *The Civilisation of the Renaissance in Italy*, tr. S. G. C. Middlemore, London and New York, 1928, pp. 139-53, has dealt with the idea of fame. Owing in part to Burckhardt's influence, many would say that the sense of the author was shaped largely by the rise of humanistic individualism and by the imitation of ancient writers like Horace who boasted that their works would outlast their own times; hence they might say that Chaucer's awareness of himself as a writer is a harbinger of the Renaissance. But in fact the sense of the author antedates the revival of the classics and the rise of humanism; it is quite possible to regard it as a cause, rather than a result, of the "revival of learning".

[10] *Troilus and Criseyde*, v, 1786-92, *The Works of Geoffrey Chaucer*, ed. F. N. Robinson, 2nd edn., London, 1957. All quotations are from this edition.

[11] Robinson, p. 837.

[12] "The Knight's Tale", A 3055-6.

labours; still, the labours are not poetical ones and Chaucer is not speaking of himself. On the whole it does not appear to me that Chaucer put more stock in lasting fame than did any late medieval author; he does not claim to confer fame on others, and his hopes of fame for himself are suggested only with the utmost modesty. In the Introduction to "The Man of Law's Tale" the lawyer mentions Chaucer by name and reels off an impressive bibliography of his works, but he takes a rather condescending tone towards the poet, who he says "kan but lewedly On metres and on rymyng craftily",[13] and prefers him to Gower only because he is more moral. Again, the passage hints at Chaucer's hope of fame, but it is sardonic indeed to make one's critics speak the Esperanto of stuffed shirts.

Another aspect of the changing sense of the author in the late Middle Ages comes about as the result of technological progress. In the earlier Middle Ages a manuscript was read by few and copied seldom, but with the rise of the professional scriptoria in the fourteenth century and the invention of printing in the fifteenth, the writer could begin to imagine an audience going unpredictably beyond his immediate milieu. People could then conceive of the writer as having power to address and influence an ever increasing body of readers – a "public".[14] The writer could imagine himself no longer a scribe, a maker of books or a transmitter of authorities, but the originator of an irreversible process. Here again Chaucer is in the transitional stage of an important cultural change. Certainly in *Troilus* he takes the position of a scribe or pedant transmitting from an "authority" matters of which he claims no personal experience. This was generally his pose in his earlier poems.[15] On the other hand, it is distinctly a pose. Chaucer might not have made extravagant claims for the originality of *Troilus*, but it is clear that he felt he had created something. Seeing himself as the originator rather than the transmitter in a process of publication through copying, he even expresses anxiety over the accuracy of the process:

[13] "Man of Law", B[1] 47-8.
[14] The *OED* reports the earliest uses of the word in the fifteenth century, but in this sense not before the sixteenth century.
[15] See Dorothy Bethurum, "Chaucer's Point of View as Narrator in the Love Poems", *P.M.L.A.*, LXXIV (1959), pp. 511-20.

> And for ther is so gret diversite
> In Englissh and in writyng of oure tonge,
> So prey I God that non myswrite the,
> Ne the mysmetre for defaute of tonge.
> And red wherso thow be, or elles songe,
> That thow be understonde, God I biseche![16]

Again, in the *Canterbury Tales*, we get a sense of his hope that he will be received well by an unseen audience of readers. In the "General Prologue" he warns us,

> But first I pray yow, of youre curteisye,
> That ye n'arette it nat my vileynye,
> Thogh that I pleynly speke in this mateere,
> To telle you hir wordes and hir cheere,
> Ne thogh I speke hir wordes proprely.[17]

There is the same kind of anxious apology just before "The Miller's Tale", and here Chaucer suggests,

> whoso list it nat yheere,
> Turne over the leef and chese another tale.[18]

To be sure he wrote with oral delivery in mind, and in many ways the expectation of oral delivery coloured his style. But it is evident that he expected also to be copied by unseen hands and read by unseen readers. To some extent this is true throughout the Middle Ages: the formula "readers and hearers" is enough to suggest it.[19] Chaucer conceives of his function as we should

[16] *Troilus and Criseyde*, v, 1793-8.
[17] "General Prologue", A 725-9.
[18] "The Miller's Prologue", A 3176-7.
[19] On the tradition of oral delivery and its influence on Chaucer, see Ruth Crosby, "Oral Delivery in the Middle Ages", *Speculum*, xi (1936), pp. 88-110; "Chaucer and the Custom of Oral Delivery", *Speculum*, xiii (1938), pp. 413-32; and B. H. Bronson, "Chaucer's Art in Relation to his Audience", *Five Studies in Literature*, Berkeley, Calif., 1940, pp. 1-53. For an excellent analysis of Chaucer's estimate of himself in relation to his audience, see Rosemary Woolf, "Chaucer as a Satirist in the General Prologue to the *Canterbury Tales*", *Critical Quarterly*, i (1959), pp. 150-7. It is not necessary to suppose that the printing press and silent rapid reading caused modern writers to stop thinking in terms of oral delivery. Writers still read orally, if only to their wives, and they may well imagine themselves speaking aloud as they compose. We write "I should like to say" and similar expressions without imply-

expect a writer of the fourteenth century to do – with an increased sense of an unpredictable and irreversible process of communication going beyond his milieu and beyond his time, but with nothing like the feeling which the printing press was to encourage.

These changes in the idea of authorship – this steadily increasing expectation of being read and admired – created a corresponding change in the idea of anonymity. In the earlier Middle Ages anonymity was a mark of the scribe's or writer's humility: it showed his deference to the "authorities" he transmitted. He viewed himself as a mere agent in a process of transmission and preservation. Writers who mention their own labours often deprecate them – one thinks of Einhard, who tells us that although his powers are almost nil he is willing to risk the opinion of the world in order to preserve the deeds of Charlemagne. By the twelfth century we can find a writer like Bernard of Morval, in the prose dedication of his *De contemptu mundi*, asking for criticism and defending his use of rhyme on the ground that it commends moral precepts more readily to the mind. Bernard argues, too, that the Bible contains lyrics and quotes Horace that writing should instruct and delight. He claims to have been inspired by a vision, and boasts of his ability in sustaining the metrical pattern at such length. All this sounds very modern for a twelfth-century monk writing at Cluny, and Bernard injects much of his own strong personality into his indignant denunciation of the evils of his time. Yet he does absolutely nothing to preserve his name: it is mentioned only in the salutation of his abbot. The scribe did not help matters, for it is uncertain that the author wrote "Bernardus Morvalensis" rather than "Morlanensis" or "Morlacensis". Nor has anyone discovered what Morval might have been.[20]

ing oral delivery. Language is by nature spoken, and a writer who writes with any degree of fluency is bound to "hear" spoken discourse as he writes. The difference between medieval and modern in this respect, as in others, is a matter of degree. *Cf.* Jordan, "Chaucer's Sense of Illusion", p. 21, n. 3. On the oral-aural component in western culture see M. McLuhan, *The Gutenberg Galaxy: The Making of Typographic Man*, Toronto, 1962; W. J. Ong, *Ramus. Method, and the Decay of Dialogue*, Cambridge, Mass., 1958, and *The Barbarian Within*, New York, 1962, esp. pp. 68-87, 220-9.

[20] See Bernard of Morval, *De contemptu mundi: A Bitter Satirical Poem of*

By Chaucer's time, of course, writers are much less reserved about mentioning their own names. A fashion has taken shape. The new interest in names of writers is reflected by the appearance, in the early fifteenth century, of the *De scriptoribus ecclesiasticis* by Johannis Trithemius, a biographical dictionary which contains chiefly dates, lists of works, and stereotyped praise of each man's piety and learning. Chaucer himself likes to name authors and praise them. At the same time, anyone who has worked with fifteenth-century manuscripts will know that while the names of authors may be more frequently recorded than in previous times, there are still many manuscripts which omit altogether the writers' names. It would be interesting to have some statistics about the decline of anonymity after the fourteenth century. What is important, however, is the increasing sense of the author: when curiosity about the author could be assumed as a normal attitude among readers, it permitted the author to use anonymity not merely to avoid criticism or persecution, but to whet the interest of his public. *Gulliver's Travels* is the classic example: the reader is purposely led to seek out in the text the true views of the anonymous author which lie behind the literal statement of the pseudonymous one. It is the sense of the author, considered as a cultural phenomenon, which makes possible a tension between the persona or narrator and the understood or felt personality of the author. And Chaucer is the first English poet to use the full artistic possibilities of this masked presentation of self.

3

Chaucer saw himself, then, as an originator of literary works who could hope for a continuing audience and reputation. He speaks of himself with modesty and, usually, with self-deprecating humour: but he does not seek anonymity – indeed, he provides us, in the Prologue to the *Legend of Good Women*, in the Retraction to the *Canterbury Tales*, and in the Introduction to "The Man of Law's Tale", with lists of his writings. He did, however, mask his personality. This seems like a kind of anonymity, but it is not anything like the simple, impenetrable anonymity of, say,

3000 Lines upon the Morals of the XIIth Century, ed. H. C. Hoskier, London, 1929, pp. xv, xxii, xxxv-ix.

the *Gawain*-poet. We should do better to call it masquerade.[21]

What is distinctive in this element of Chaucer's style begins, perhaps, with the *House of Fame*. Here the narrator is actually called "Geffrey"; he is a plump, bookish fellow with little experience in the high courtly practices of love. The portrait is humorously autobiographical – for our author is a bourgeois, a customs-clerk; and his audience is composed of knights and ladies, or of people like himself who are knowledgeable about court fashions. What *is* out of character, of course, is the narrator's obtuseness and insensitivity. This, I suspect, was a humorous development of the half-comprehending, naïve reactions which one finds in the conventional "dreamer".[22] Such a narrator serves the artistic function of throwing attention on the subject-matter: the audience perceives the *meaning* of the facts, while the narrator does not. And of course it is high comedy for the writer to adopt the mask of a fool when his artistry shows him to be anything but.

The device is essentially the same in *Troilus*, but there are refinements. The narrator is a devotee of books, and a "servant of the servants of love". He himself is unsuccessful as a lover, because of his "unliklynesse", yet he stands in wide-eyed and sometimes envious admiration of the affair as he transmits it from his "auctor". He is no longer the conventional dreamer of the earlier poems – he is a *reader*. What Professor Bloomfield has brilliantly described in his article on "distance and predestination" in *Troilus*[23] is, after all, the common experience of those who read: the alternation between emotional involvement in the illusion and aesthetic distance from it. The "narrator" of *Troilus*, this reader with his old book in hand, is therefore like ourselves: we are "reading Lollius with him". He is closer to the events than

[21] See Ruth Nevo, "Chaucer: Motive and Mask in the 'General Prologue' ", *Modern Language Review*, LVIII (1963), pp. 1-9.

[22] On the early development of the device see Bethurum, "Chaucer's Point of View . . .", pp. 511-16; A. L. Kellogg, "Chaucer's Self-Portrait and Dante's", *Medium Aevum*, XXIX (1960), pp. 119-20; D. M. Bevington, "The Obtuse Narrator in Chaucer's *House of Fame*", *Speculum*, XXXVI (1961), pp. 288-98; and C. A. Owen, Jr., "The Role of the Narrator in the 'Parlement of Foules' ", *College English*, XIV (1953), pp. 264-9.

[23] M. W. Bloomfield, "Distance and Predestination in *Troilus and Criseyde*", *P.M.L.A.*, LXXII (1957), pp. 14-26. *Cf.* E. T. Donaldson, *Chaucer's Poetry*, New York, 1958, p. 966.

we are (for he has already read the book from which he draws his tale), but he is willing at times to remove himself from our attention and let us look on directly with him as the story unfolds.

Pandarus is a kind of mirror image of this narrator. He, too, is an unsuccessful lover, taking a vicarious enjoyment in place of a real one. He reacts to the story quite as the narrator does – fearful for Troilus, eager over the progress of the affair, exercised in the consummation scene, helpless and dejected by the way things turn out. And, as the narrator manipulates the events of his story, Pandarus manipulates the events themselves. But the similarities between Pandarus and the narrator all merely emphasise one enormous difference between them. Pandarus is a pagan who believes in a pagan philosophy of *carpe diem* ("cache it anon", he says at one point), whereas the narrator is a Christian. Pandarus is of their time, the narrator of ours. Hence Pandarus is of no use when things go wrong. His morality, which consists chiefly of the notion that one should take advantage of Fortune while one may, can provide no better consolation for Troilus than another affair. He "stant, astoned of thise causes tweye, As stille as ston; a word ne kowde he seye".[24] At the end, the narrator, like any reader, sees a lesson in the story shaped by his own age and culture: he is a Christian, and he learns from his story the error of "payens corsed olde rites", though he had been carried away at first by enthusiasm for them.

Now this narrator, this reader and learner, *is Chaucer*. We learn this from the epilogue, where he speaks in his own person – "Go, litel bok, go, litel myn tragedye". To say that the narrator goes off stage at the end and Chaucer steps on to speak the envoy *in propria persona* is simply to misread the text. At the end of the envoy, after expressing his worries over the diversity of English, Chaucer says "But yet to purpos of my rather speche"[25] and then, going back to what he had been saying, "The wrath, as I bigan yow for to seye . . . ".[26] What is this if not an explicit statement that the "I" of the epilogue is identical with the "I" who has told the story? We could, of course, say with Professor Jordan that the

[24] *Troilus and Criseyde*, v, 1728-9.
[25] *Op. cit.*, v, 1799.
[26] *Op. cit.*, v, 1800.

narrator *becomes* Chaucer at the end.[27] But what would be the point? Do we not rather discover here, if we had any doubt before, that it was Chaucer speaking all along? It was Chaucer the enthusiast of courtly love, who is now convinced that Christian love is best. And why is this so different from the real live Chaucer of the fourteenth century? We know that he *was* a lover of books. And he *did* have a certain "unliklynesse" as concerns courtly love: it was aristocratic behaviour and he was not an aristocrat. At least for a time he did take the poetry of courtly love seriously. But also, quite early in his career, he began to search for other materials and other styles. And he wrote Christian poems throughout his life. One cannot really find anything in *Troilus* (except for his reading of "Lollius") which makes the narrator *factually* different from Chaucer the man. The difference is a matter of tone. It is the humorous exaggeration of his bookishness and "unliklynesse" that makes him seem different from the presumably "real" Chaucer of the epilogue – the Chaucer we *think* we know.

This element of humorous and exaggerated self-presentation is carried a step further in the narrator of the *Canterbury Tales*. In *Troilus* Chaucer unmasks himself at the end, but in the *Canterbury Tales* he avoids any direct self-revelation, except in the Retraction. Rather than unmask himself, he unmasks the pilgrims. And his knowledge of them is based upon direct observation.[28] He is not a "dreamer" here, nor a "reader" either; he is a returned traveller. Now returned travellers always have a certain air of omniscience. When the narrator says, as he does of the Merchant, "Ther wiste no wight that he was in dette",[29] we do not have to think it out of character or charge it up to an omniscient author: returned travellers report gossip and surmises along with facts. Who has not endured their enthusiasm? It is the most natural kind of storytelling in the world, utterly realistic and utterly convincing.

[27] R. M. Jordan, "The Narrator in Chaucer's *Troilus*", E.L.H., xxv (1958), p. 255.

[28] On the narrator's stance in the "General Prologue", see R. Baldwin, *The Unity of the Canterbury Tales*, Copenhagen, 1955, pp. 55-7, and E. H. Duncan, "Narrator's Points of View in the Portrait-sketches, Prologue to the *Canterbury Tales*", *Essays in Honor of Walter Clyde Curry*, Nashville, Tenn., 1954, pp. 77-101.

[29] "General Prologue", A 280.

As a dreamer in the earlier dream-poems, Chaucer had been reporting what was an illusion to begin with; as a reader in *Troilus*,
he claimed only to be translating and adapting an old story. But
in the *Canterbury Tales* he claims to be reporting real events in
which he has been a participant, things he can remember. And
yet, while he claims this, we enter into the most improbable
illusion in the world: that people can tell tales in rhymed verse as
they ride on horseback in a group – through open country.

What this means is that the "fictional illusion" of the *Canterbury
Tales* is less real and less convincing, despite its contemporaneity,
than the intense events of the ancient, doomed city in *Troilus*. All
that was far and strange in Troy was made to seem near and real:
but on the way to Canterbury, something in the author himself
endues the familiar world of his audience with a strangeness. As
we read the "General Prologue" we perceive that the author does
not think what the narrator says. Our curiosity about the author
is brought into play; we wonder about his real opinions. Chaucer
even throws dust in our eyes by telling (as pilgrim) a dull tale like
"Sir Thopas", which we know he intends (as poet) to be a spoof,
then following it with the quite serious "Melibee". Again, he titil-
lates our sense of the author by having the Man of Law drop his
name and also discourse on his works. Indeed, he conceals himself so skilfully that we continue, almost six centuries later, to
argue about what he really thought. For just as soon as Chaucer
the returned traveller is removed from the scene, just as soon as
we are listening directly to one of the pilgrims, we think we
detect Chaucer the man in the pilgrim's words. For example,
when we read "The Miller's Tale" we are delighted by all the
echoes of "The Knight's Tale" in it. Is the Miller poking fun at
"The Knight's Tale" or is Chaucer poking fun at it? Or is
Chaucer poking fun at the Miller for not understanding the
Knight's high seriousness? or is it all three at once? And even in
"The Knight's Tale", for all its high style, we are faced with lines
like these on Palamon's imprisonment:

> And eek thereto he is a prisoner
> Perpetuelly, noght oonly for a yer.
>   Who koude ryme in Englyssh proprely
> His martirdom? for sothe it am nat I;

Therfore I passe as lightly as I may.
It fel that in the seventhe yer, of May
The thridde nyght, (as olde bookes seyn,
That al this storie tellen moore pleyn) . . .[30]

Is the Knight merely being humble? If so, why the reference to rhyming? Or is the Knight being ironic, making fun of his own tale? Or is it Chaucer himself speaking? – and if so, is he making fun of the Knight or of himself? We want to say to Chaucer, as the Host does, "What man artow?" But it is an essential part of the style of the *Canterbury Tales* that no real answer to the question is ever given. And it is probably time we stopped trying to decide who is speaking where.

What I am arguing is that Chaucer the man is present in the *Canterbury Tales* not "objectively" through any explicit representation, but dynamically – through an implied relationship between himself and his audience. And his role is precisely what it must have been in reality – that of a bourgeois addressing his social betters. From all the biographical facts which we know about Chaucer, exactly two major ones emerge: that Chaucer was a bourgeois who successfully established himself as a civil servant, and that he was a poet who wrote for the court. His aristocratic audience, which certainly admired him, would still have looked upon him as a social inferior. In such a milieu a man of wit is on guard not to show any bourgeois vices – literal-mindedness, uncritical gregariousness, pedantry, naïveté, inexperience, or pretentiousness. It is the perennial problem of the bourgeois: he does not want to appear bourgeois in the eyes of the upper class, but he knows that the most bourgeois thing he can do is to show discomfort about his status, or, worse, deny it. I can think of only two ways to get out of the dilemma. One is good-natured clowning with an edge of modest self-deprecation; the other is to be a sober, useful fellow and let your betters like you for what you are, not what you say you are. In the *Canterbury Tales*, and to an extent in the earlier poems, Chaucer adopts both these attitudes. He presents himself in the "General Prologue" as an exaggerated bourgeois type – uncritical, affable, admiring the rich and powerful, even impressed with successful thievery. He presents with

[30] "The Knight's Tale", A 1457-64.

humour exactly those bourgeois qualities which the average
bourgeois would conceal from aristocrats, makes them into an
elaborate joke, and parades it before the court. In doing so he
tactfully conceals his wit, his intelligence, his learning, his
philosophical depth, his wisdom – traits which could hardly have
escaped any member of his audience. To make it easier, he pokes
gentle fun at other bourgeois – the sober Man of Law, for example,
or the genial Franklyn. His own tale of Sir Thopas illustrates the
method perfectly. He presents himself as a bourgeois dunder-
head attempting to tell an aristocratic tale of knightly deeds. And
in the tale itself the joke revolves around the notion of a Flemish
bourgeois ineptly playing knight. The real and necessary
implication is that Chaucer himself really sees it all not from any
bourgeois point of view but from that of true knights and ladies.
He leaves his audience to assume that he is indeed *au courant* with
their aristocratic attitudes. In a word, he leaves the audience *to
create him in their own image*. In *Troilus*, the narrator carries on a
kind of running dialogue with us the audience, implies what kind
of an audience he thinks we are and draws us into the poem so
that we become a part of its reality.[31] But in the *Canterbury Tales*
Chaucer does something different: he draws the audience into the
work not by engaging in a dialogue with us but by expecting us
to infer what he thinks, to project ourselves into the role of the
implied author, to overreach ourselves and become one with him.

I will venture a step further and suggest that in one fundamental respect the naïve narrator is wiser, has a truer vision, than
this "implied author" with whom we align ourselves – that in the
narrator Chaucer has isolated and presented one important trait
of his own personality, his interest in people and his tolerant
humanity.[32] Everyone is accustomed to say that through the
narrator Chaucer presents the surface appearance and lets the
pilgrims themselves show the underlying reality. But is it not
equally true that the wide-eyed narrator, blind as he may be to the
vices of his companions, sees the good side of them with a strange
clarity? This – if you care to be allegorical – is quite consistent
with medieval theology. Chaucer had it from St Augustine that

[31] See R. O. Payne, *The Key of Remembrance: A Study of Chaucer's Poetics*,
New Haven and London, 1963, pp. 227-32.
[32] My point is anticipated by Donaldson, "Chaucer the Pilgrim", p. 936.

all created things are fundamentally good – that evil is parasitic, a deprivation of goodness rather than an entity; that one should on this account "hate the vice but love the man". So, in the masquerade of the literal-minded, gregarious pilgrim, Chaucer plays a kind of Holy Fool who stumbles into Christian charity unawares. We, with the implied author, perceive his intellectual errors, but his foolish generosity infects us all the same. Through it we are made to see – in the Monk, say, or the Pardoner – the created man beneath the canker evil.

If I am right in this, then Chaucer's fragmented self-presentation leads us to grasp two truths at once – that evil lurks beneath good appearances, but that good lies beneath evil. The pilgrimage begins with the narrator's doubtful notion that everything and everyone is good. It ends with a sermon whose point is that we should look to our own sins; and, in the Retraction, Chaucer makes his own act of penance. For Chaucer's own audience I should not be surprised if this had finally the effect of making some of them look within themselves and examine their own lives as Christians. To a degree Chaucer's audience might also have wondered about the elusive Chaucer himself – which pilgrims he liked, or thought absurd, or condemned. Since Boswell's time it is much more our tendency to wonder of the author "What man artow?" and to go in search of him. It would be good to know more facts about him, but finally the most relevant information we can have comes from the style of his works. The Chaucer of biographical documents, the Chaucer of the customs-house, may indeed have been literal-minded, uncritical, bookish, and fat – what might we not say, if we cared to collect anecdotes, about the Wallace Stevens of the insurance company or the T. S. Eliot of the publishing house? The Chaucer we know is a creation of our response to his works. For all that he is no less the *real* Chaucer. This is true for a reason which, as exegetes, we sometimes set aside, but which as humanists we always assume: that for every man who creates great poems there is an infinite truth, of grandeur and terror, in the adage *style is the man himself* – that there must be in him, and in those who would read him, all of the human possibilities which can be realised in his works.

R. W. V. Elliott

CHAUCER'S READING

Had Chaucer been invited to name his favourite recreations for a fourteenth-century *Who's Who*, he would no doubt have included travelling, dreaming, and reading. His travels, as far as we can tell from the data amassed by his biographers, were mainly of a professional nature, both on the continent of Europe and around England and perhaps Ireland:[1] but by opening up new literary as well as geographical vistas they exerted considerable influence upon Chaucer's development as an artist. His interest in dreams was both a scientific and a literary one, in dreams as natural phenomena and as modes of experience; and from the *Book of the Duchess* to "The Nun's Priest's Tale" the fascination persisted, as did the eagerness to discuss and explore. Dreams were indeed to Chaucer not merely the recreation of idle or speculative hours but a lifelong preoccupation, and to illustrate the close links between this preoccupation and Chaucer's interest in books will be one of the main aims of the present chapter. For books served Chaucer not merely, in Bacon's words, "for delight, for ornament, and for ability", but as authorities, as courts of appeal, in a continuing debate played out in the pages of his poems by a succession of characters animal, human, and divine.

There were, it must be remembered, physical obstacles to Chaucer's seemingly insatiable appetite for reading which life in

[1] It has been suggested that during the undocumented years of Chaucer's life between 1360 and 1367 he may have attended the Duke of Clarence in Ireland. See, for example, N. Coghill, *The Poet Chaucer*, London, 1949, p. 6. For different views on the "lost six years" *cf.* J. L. Lowes, *Geoffrey Chaucer*, London, 1934, p. 41, or G. Williams, *A New View of Chaucer*, Durham, N.C., 1965, pp. 42-4. For full documentary evidence of Chaucer's travels see M. M. Crow and C. C. Olson, *Chaucer Life-Records*, Oxford, 1966.

the fourteenth century inevitably imposed and from which we
in the paper-back plethora of the neon-lit twentieth are merci-
fully free. Books were rare and expensive, prized possessions,
and the laborious copying in manuscript was not entered upon
lightly. Moreover, nights were dark and time for reading was as
precious as the book itself. Like Keats's Bertha in *The Eve of Saint
Mark* straining to read

> with forehead 'gainst the window-pane,

so Chaucer has left us a picture of nightfall interrupting his bed-
time reading in the preamble to the dream of the *Parlement of
Foules*:

> The day gan faylen, and the derke nyght,
> That reveth bestes from here besynesse,
> Berafte me my bok for lak of lyght.[2]

But while Bertha "struck a lamp from the dismal coal" and continued to read, Chaucer settles down to metamorphose into a
dream the *Somnium Scipionis* of Cicero which he had just been
reading. What he does not tell us, unfortunately, is which version
of the *Somnium* was before him, and we must constantly recall
R. A. Pratt's reminder that "medieval readers studied not the
purified texts reconstructed for us by the editors, but instead
made use of corrupt forms of classical and of medieval texts".[3]
Much of Chaucer's knowledge of older literature – and the
Somnium Scipionis with Macrobius's Commentary may well have
been a case in point – presumably derived from popular medieval
textbooks, literary readers, anthologies in which selections from
the classics rubbed shoulders with arithmetical or astronomical
treatises. Hence, at times when Chaucer's literary allusiveness
most compels our admiration at his wide erudition, he may be
simply recalling from some such textbook a piece of literature
"long familiar both to him and to much of his audience"[4]
nurtured on the same fare.

---

[2] *Parlement of Foules*, 85-7, *The Works of Geoffrey Chaucer*, ed. F. N. Robinson,
2nd edn., London, 1957.

[3] R. A. Pratt, "The Importance of Manuscripts for the Study of Medieval
Education as Revealed by the Learning of Chaucer", *Progress of Medieval and
Renaissance Studies in the U.S.A. and Canada*, Bulletin No. 20 (1949), p. 48.

[4] R. A. Pratt, "Chaucer's Claudian", *Speculum*, xxii (1947), p. 429.

To remember the physical circumstances of Chaucer's reading only enhances one's admiration for his studious pertinacity amid all the distractions and preoccupations of a busy life; while to be aware of the nature of the material to which he had access need not diminish one whit the modern reader's respect for a truly educated, cultivated, urbane, medieval mind. And this despite the fact that it is not difficult to pick holes in Chaucer's learning, for he is certainly guilty of errors and inaccuracies "which, if committed by a modern author, would be held up by hostile critics as convincing evidence that he had failed to master the rudiments of knowledge".[5] But to ascribe such blunders to Chaucer's "failure to read his originals aright"[6] is both to overlook R. A. Pratt's aforementioned caveat, and to forget that Chaucer must have been more often than not working from memory. For the modern scholar writing in a flat at Aldgate the Reading Room of the British Museum is within comfortable reach; for Chaucer writing in his flat at Aldgate there were at best

> at his beddes heed
> Twenty bookes, clad in blak or reed,[7]

and, apart from these, whatever he carried in his head. In any case, Chaucer was writing poetry, not doctoral dissertations; and his poetry was frequently intended for specific audiences to whom the pleasure to be derived from some literary echo or from the evocation of a familiar name meant more, one may assume, than the scholarly accuracy looked for by the modern critic. It is certainly true that "within the limits of his day he was, like most great poets, an astonishingly learned man, though not in the strict sense a scholar".[8]

How much of Chaucer's learning was acquired in his youth and adolescence is impossible for us to know, but probably already at school he would have had the opportunity to read quite extensively,[9] and it is possible that his acquaintance with some of the

[5] T. R. Lounsbury, *Studies in Chaucer*, London, 1892, II, p. 181.
[6] *Op. cit.*, p. 183.   [7] "General Prologue", A 293-4.
[8] D. S. Brewer, "The Relationship of Chaucer to the English and European Traditions", *Chaucer and Chaucerians*, London and Edinburgh, 1966, p. 35.
[9] It is not known where Chaucer went to school, but it may well have been at St Paul's Almonry in the Vintry, near his father's tenement, a school which

popular Middle English romances went back to his years of service, from 1357 onwards, in the Ulster household. D. S. Brewer has recently argued persuasively for a close connexion between the manner of these romances and some of the metrical and stylistic features of Chaucer's earliest poems. If these romances are indeed "the source of his first poetic nourishment",[10] it is important to revise the traditional account of Chaucer's literary genesis to the extent of prefacing an "English period" to the so-called French and Italian "periods" covering the composition of his works from the *Book of the Duchess* to *Troilus and Criseyde*.

The concept of "period" in Chaucer's development, although rather discredited among modern critics, can be a helpful one provided it is not applied too rigidly. For it is true that Chaucer appears to have responded with particular alacrity to the stimuli offered by his most recent reading, which would be mainly French or Italian books as a result of his several journeys. Yet the influences at work in the shaping of all his major poems were manifold. The *Book of the Duchess*, for example, has long been recognised as strongly indebted to poems by Guillaume de Machaut as well as to the *Roman de la Rose* and other French sources, yet its style, as Brewer has indicated, has strong English affinities, and the total work is, for all its indebtedness and immaturities, genuinely and originally Chaucerian in several important respects.

The same is true of later, maturer poems like "The Knight's Tale" and *Troilus and Criseyde*, based respectively on Boccaccio's *Teseida* and *Filostrato* with which Chaucer probably became acquainted during his journeys to Italy in 1372 and 1378. Neither poem, however, is a slavish copy of an Italian original, for Chaucer here as in all his work drew upon much and varied earlier reading: Ovid, Statius, Boethius, and the *Roman de la Rose*, for example. Up to the inception of the *Canterbury Tales* Chaucer's creative process seems to have followed a pretty regular pattern: a burst of creative energy, fired by recent perusal of a particular work, stimulated an imagination nourished by the accumulated learning of years of avid reading. The result in every case is a typically

possessed in the fourteenth century many of the books that Chaucer had read. See the list in E. Rickert, *Chaucer's World*, London, 1948, pp. 121-6.

[10] Brewer, *Chaucer and Chaucerians*, p. 4.

Chaucerian amalgam of "source", *auctoritees, olde bokes*, and Chaucer's own inimitable genius. Hence the study of Chaucer's reading is valuable "not simply to trace the history of an idea, still less to imply any plagiarism or barrenness of invention. . . . It is to divine what an author saw in his original and what he saw beyond it".[11]

The range of Chaucer's reading embraces works in four languages – English, Latin, French, and Italian – and may be divided into intimate and nodding acquaintance. There are many authors in the second group, like Horace, Juvenal, and Persius, some of whom Chaucer may have known directly, others only from textbooks and anthologies.[12] Taken together they make an impressive list, however scanty Chaucer's knowledge may have been in individual cases. In Eleanor Hammond's *Chaucer: A Bibliographical Manual* they occupy the greater part of the thirty pages devoted to Chaucer's sources,[13] and more recent scholarship has added further possible material. Thus it has been suggested that among English works Chaucer may have known *Mandeville's Travels* and *Sir Gawain and the Green Knight*,[14] although their influence on his work is admittedly slight.

The attentive reader of Chaucer will not take long to discover that there is a handful of works which exerted a much more profound and lasting influence upon his poetry than those of nodding acquaintance so readily echoed, alluded to, or paraded *en passant*. They include works in the three foreign languages with which Chaucer was familiar and range from textbooks on

[11] Coghill, *The Poet Chaucer*, p. 70.

[12] While Juvenal is twice mentioned by name (in *Troilus and Criseyde*, IV, 197, and "The Wife of Bath's Tale", D 1192) Horace and Persius are not. Both Lounsbury and Skeat argue that Chaucer knew Horace only indirectly. Juvenal and Persius were represented in the library of St Paul's School, but Chaucer's indebtedness to them is so slight as to make close firsthand acquaintance unlikely. Only line 721 of the Prologue to "The Franklin's Tale" has been traced to Persius's *Satires*, mainly on the strength of the marginal quotation of the three relevant Latin lines in two of the best manuscripts of the *Canterbury Tales*. *Cf.* Lounsbury, *Studies in Chaucer*, p. 264.

[13] Eleanor P. Hammond, *Chaucer: A Bibliographical Manual*, New York, 1933, pp. 75-105.

[14] See Josephine W. Bennett, "Chaucer and Mandeville's Travels", *Modern Language Notes*, LXVIII (1953), p. 531 ff., and R. W. Frank, Jr., "Chaucer and the Gawain-poet: A Conjecture", *op. cit.*, p. 521 ff.

the art of poetry and on the "colours" of rhetoric to works of art
of the highest order, like Dante's *Divine Comedy*. Among Italian
writers it was Dante and Boccaccio who most influenced Chaucer's
work, although, as Wolfgang Clemen argues, "any influence felt
must have been of a very indirect and special kind, far removed
from what is understood by 'imitation' ".[15] One need only
compare the *Divine Comedy* with the Chaucerian poem which it
inspired, the *House of Fame*, to be acutely conscious of the differences in scale, manner, and "high seriousness", "between the
austerity of the one and the other's buoyant and exhaustless zest in
life; between an intensity like white flame, set over against an
unrivalled lightness of touch; between a remorseless com-
pression which packs stanzas into lines, lines into words, as
contrasted with a lavishness for which Dryden's 'Here is God's
plenty' is the only phrase; between a passion for the minutest,
most circumstantial record of contemporary incidents, and a
supreme indifference to such particulars".[16] If Dante did suggest
details of narrative or expression to Chaucer, these form the least
part of an influence which was rather an intellectual and imaginative excitement of the sort to which Chaucer so readily responded.

Not that Chaucer spurned the plots and stories offered to him
by some of his favourite authors. On the contrary, where he
found an opulence of stories, as in the works of Ovid, he "borrowed" lavishly. The story of Ceyx and Alcyone in the *Book of the
Duchess* (also used in Gower's *Confessio Amantis*) and several of the
stories in the *Legend of Good Women* have their sources in Ovid,
besides numerous other passages in Chaucer's poems which
declare his obligation to the Roman poet.[17] The Middle Ages
placed no great premium upon invention of plot; what mattered
was rather the manner of the telling than originality of the tale,
so that Chaucer was by no means alone in turning to new use
what he found in his books, or (to borrow a familiar phrase from
his father's profession) in pouring new wine into old bottles.

[15] W. Clemen, *Chaucer's Early Poetry*, tr. C. A. M. Sym, London, 1963,
p. 70.
[16] J. L. Lowes, *Geoffrey Chaucer*, p. 103.
[17] Internal evidence is convincing that Chaucer knew Ovid's work at
first hand, and a copy of the *Metamorphoses* is known to have been among the
books in St Paul's School.

Two works remain to be singled out from Chaucer's reading as of special significance: the *Roman de la Rose* and Boethius on the *Consolation of Philosophy*. Both of these Chaucer himself translated into English and no doubt the process of translation helped to foster an intimacy with the originals which is evident throughout the whole of Chaucer's work. Few great English writers display so patently an intellectual indebtedness to the work of lesser men than Chaucer does to Jean de Meun and to Boethius. Whether the extant Middle English version of the *Romaunt of the Rose*, as printed in Robinson's edition, is the one Chaucer acknowledges to have made in the Prologue to the *Legend of Good Women*,[18] is immaterial to our discussion, although, in Robinson's words, "the whole work, if not Chaucer's, is conspicuously Chaucerian".[19] Little doubt attaches to the authenticity of the *Boece*, although its prose style suffers in comparison with those passages from the *Consolation* which Chaucer rendered and expanded into verse in "The Knight's Tale" and in *Troilus and Criseyde*. In these Chaucer succeeds in subordinating the philosophy to the poetry in such a way that the reader, far from being disturbed by their presence, should be able to accept them as integral to Chaucer's purpose. This view has not always been accepted by readers of *Troilus and Criseyde*, in particular, some of whom regard Troilus's famous soliloquy on predestination and free will[20] as a later and rather inept addition on Chaucer's part. It may well be a later addition, but I agree wholly with R. K. Root's view that "the ideas of Boethius are taken over not merely as poetical elaborations of Chaucer's theme; they are sum and substance of the deeper significance which he sees in the story of the tragic love of Troilus".[21] In the *Boece* itself, on the other hand, Chaucer endeavoured above all to make himself – and his *auctour* – understood even to the point of prolixity. The result is indifferent prose, but the process of writing it undoubtedly impregnated Chaucer for life with the Boethian philosophy.

There is not a major poem of Chaucer's which does not draw on the *Consolation of Philosophy*, and some of his minor ones – *The*

---

[18] *Legend of Good Women*, F 329, G 255.
[19] *The Works of Geoffrey Chaucer*, ed. F. N. Robinson, p. 564.
[20] *Troilus and Criseyde*, IV, 958 ff.
[21] *The Book of Troilus and Criseyde*, ed. R. K. Root, Princeton, 1926, p. xli.

Former Age, Fortune, Truth, Gentilesse, and *Lak of Stedfastnesse* – are
directly inspired by it.[22] Chaucer does not follow the reasoning
of Boethius in every particular, but he accepts his important
concept of the principle of love as the binding force of all created
things (the theme of the song of Troilus in *Troilus and Criseyde*),[23]
and his central belief that "the nature of thinges ne took nat hir
begynnynge of thinges amenused and inparfit, but it procedith of
thinges that ben alle hole and absolut",[24] which is restated in the
final speech of Theseus in "The Knight's Tale":

> For nature hath nat taken his bigynnyng
> Of no partie or cantel of a thyng,
> But of a thyng that parfit is and stable.[25]

The further one descends from this "whole and absolute"
centre, the more one is confronted with the things imperfect and
corrumpable[26] which constitute human experience and which only
faith, through the agency of wisdom, can see in their true relationship to the divine providence. To the continuing medieval debate
on God's foreknowledge and man's free choice, which is closely
bound up with these Boethian arguments, and to the discussion of
the place of an unpredictable Fortune in this scheme of things,
Chaucer contributed his share, even though he must have been
sorely tempted at times to give up philosophical questions in
despair and to exclaim as he did in "The Nun's Priest's Tale":

> I wol nat han to do of swich mateere;
> My tale is of a cok.[27]

To see how Chaucer's thinking was fertilised and ordered by
the *Consolation of Philosophy* is to understand his eager response to

[22] See especially B. L. Jefferson, *Chaucer and the Consolation of Philosophy of Boethius*, Princeton, 1917, and J. Koch, "Chaucers Boethiusübersetzung: Ein Beitrag zur Bestimmung der Chronologie seiner Werke", *Anglia*, XLVI (1922), pp. 1-51. T. A. Stroud, "Boethius's Influence on Chaucer's *Troilus*", *Modern Philology*, XLIX (1951), p. 2, refers to Boethius as "a basic stimulant to Chaucer's creative imagination".
[23] *Troilus and Criseyde*, III, 1744 ff.
[24] *Boece*, III, Prose 10, 25-8.
[25] "The Knight's Tale", A 3007-9.
[26] *Op. cit.*, A 3010.
[27] "The Nun's Priest's Tale", B² 4441-2.

the portion of the *Roman de la Rose* written by Jean de Meun, for here was another vital contribution to the intellectual climate of the Middle Ages with which Chaucer's act of translating had made him closely familiar. The influence of de Meun's scholarship (he, too, had translated Boethius), of his wide-ranging interests in theology, philosophy, and the sciences, as well as of his critical, often satirical, attitudes can be traced, like the influence of Boethius, throughout Chaucer's poetry.[28]

But it is to the first part of the *Roman*, the work of Guillaume de Lorris, that Chaucer owed his initiation into the garden of love entered through the curtain of sleep. Chaucer's response was immediate, and once established in the *Book of the Duchess* the connexion between *bokes* and dreams remained firm. He already knew something of "Macrobeus" in the *Book of the Duchess*:

> He that wrot al th'avysyoun
> That he mette, kyng Scipioun,
> The noble man, the Affrikan,[29]

which is not strictly correct and was in due course put right in the *Parlement of Foules*:

> This bok of which I make mencioun
> Entitled was al thus as I shal telle:
> "Tullyus of the Drem of Scipioun",[30]

and by the later reference to "Macrobye" in the same poem. It is the mention of Macrobius, the Freud of the Middle Ages, which suggests that from the outset Chaucer was interested not merely in the dream form as a poetic device, but in the nature of dreams, their significance, and their relationship to other modes of experience. To manipulate dreams was to employ a useful key to a variety of poetic experience; hence the dream-poems. To understand dreams was one way of exploring the mysteries of the universe, possibly no less authoritative than the wisdom of *olde bokes* held in such high esteem by the medieval world; hence the discussions and speculations about dreams in Chaucer's poems.

As a literary form the dream-vision possessed a number of

---

[28] See especially D. S. Fansler, *Chaucer and the Roman de la Rose*, New York, 1914.

[29] *Book of the Duchess*, 285-7.   [30] *Parlement of Foules*, 29-31.

artistic possibilities, some of which were well established by the time Chaucer came to make use of them. What was new, however, was Chaucer's use of his reading both to set the scene and to launch his dreams: "thus early we find Chaucer setting himself apart from his fellows as a *reading* man; and throughout his work he never lets us forget the fact".[31] In the *Book of the Duchess* the poet combats sleeplessness with the help of "a book, a romaunce",[32] and the tale that he reads acts as an appropriate prologue to the dream-encounter with the Black Knight. In the *Parlement* the reading of the *Somnium Scipionis*

> gan me so delite,
> That al that day me thoughte but a lyte,[33]

and accounts for the appearance of "this forseyde Affrican"[34] as the guide in the subsequent dream. The *House of Fame* opens with a rapid survey of medieval dream-lore in which Chaucer remains characteristically non-committal. The discussion, however, leads naturally into the dream-vision itself, and this time it is within the dream that he makes use of a particular book, Virgil's *Aeneid*, devoting almost the whole of the first Book of his poem to the episode between Aeneas and Dido. It is not until the second book that reference is made by the Eagle to Chaucer's reading habits:

> For when thy labour doon al ys,
> And hast mad alle thy rekenynges,
> In stede of reste and newe thynges,
> Thou goost hom to thy hous anoon;
> And, also domb as any stoon,
> Thou sittest at another book
> Tyl fully daswed ys thy look,
> And lyvest thus as an heremyte.[35]

The last of the dream-visions, the *Legend of Good Women*, opens with a vindication of books and a ready admission that

---

[31] B. H. Bronson, *In Search of Chaucer*, Toronto, 1960, p. 36.
[32] *Book of the Duchess*, 47-8.
[33] *Parlement of Foules*, 27-8.
[34] *Op. cit.*, 120.
[35] *House of Fame*, 652-9.

> as for me, though that I konne but lyte,
> On bokes for to rede I me delyte,
> And to hem yive I feyth and ful credence,
> And in myn herte have hem in reverence
> So hertely, that ther is game noon
> That fro my bokes maketh me to goon,[36]

except that, Chaucer goes on, he will put his book aside to hear the birds sing and watch the flowers grow on a May morning. In the F-version of the Prologue to the *Legend* he does just this, then goes home and dreams himself back on to his daisy meadow; in the G-version these prolegomena are somewhat re-arranged, but the end result is the same.

One of Chaucer's innovations then in these poems was to employ his reading as "a natural gateway from the active life to the contemplative, from waking to dreaming; and probably he thought of himself as unusual in this regard".[37] But there were others: "The essential point is that Chaucer saw new poetic and artistic possibilities in the use of the dream. He links it with reality and with the preceding action, he deliberately uses the illusion inherent in the dream and he portrays his own second self within this dream world. Artistic problems of specific nature thus arose which Chaucer solved in his own way: the transition into the dream-state, the relation between the dream and reality, the rendering of 'dream psychology' ".[38] Both Bronson and Clemen rightly stress the close connexion in Chaucer's dream-poems between the waking – and reading – world and that of the dream. To be relevant, the world of the dream-poem had to be close to the waking world and to have its roots in it, but to allow full scope to the vision it had to be different, with laws and mechanics of its own. The differences are to some extent pointed by the metamorphosis of Chaucer the poet into the sometimes slow-witted, sometimes enigmatic, generally monosyllabic "second self" of the dreams, as in the *House of Fame*, where the mono-syllabic responses offered by the passenger to the lectures given by his aerial guide are continued as long as the flight lasts:

---

[36] *Legend of Good Women*, F 29-34.
[37] Bronson, *In Search of Chaucer*, p. 36.
[38] Clemen, *Chaucer's Early Poetry*, p. 27.

"Gladly", he says in line 605; "noo, helpe me God so wys", in
700; "yis", in 864; "wel", in 888; "nay", in 913. The adoption of
such poses enables the poet to dissociate his waking self from
what happens, from what is said and done in the dream; to be
both involved and on the fence, committed and non-committal.
The ambivalence as well as the inherent lack of commitment, no
less than the potential irony, seem to have suited Chaucer's
temperament, as far as we can judge this, admirably. It also
helps in the creation of worlds of make-believe into which
dreamer and audience could be projected without any difficulty
and with the minimum suspension of disbelief. To one nurtured,
as Chaucer was, on the *Roman de la Rose* and the love-visions of
other medieval poets, the dream was the obvious portal into the
world of courtly allegory in which the whole traditional "machin-
ery" of *fine amour* could be brought to life in settings both
sufficiently close to, and sufficiently removed from, the world of
real love and sex and *harlotrie*, for the connexions between them
to remain palpable without being too insistent. That Chaucer
dispensed with most of the personified abstractions of the
allegorical tradition, a development possibly suggested by his
reading of Machaut and Froissart, does not really affect the
argument. Admittedly, the *Book of the Duchess* could conceivably
have dispensed with the dream, but Chaucer was by no
means ready yet for such dispensing; and in any case the dream
afforded just the detachment and element of impersonality
advisable for a young poet tackling a topical theme involving
a noble patron. On the other hand, the *Parlement of Foules* could
not have dispensed with the dream any more than could the
House of Fame: the other worlds in both poems were as yet too
otherworldly for the narrator to venture to plant them into the
broad, realistic glare of waking daylight, although it is certainly
true that the audience of the later fourteenth century would have
been readier to accept such changes than an audience of two or
three generations earlier might have been.[39] In "The Merchant's
Tale", which provides the most comically picturesque cuckolding
in all English literature, the presence of Pluto and Proserpina and
their train of fairies in the very real garden in which May is dis-
porting herself with Damyan up a peartree is, to say the least,

[39] *Cf.* Clemen, p. 12 ff.

incongruous. It could easily have ruined a good tale. Even
Shakespeare takes care to put his fairy folk into a midsummer
night's dream. That it comes off in "The Merchant's Tale" is a
tribute to Chaucer's ability to handle such matter convincingly
within the new context which he had created for himself in the
Canterbury Tales.

Whether Chaucer himself believed in fairies, or in the possi-
bility of air transport,[40] or of understanding the language of
birds, we shall never know for certain; it seems unlikely, however.
But he clearly regarded dreams as a method of personal exploration, as a genuine mode of individual experience. Hence his
"scientific" interest in their causes, characteristics, and possible
significance. His reading of Macrobius had taught him the latter's
classification of dreams, echoed in the opening lines of the
House of Fame; other sources, including again the *Roman de la Rose*,
added further opinions.[41] For the moment, however, Chaucer
reserves his own opinion:

> But why the cause is, noght wot I.[42]

He is rather more ready to accept a direct link between waking
and dreaming in the *Parlement of Foules* in lines as familiar as
Mercutio's in *Romeo and Juliet*, I, iv, 71-5, about Queen Mab:

> And in this state she gallops night by night
> Through lovers' brains, and then they dream of love;
> O'er courtiers' knees, that dream on curtsies straight;
> O'er lawyers' fingers, who straight dream on fees;
> O'er ladies' lips, who straight on kisses dream . . .

while Chaucer says:

> The wery huntere, slepynge in his bed,
> To wode ayeyn his mynde goth anon;
> The juge dremeth how his plees been sped;

[40] Chaucer's reading had made him familiar with several well-known
medieval heavenward journeys apart from Dante's in the *Divine Comedy*, two
of which, Martianus Capella's *De Nuptiis Philologiae et Mercurii* and Alanus
de Insulis' *Anticlaudianus*, are mentioned in the *House of Fame*, 985-6.

[41] See especially W. C. Curry, *Chaucer and the Mediaeval Sciences*, rev. edn.,
New York, 1960, chaps. VIII and IX.

[42] *House of Fame*, 52.

The cartere dremeth how his cartes gon;
The riche, of gold; the knyght fyght with his fon;
The syke met he drynketh of the tonne;
The lovere met he hath his lady wonne.[43]

But the problem which most interested Chaucer was the value of dreams as evidence; for the rival claims of authority, as contained mainly in *olde bokes*, and of what we should now call empiricism are a persistent theme in the early poems, and one that persists through to the *Canterbury Tales*. In the *House of Fame* this theme is first seriously explored: Clemen calls it "the conflict between *auctoritee* and *truth*, between what is handed down and a man's personal experience";[44] and this, rather than love or fame, seems to me the unifying theme of the poem. "The poet will, for once", writes John Lawlor, "be freed from dependence upon the authorities, the books which he must pore over in Aldgate. Now he may know by experience, rarest of opportunities".[45] The opportunities were not so rare, as Chaucer's dreams show, but for once the poet's other self, if not his real self, was indeed free to explore for himself. By all means, says Chaucer,

> Rede Virgile in Eneydos
> Or the Epistle of Ovyde,[46]

but his other self is ready to "goo out and see";[47] and the Eagle, ready enough to cite "Aristotle and daun Platon",[48] is no less ready to provide "preve by experience".[49] Authority, in this case Martianus Capella and Alanus de Insulis, is not accepted unreservedly, and when Chaucer sees "the preve" there is the novel satisfaction of a theory personally verified:

> And than thoughte y on Marcian,
> And eke on Anteclaudian,
> That sooth was her descripsion
> Of alle the hevenes region,
> As fer as that y sey the preve;
> Therfore y kan hem now beleve.[50]

---

[43] *Parlement of Foules*, 99-105.   [44] Clemen, *Chaucer's Early Poetry*, p. 113.
[45] J. Lawlor, "The Earlier Poems", *Chaucer and Chaucerians*, p. 48.
[46] *House of Fame*, 378-9. *Cf.* also 447-50.
[47] *Op. cit.*, 476.   [48] *Op. cit.*, 759.
[49] *Op. cit.*, 878.   [50] *Op. cit.*, 985-90.

It is of course true that the whole process could be dismissed as absurdly circular, for had it not been for reading Martianus and Alanus in the first place Chaucer could not have described such details as he found there which he then "proves" correct by experience: but what matters is the tenor of the debate, if we can call it that, the earnest weighing up of books against observation. In the *House of Fame* it all leads up to the "man of gret auctoritee" who enters in the last line of the unfinished poem. There is a tinge of irony about these words after what has gone before – after the emphasis upon personal proof, the implication that "auctoritee" alone may not suffice, the mingling of truth and falsehood and the doubts cast on the reliability of fame in the third Book. That the poem breaks off here, unfinished like so many other enterprises of Chaucer's, does not matter all that much: the central point of the poem, I think, had been made, and whatever the "man of gret auctoritee's" pronouncement was to be, which everyone was stampeding to hear, it could not now be taken without a pinch of salt.

As Chaucer continued to read,[51] so he continued to ponder, as in the *Parlement of Foules*:

> For out of olde feldes, as men seyth,
> Cometh al this newe corn from yer to yere,
> And out of olde bokes, in good feyth,
> Cometh al this newe science that men lere;[52]

and if this seems like a step back towards acceptance of traditional authority, even more so does his realisation in the Prologue to the *Legend of Good Women*, accompanied by an appropriate "God wot" or two, that some things cannot be proved, that some beliefs cannot be tested, "by assay". Instead, there is no choice but to "yive credence" to books, a phrase sufficiently repeated in the opening of the *Legend* to make its point:

> But wherfore that I spak, to yive credence
> To olde stories and doon hem reverence,

[51] The moment he awakes from his dream in the *Parlement of Foules* Chaucer reaches for "othere bokes . . . To reede upon" (695-6).

[52] *Parlement of Foules*, 22-5. Cf. J. A. W. Bennett, *The Parlement of Foules: An Interpretation*, Oxford, 1957, p. 30 ff.

And that men mosten more thyng beleve
Then men may seen at eye, or elles preve.[53]

This point of view can be regarded as much a paean on books
as a vindication of "auctoritee" over empiricism, at least in
certain cases. But it can also be regarded as a final attempt to
justify dreams as an empirical tool; for Chaucer is about to embark
once more on a dream-vision in which he himself will be ex-
periencing strange things in the garden of love. Hence the
speculations about the nature of dreams are seen to take on a
particular significance in the context of this other speculation
about the relative merits of "preve" and "auctoritee", particularly
the authority of *old* books, for the "most precious books were
likely to be the oldest books".[54] If what happens in certain kinds
of dream *has* "significacioun", then what Chaucer claims to have
experienced in some of his visions at least takes on a more
important meaning: thus the dream of the *House of Fame* would
certainly be regarded as a *somnium coeleste* which "is never without some significance which the celestial intelligences wish to
impress upon the mind of the sleeper",[55] and that of the *Legend
of Good Women* has a strong claim to be put into the same category.

But Chaucer was a poet, not a scientist or psychoanalytic
investigator, and moreover before he wrote the *Legend of Good
Women* something very important had happened: he had written
Troilus and Criseyde. He had discovered, in the writing of *Troilus,*
the superfluousness of allegory and the limited appeal of its
abstractions and artificialities as well as, by corollary, an interest
in people and the importance of personal observation of people.
Not that he abandoned his reading, of course; he never, as far as
we can tell, did so. On the contrary, *Troilus and Criseyde* owes
much to Boccaccio and to Boethius, as we have seen, besides a
dozen or more other writers from Ovid to Machaut, and there is
an almost embarrassing recurrence of acknowledgments to "myn
auctour", to "bokes" and "wise clerkes" and to individual

[53] *Legend of Good Women*, F 97-100. *Cf.* also the opening lines of the poem,
F 1-39.
[54] Bronson, *In Search of Chaucer*, p. 93.
[55] Curry, *Chaucer and the Mediaeval Sciences*, p. 207, and *cf.* pp. 238-9.

writers.[56] Nor had Chaucer lost his interest in dreams, but this is now made wholly subservient to the story, so that the anxieties of Troilus and Pandarus's

> A straw for alle swevenes signifiaunce!
> God helpe me so, I counte hem nought a bene![57]

are fittingly in character, and, as later in "The Nun's Priest's Tale", the truth of the dream is merely a part of a greater total design. Despite Chaucer's heavy dependence on his reading, however, and the continuing interest in dreams, *Troilus and Criseyde* represents the first significant defeat in the Chaucerian "battle of the books", and the *Legend of Good Women* the last spurious victory. If the *Legend* had been Chaucer's last poem, we should have had to deduce that, despite *Troilus*, he never outgrew the dream-poem, that he never found full satisfaction in another mode of communicating his experiences, his ideas, and his ironies, or, for that matter, of utilising and parading his considerable learning. But the *Legend* was not Chaucer's last poem, and the *Canterbury Tales* shows just how effective the emancipation from dream-vision was to be.

The *Canterbury Tales* is Chaucer's most encyclopaedic work. To some extent the evidence of his reading in his earlier poems had of course prepared us for this: Machaut, Froissart, Ovid, "al the story of Troye", and the *Roman de la Rose* in the *Book of the Duchess*; Macrobius and Virgil and Dante in the *House of Fame*; Cicero and Macrobius, Alanus de Insulis and the *Roman* in the *Parlement of Foules*;[58] Boccaccio and Boethius and the rest in *Troilus and Criseyde*; Ovid, Virgil, Boccaccio, Froissart, and Deschamps in the *Legend of Good Women*. But the final harvest was to come, as Chaucer gathered his material for the Canterbury pilgrims and their tales, and there is no better way to gauge its wealth than to study that indispensable contribution to Chaucerian scholarship, the *Sources and Analogues of Chaucer's Canterbury Tales* edited

[56] Cf., for example, *Troilus and Criseyde*, I, 146, 394, 1002; II, 18, 49, 700; III, 91, 450, 1196, 1429, 1691; IV, 1415; V, 799, 1044, 1051, 1478, 1753.
[57] *Op. cit.*, V, 362-3.
[58] The various sources of the *Parlement* are conveniently summarised in *The Parlement of Foulys*, ed. D. S. Brewer, London and Edinburgh, 1960, p. 38 ff.

by W. F. Bryan and Germaine Dempster,[59] and to keep an eye upon F. N. Robinson's scholarly annotations in his edition of Chaucer's *Works*.

But the *Canterbury Tales* is of course much more than a final depository of Chaucer's lifetime's reading. It is a superb creation in which not a few of the preoccupations of the earlier poems are resolved. The change from the manner of the dream-visions was of course a fundamental one, yet it was also a relatively simple one, for if the dream-poem is imaginative fiction at a double remove through the sleep barrier, the *Canterbury Tales* is imaginative fiction at a double remove without the sleep barrier. Chaucer had discovered what Charles Lamb was much later to express in the words "the true poet dreams being awake". But there is this further difference: in the dream-poem the interest centres on the further remove, the dream experience. The narrative framework is less important. In the *Canterbury Tales* the interest is more evenly divided between the dramatic framework and interplay involving the pilgrims, and the tales themselves. For those readers who find the tales on the whole less interesting than the pilgrimage itself and the "sondry folk" going on it, the shift of emphasis is even more complete.

Moreover, Chaucer succeeded in dispensing with the mechanics and artificialities of the dream-poem without sacrificing any of its real merits. By including himself among the pilgrims Chaucer is able to retain that other self that contributed so much to the earlier poems, and to retain the pose there adopted. We saw its early maturing in the *House of Fame* and we now see the rich harvest in the tale of Sir Thopas. The poet-pilgrim, the maker of all the other tales, of the pilgrims even, of the very pilgrimage itself, is, as G. K. Chesterton pointed out, the only one who cannot tell a decent tale in verse. All he can do is to piece together what he can remember of those rhymed romances, whose style provided "the very true gallop"[60] of his earliest poems, and produce as much abominable doggerel as his fellow-pilgrims can stand.[61]

[59] *Sources and Analogues of Chaucer's Canterbury Tales*, ed. W. F. Bryan and G. Dempster, Chicago, 1941.

[60] Brewer, *Chaucer and Chaucerians*, p. 6.

[61] See G. K. Chesterton's excellent discussion of this episode in his *Chaucer*, London, 1932, Chap. I.

And when the disgusted Host puts an end to it with his characteristic

Namoore of this, for Goddes dignitee,[62]

Chaucer snatches the opportunity to "publish" what was probably the result of his most recent reading, his translation of the *Livre de Melibée et de Dame Prudence* of Renaud de Louens. He calls it, with ironic modesty, "a litel thyng in prose", but probably W. P. Ker expressed the modern reader's reaction to "The Tale of Melibee" more accurately when he called it "a thing incapable of life, under any process of interpretation, a lump of the most inert 'first matter' of medieval pedantry".[63] The irony is of the same kind as in Alceste's remark in the *Legend of Good Women*,

Al be hit that he kan nat wel endite,[64]

but the joke is so much larger. This, as Chesterton said, is "laughter in the grand style, *pace* Matthew Arnold";[65] and if the dream-poem gained something from its greater objectivity, its element of otherworldliness, this incident in the *Canterbury Tales* gains from the very opposite, its immediacy, the direct involvement of reader or audience, of poet and pilgrims. This is where fact and fiction, the poet making and the poem made, merge as they could not have done in the dream-poem, despite all Chaucer's attempts to elevate his dream experiences to the status of "preve".

And yet the particular arrangement of the *Canterbury Tales* still allows that further remove into worlds of make-believe in which Chaucer's reading could be put to such fruitful use. The tales-within-the-tale afford a method of escape into worlds of faerye, mythology, and wonder as marvellous as anything in the dream-visions, worlds in which animals talk, ladies change shape, rocks disappear, magic horses and rings function, and fairies walk. On the other hand, the world of love is subjected in the *Canterbury Tales* to a much closer and more critical scrutiny than ever it was in the daisy meadows and dream gardens of the earlier poems,

---

[62] *Canterbury Tales*, B² 2019.

[63] W. P. Ker, *Essays on Medieval Literature*, London, 1905, p. 78.

[64] *Legend of Good Women*, F 414.

[65] Chesterton, *Chaucer*, p. 20.

excepting only *Troilus and Criseyde*. The result is the varied literature of love in the *Canterbury Tales* in which Chaucer's considerable reading on the subject is reinforced by personal experience and mature observation, and we can see, with the earlier poems in mind, how much Chaucer's interest has shifted from allegory and abstraction to actuality, from books to real life, from *fine amour* to the whole gamut of love and sex which extends from the courtly romance of "The Knight's Tale" to the "harlotrie" of the Miller's and the Reeve's. Old January and young clerk Nicholas, Dorigen and Arveragus are the true heirs of Troilus and Criseyde, not Alceste and the heroines of the legends who somehow managed, almost anachronistically, to step in between.

But perhaps the true successor to the dream-poems is "The Nun's Priest's Tale"; not merely because, once more, Chaucer is concerned with dreams, but because it comes closest among the *Canterbury Tales* to what the earlier vision poems tried to do. The secret of "The Nun's Priest's Tale" is Chaucer's daring obliteration of the boundaries between animal fiction and the human truths it illustrates. It allows a constant changing of viewpoint and altering of dimensions which would have been much more awkward, if not unmanageable, in the semi-animal, semi-human world of the *House of Fame* or the *Parlement of Foules*. It allows the leaping to and fro between the cock and the hen, the husband and wife, the courtly hero-lover and his paramour; it allows the mingling of the comic and the serious; the skirting along the edge of "tragedye" to the final, happy "solas" – the real answer to the Monk's gloomy tirade which went before. Chaucer found in the course of his reading the ancient Aesopian fable of the fox and the crow metamorphosed into the medieval story of the fox and the cock, possibly in the *Ysopet* of Marie de France, more likely in the French *Roman de Renart*, and he made it the vehicle not merely for an impressive display of learning, but, more importantly, for the expression of a genially ironic view of life organised in a wholly delightful poem.

In "The Nun's Priest's Tale" something remains of the oblique vision of the earlier poems in which the dream was a door to faerye and to allegory, to the garden of love and to some of the mysteries of life, seen as through a glass. "The Nun's Priest's

Tale" is no longer a dream-poem, but Chauntecleer's dream is central to it: the debate on dreams still goes on, as does that other one concerning authority and "olde bokes" *versus* empiricism. Chauntecleer represents the former; he fires off a heavy fusillade of authorities and examples to prove the "significacioun" not only of his dreams but of all dreams:

> By God, men may in olde bookes rede
> Of many a man moore of auctorite
> Than evere Caton was, so moot I thee,
> That al the revers seyn of this sentence,
> And han wel founden by experience
> That dremes been significaciouns
> As wel of joye as of tribulaciouns
> That folk enduren in this lif present.
> Ther nedeth make of this noon argument;
> The verray preeve sheweth it in dede.[66]

Experience and proof are still subservient to "olde bookes", and with this wholly bookish view the practical hen, Pertelote, cannot agree. Her point of view is rather that of the Wife of Bath:

> Experience, though noon auctoritee
> Were in this world, is right ynogh for me.[67]

Nevertheless, she (or rather Chaucer) was familiar with the textbooks on medieval science and is capable both of diagnosing the nature of Chauntecleer's "sweven" and of prescribing the appropriate remedy. As far as the dream is concerned, either disputant could be indeed right, for "Pertelote's contentions are well founded when the dream is a *somnium naturale*; Chauntecleer's claims are undeniable when the vision is a true *somnium coeleste*".[68] The end of the poem proves Chauntecleer right, yet it is characteristic of Chaucer's mature poetic achievement that somehow, as in the dénouement of "The Knight's Tale", he reconciles the seemingly irreconcilable and leaves his reader persuaded that Pertelote was right too. For if we are anxious about the fate of the

---

[66] "The Nun's Priest's Tale", B² 4164-73.
[67] "The Wife of Bath's Prologue", D 1-2.
[68] Curry, *Chaucer and the Mediaeval Sciences*, p. 220.

lovable, conceited, chicken-livered cock, we are caught up no less in sympathy for his favourite hen as, at the end

> sovereynly dame Pertelote shrighte
> Ful louder than dide Hasdrubales wyf,
> Whan that hir housbonde hadde lost his lyf.[69]

It is because Chaucer was no longer dealing with abstractions in the *Canterbury Tales* but with people that such reconciliation becomes possible, even where, as in "The Nun's Priest's Tale", the people are farmyard fowls. In this tale Chaucer is still speaking figuratively, albeit in mock-heroic mode, but his art is no longer confined within the bounds of his earlier reading of love allegories and dream-visions. The pretty May-garden of the *Roman de la Rose* has become the poor widow's yard, and just beyond the make-believe world in which Chauntecleer reigns over his harem like a royal prince or a "grym leoun", there is a cabbage patch with a preying fox lurking in it and the real world of frugal meals and hard country chores in which the capture of a barnyard fowl by a marauding fox is a major catastrophe. The difference between "The Nun's Priest's Tale" and the dream-poems is that there is no curtain of sleep to divide these worlds. The world of imagination, in which animals talk and in which they behave not only like ordinary beings but like extraordinary ones, and the "real" world of poverty and hard work and suffering and treachery and vanity and absurdity – and comedy – are after all one and indivisible. Hence there is no going to sleep at the beginning of "The Nun's Priest's Tale" and no awakening at the end; hence there are no boundaries between the learned cock's disquisitions on dreams and his strutting about the barnyard pecking at the corn. Life and learning, books and experience, have become one.

"The Nun's Priest's Tale" may thus be regarded as one of the summits of Chaucer's artistic career in its fusion of fantasy and realism, of animal fable and human truth, of "auctoritee" and experience. It illustrates *in parvo* the achievement of the *Canterbury Tales* as a whole, the inimitable Chaucerian harmony of book-learning and of a genial, tolerant, but nonetheless penetrating, view of humanity. The brief glimpse at the end of the *House of Fame* of "shipmen and pilgrimes" had become the broad vision of

[69] "The Nun's Priest's Tale", B² 4552-4.

the Canterbury pilgrimage. And if we look in vain for the naïve other self in "The Nun's Priest's Tale" it is because of all the pilgrims the Nun's Priest answers most clearly to our impression of the genuine Geoffrey Chaucer: not the dull-witted dreamer who could not "endite", nor the "elvish", bookish, abstracted pilgrim who perpetrated the tale of Sir Thopas and went to town on "Melibee", but the witty, genial, learned man whose imprint is stamped like a trademark on his poetry. In the "General Prologue" the Nun's Priest has no portrait; in the links preceding and following his tale we learn only a little about him, and Harry Bailly the Host is not the most reliable of informers. His reference in the Epilogue to "this gentil preest" as perhaps a bit of a lady-killer[70] may be no more than a sly dig at the priest's travelling in attendance upon the lady Prioress. We learn little of his looks and less of his character from these few lines. But we learn much about his wit and skill, his tolerance and genial optimism and, not least, his wide reading and rich learning, from his tale. Paradoxically, the Nun's Priest's story of the farmyard animals is perhaps the most human of all Chaucer's Canterbury tales. And it is no coincidence surely that so many of the seeds scattered throughout the earlier poems have come to fruition in this poem: the speculations about dreams; the "debate" between authority and experience; the connexion between realistic truth and imaginative truth; the reading of all those books in English and Latin and French and Italian over which "Chaucer's mind moved like a magnet";[71] and not least the creation of character, as in the inimitable portrait of Chauntecleer which combines the learned pedantry of the eagle in the *House of Fame* and the garrulousness of the goose in the *Parlement* with the comic humanity of Pandarus. Chaucer had come a long way, and his reading both in his "olde bokes" and in the pages of experience had borne rich fruit indeed.[72]

[70] Epilogue to "The Nun's Priest's Tale", B² 4637-49.

[71] Lowes, *Geoffrey Chaucer*, p. 114.

[72] It is a pleasure to acknowledge my indebtedness to Miss P. R. Eaden for assistance with this chapter.

Francis Lee Utley

CHAUCER AND
PATRISTIC EXEGESIS[1]

At first, faced with so controversial a book as Robertson's *A Preface to Chaucer*,[2] one is tempted to dismiss it simply as a strange hodgepodge of patristics and puzzle-solving, insulting to the community of scholars and, indeed, to the twentieth century itself. Of two major reviews that came my way some time ago, Robert O. Payne's finds the book "neither logically compelling nor rhetorically convincing".[3] The author of the other, R. E. Kaske, is vastly more sympathetic, being one of our leading patristic exegetes; but his gentle charges of philological deficiency, failure to see Chaucer's human commitment to his characters, facile polarities, and ironies with nothing to ironise are the more damning because he grants that Robertson's critics could do with more "first-hand acquaintance with the Biblical commentaries and other exegetical texts whose relevance they are disputing".[4] The book cannot therefore be dismissed with a word. Allegorical exegesis of medieval secular and religious poetry, which has pre-empted more than one session of the English Institute[5] and several Old English, Middle English, and Chaucer discussion groups of the

[1] [Reprinted from *Romance Philology*, xix (1965), pp. 250-60. Original title, "Robertsonianism Redivivus".]

[2] D. W. Robertson, Jr., *A Preface to Chaucer: Studies in Medieval Perspectives*, Princeton, 1962. See also the earlier discussions of Robertson's book in *Romance Philology* by J. Misrahi (xvii, pp. 555-69) and W. Matthews (xvii, pp. 634-42).

[3] R. O. Payne, *Comparative Literature*, xv (1963), pp. 269-71.

[4] R. E. Kaske, *E.L.H.*, xxx (1963), pp. 175-92.

[5] See *Critical Approaches to Medieval Literature: Selected Papers from the English Institute, 1958-9*, ed. Dorothy Bethurum, New York, 1960, pp. 1-82.

69

Modern Language Association, is apparently here to stay whether we like it or not. It shares its viability with Jungian archetypes, myth criticism, personae, configurations, social realism, and other post-Hegelian modernities.

The book is massive, comprehensive, provocative, and infuriating. It demands honest summary, though such summary is difficult. The title itself is misleading: the perspective is Robertsonian rather than medieval, and Chaucer, though a leitmotif, receives no proper preface. The final paragraph puts us off with the following promise:

> So far as Chaucer is concerned, we may as well recognize the fact that he was a Christian poet. Not much has been said in this book about his artistry, except in passing. But if we consider the aesthetic presuppositions of his time, the stylistic limitations of his work, and the literary techniques he inherited from the classical traditions and from St. Paul, we should be in a position to judge the artistry with which he presented what he had to say to his own audience. That, however, is a subject for another volume.[6]

But it is this volume which is before us. If I approach it in my own way, as a proper division of labour with Payne and Kaske and a cloud of other witnesses, I hope Robertson in his besieged Joyous Garde may forgive me. There will be some chaffing since chaff is a form of charity.

The first chapter, on "Medieval and Modern Art", is overtly anti-modernist, though it uses a number of clichés from modern criticism. Robertson seems unaware that three decades of New Humanists and New Critics have avowed anti-romanticism; though Murray Krieger and Frank Kermode have seen the demon lurking in the underwater portion of the iceberg.[7] He further assumes that his critics are uninterested in allegory or patristic exegesis. While it is true that some of us might prefer St Augustine and John the Scot to the *Glossa Ordinaria*,[8] simply because they might be more the equals of the Dante, Boccaccio, and Chaucer they are supposed

[6] Robertson, *A Preface to Chaucer*, p. 503.

[7] Murray Krieger, *The New Apologists for Poetry*, Minneapolis, 1956; Frank Kermode, *Romantic Image*, London, 1957.

[8] See *Patrologia Latina*, p. 114, col. 94.

to have influenced, we must make it very clear that patristics has, for twenty years, been a major ancilla to secular interpretation and criticism. It is Robertson's attitude and results which disturb us. When a scholar declares: "I have found out something interesting which I would like you to share with me", we listen. But when a Jungian or a Robertsonian says, "I have special and arcane knowledge and I will make utterance, though I doubt whether you have the experience or the erudition to follow me", we are likely to take him at his word and turn away.

In the Introduction Robertson calls the roll of modern heresies: aesthetic relativism, evolutionism, Zeitgeist, Hegelian polarities, Marxism, romanticism. For all these he would substitute a nostalgically simple medieval world-picture of order and hierarchy. The "paganism" of *Beowulf* and of twelfth-century Platonism is a delusion; paganism is simply the proper placing of the fleshly and the obscene in the Great Chain of Being, for the Middle Ages are neither Puritanical nor Manichean. Yet the two loves, *cupiditas* and *caritas*, resist synthesis or reconciliation; the upward ascent is not by Hegelian dialectic but only by grace. Above all, the Middle Ages do not seek, as modernity does, for aberrant states of mind: "In William Faulkner's *The Hamlet*, for instance, a work of undeniable artistic merit and considerable moral gravity, we are led to respond sympathetically to an idiot's amorous affection for a cow".[9] Finally the chapter contains a summary of the reasons why medieval literature is neither dramatic nor dialectic: its strong emotion is stylised, its conventional language evokes thought rather than emotion, its objective accounts of a psychological state like the lover's malady lack affective value, and dramatic action and tensions are absent.

Chapter II, on "Some Principles of Medieval Aesthetics", sounds a disagreement with the "imbalances" of de Bruyne's neglect of St Augustine.[10] Medieval allegory and exegesis are intellectual, not affective; their goal is wisdom, not eloquence – the solution to an enigma rather than exaltation. Masculine Reason is preferred to feminine Sensuality; beauty is for instruction only in the avoidance of the Triple Temptation: suggestion, delectation, consent. Andreas Capellanus, Chrétien de

[9] Robertson, p. 42.
[10] E. de Bruyne, *Etudes d'esthétique médiévale*, 3 vols., Bruges, 1946.

Troyes, Guillaume de Lorris, and Jean de Meun were talking not about courtly love, but about the Triple Temptation. Since neither Palamon nor Arcite is a "courtly" lover, "The Knight's Tale" is didactic in purpose. Arcite meets his death "through the action of an infernal fury (a wrathful passion) sent up by Pluto (Saturn) at the instigation of Saturn (Time, who consumes his 'children'), who was, in turn, prompted by Venus (Concupiscence)".[11] One wonders why Palamon, the real idolater, who identified Emily with Venus, managed to save his life and get the girl. Apparently half an allegory is better than none.

Equally didactic is "The Merchant's Tale". None of us would disagree that January is full of "delectatio cogitationis". Yet, though the old man urges himself on with Dan Constantyne's aphrodisiacs and with all the "consent" in the world, we see no performance in him. One wonders what this may mean, allegorically. Once more proceeding to the nature of beauty with St Augustine as a Dantean guide, Robertson discusses its relationship to order, proportion, harmony, symmetry, numerology, and the music of the spheres. Symbolic of a lower order of music are the Olde Daunce and the bagpipe, the latter a kind of obscene visual pun, with iconographic as well as Chaucerian examples.

In the next chapter, on "Late Medieval Style", the author provides a thoroughly illuminating account of the juncture between poetry and the plastic arts, icon and topos. Samson, Hercules, and Ulysses become types of Christ in the Romanesque period, with its skilled use of the classics, its lack of affectation and its realism, its formalism and its artificiality. Monsters and gargoyles symbolise the beastly sins, the souls devoid of reason. Though Robertson slightly confuses the chronology by a long illustration from the fourteenth-century Robert Holcot, he proceeds successfully to other Romanesque traits: lack of subjective feeling, the limits of the frame, the intentional lack of perspective. The climactic literary parallel, the *Chanson de Roland*, is convincing. Next we have a section on Gothic, which stresses order and organisation, increased didacticism, and a very flexible new iconography. A little dog, symbolic of sensuality, emerges from the art of the period. Surprisingly enough, Robertson has

[11] Robertson, p. 110.

not tied him to Tristram's Petitcrieu,[12] whose very name seems significant of the *ragerie* of the iconic canine. The *Roman de la Rose* climaxes the section. Finally we have the English fourteenth century, with new Perpendicular icons, and a treatment of Chaucer's English, French, and Italian literary background, and of icon and figura in the *Canterbury Tales*. Chaucer's genius transcends his age in his turn to Romance versification, his easy colloquial rhythms, his wealth of significant (allegorical) detail, his unfailing sense of humour, which derives from true detachment and not from a modern "release of tension".[13] Likewise Chaucerian are his "Englishness", his conservatism, his exuberance and informality, his implicit rather than explicit unities, his digressiveness, his preference of the virtuous to the heroic. Though we may cavil at details, particularly in the last pieces of Chaucerian Englishry, since it is hard to square with Chaucer's uniqueness as a writer of English *fabliaux*, uncommon until the sixteenth century, I am convinced that this is Robertson's best chapter. Perhaps it is because he has been able, for the moment at least, to abandon certain fixed positions, certain clichés of approach, into which his earlier articles[14] had trapped him. From the plastic arts he has received a fresh impulse which is less destructive to critical judgment than the unitary doctrine of cupidity and charity.

With the fourth chapter, "Allegory, Humanism, and Literary Theory", we return to the *parti pris*. Why do we moderns distrust allegory? We like "symbolism" better; we think humanism is opposed to allegory (are not Petrarch, Ficino, and Erasmus humanists?); our modern philological methods cannot detect allegory or irony; and we think medieval allegory was discarded by the Renaissance (though its origins are classical and its life in

[12] Gottfried von Strassburg, *Tristan*, tr. A. T. Hatto, Baltimore (1960), pp. 249-56 (section 24).

[13] Robertson, p. 277.

[14] *E.g.* "Historical Criticism", *English Institute Essays, 1950*, ed. A. S. Downer, New York (1951), pp. 3-31; "Some Medieval Terminology, with special reference to Chrétien de Troyes", *Studies in Philology*, XLVIII (1951), pp. 669-92; "The Doctrine of Charity in Mediaeval Literary Gardens: A Topical Approach through Symbolism and Allegory", *Speculum*, XXVI (1951), pp. 24-49; "The Subject of the *De amore* of Andreas Capellanus", *Modern Philology*, L (1953), pp. 145-61; "Why the Devil wears Green", *Modern Language Notes*, LXIX (1954), pp. 470-2.

the Renaissance was vigorous). To properly inform us (and he does so, though he misses Philo Judaeus in the genealogy of allegory), Robertson discusses the commitments of St Paul, Christian Platonism, St Augustine, John the Scot, St Thomas Aquinas, Robert Holcot, Richard de Bury, and Berchorius. Countering the claim of Robert Frank,[15] Morton Bloomfield,[16] and others that the later Middle Ages saw a decline of multi-levelled spiritual interpretations, he discounts the Aristotelian lack of friendliness toward certain kinds of exegesis and asserts the value of patristic allegory for Chaucer. He provides a welcome discussion of Chaucer's four exegetes: the Wife of Bath, "rigorously carnal and literal";[17] the Summoner's Friar, who "represents hypocrisy";[18] the Pardoner, typifying "those who deny the spirit of Christ beneath the letter of the text *radix malorum est cupiditas*";[19] and the Parson, who "neither reads his text carnally, abuses the spirit for his own interest, nor denies the validity of the spirit beneath the letter".[20] Apparently the Parson makes all clear, and there is no suggestion that the other three could be taken as satires on exegesis, or even as Chaucerian rejection of exegetical extremes. No doubt it is merely a failing of modern philology if we observe that one ought to give more weight to the authority of the Wife and the Pardoner, two of Chaucer's most original creations, than to "The Parson's Tale", which some of us still believe to be essentially raw material, not yet transformed by the Chaucerian spirit.

The next section, on Christian Humanism, purports to enlighten us about the Christian knowledge of pagan allegory and the classics. The tone of a voice crying in the wilderness and the lack of footnotes might give the impression that E. K. Rand's *Founders of the Middle Ages* had never been written. Augustine, Jerome, and John of Salisbury saved the classics for us; they even saved Ovid. Dante, Gerson, and Chaucer are all aware of the rescue: "Taketh the fruyt, and lat the chaff be stille". As far as Chaucer is

[15] R. W. Frank, "The Art of Reading Medieval Personification-Allegory", *E.L.H.*, xx (1953), pp. 237-50.

[16] M. W. Bloomfield, "Symbolism in Medieval Literature", *Modern Philology*, lvi (1958), pp. 73-81.

[17] Robertson, p. 321.   [18] *Op. cit.*, p. 331.

[19] *Op. cit.*, p. 334.   [20] *Op. cit.*, p. 336.

concerned, we are reprobate enough to suggest that there is a good deal of humour in most of the passages cited and that, in any event, the fruit is always mere morality, the tropological, rather than the anagogical or the allegorical. But on Chaucer's icono-graphy we can give Robertson good marks; nor can we cavil at this manifesto:

> A medieval poet had at his disposal various sources of figurative material: scriptural signs and concepts, moralized natural history from non-scriptural sources, and figurative materials derived from mythography or astrology and from commentaries on the classics. In addition, iconographic materials . . . were sometimes used for literary purposes.[21]

In the later Middle Ages we must distinguish between humanistic, jocular, and Rabelaisian allegory, and theological allegory resting squarely on the Scriptures.

The last chapter is almost wholly composed of Robertson's earlier articles. Its first section attacks the entire concept of courtly love, denying its presence at the court of Champagne or its espousal by Andreas Capellanus.[22] Andreas is neither a sentimentalist nor a technician of love like Vatsyana; he is orthodox (*pace* Father Denomy)[23] and a Christian humanist whose dialogues are a subtle and ironic attack on concupiscence and the love he has been thought to admire. As if this reading did not suffice to submerge deluded moderns, we are provided with another, more catastrophic still, of Chrétien's *Chevalier de la charrette*. "Gorre" means "vanity",[24] and thus the land to which Guenevere was abducted is no medieval otherworld but an abstraction for didactic purposes. (The conventional Arthurian interpretation of the place-name may be wrong: but it is charac-teristic of Robertson that he does not bother to cite it even for refutation.) His kind of revisionism leaves us with little of the original Lancelot story, which was enough of a tale of passion to

---

[21] *Op. cit.*, p. 389.

[22] Andreas Capellanus, *The Art of Courtly Love*, tr. J. J. Parry, New York, 1941.

[23] A. J. Denomy, C. S. B., "The *De amore* of Andreas Capellanus and the Condemnation of 1277", *Mediaeval Studies*, VIII (1946), pp. 118-25.

[24] Robertson, p. 448.

evoke passionate love in Paolo and Francesca and compassion for lovers in Dante. Indeed, it is always interesting to see more charity in Dante than in a modern defender of *caritas* against *cupiditas*.

The *charrette* or gallows-cart is no longer a test of Lancelot's fidelity to Guenevere, a sublime medieval example of aristocratic sensitivity and refinement, a test forced by the dwarf carter on the unwilling nobleman; it is now mere sensual unreason, symbolic of Lancelot's criminal love. When Guenevere denies the charge of adultery with Kay, her märchen-like equivocality and inconsistency vanish, and she is made by implication to condemn at the same time Lancelot's love. Lancelot's bird-lover rendezvous with Guenevere is a clerical exemplum; his perilous fiery bed and the wound in his thigh lose their folklore character and become "an indication of the heat and vigor of his passion"[25] – all on the strength of a short polemic exegesis from St Jerome. Again we have only half an allegory; since Lancelot is *alone* in his perilous bed, might we not more properly allude to St Paul's counsel that it is better to marry than to burn? Though at war with modernity, Robertson is not unwilling to borrow from certain fashionable kinds of contemporary myth criticism. Lancelot "is an inverted Redeemer who shows others how to live vainly without incurring social ostracism".[26] "Our own difficulties with Chrétien's romance arise from the fact that we insist on reading it 'as a story', so that we become vicariously involved in the hero's 'adventures' and so lose the exemplary force of the narrative".[27] Thus the Age of Adventure had no adventures, and the *roman d'aventure* is a mere delusion, a simple exemplum.

So perverse are his views that Robertson is forced to treat a fairly obvious fact as meriting surprise: "It may be true that young men who vied with one another in an effort to be courteous and amorous may have sometimes abused their graces in a quest for physical satisfaction".[28] It may, indeed! A strange sort of society in which young men would not be lusty, whatever the restraints of *fin amors* or clerical counsel. The *Lai du lecheor* was written to satirise false courtesy, says Robertson, though it is hard to see how we can have parody either here or in Andreas of a non-

[25] *Op. cit.*, p. 451.   [26] *Op. cit.*, p. 452.
[27] *Ibid.*   [28] *Op. cit.*, p. 453.

existent courtly love.[29] At last he grows aware of some such thing, and begins to admit a sort of "courteous" love; we may even call it "courtly" provided we do not confuse it with the "romantic love celebrated by poets in the nineteenth century".[30] Chaucer, however, displays little "courteous love". It is seriously treated only in the *Book of the Duchess*, which is no elegy for John of Gaunt's Blanche, but an allegorical debate between the dreamer Reason and the sorrowing Heart. "The Knight's Tale" laughs at Palamon and Arcite's love and "The Miller's Tale" laughs at Absalon; the point of "The Reeve's Tale" is much the same. We had thought that the three represented a striking example of Chaucerian ironic contrast; instead they are identical in purpose. We find the same dull grey mass of identity in the Marriage Group, where Franklin, Merchant, and Wife of Bath all share the same worship of the God of love. *Troilus and Criseyde* is "neither a tale of true love, what Jehan called love 'par amours', nor of courteous love. It is, rather, a tale of passionate love set against a background of Boethian philosophy".[31]

And so we come to Robertson's climactic piece of applied exegetical criticism, a reduction of one of the world's great tales of true love to a simple *De casibus* story with philosophical overtones. This is a rifacimento of his devastating article on "Chaucerian Tragedy".[32] A few illustrations are changed, a few crudities altered, and the place of Fortune at the outset is slightly shifted in emphasis. But we still move relentlessly in the "new "version, topic sentence by topic sentence, to the same moralistic reduction of the poem as in the earlier article. It must be one of the most wrong-headed pieces of criticism since Thomas Rymer wrote about *Othello*.

Troilus is a slave to the God of Love, a traitor to his sense of duty. Pandarus, though "a masterpiece of medieval irony",[33] is a devil, a priest of Satan.[34] His moving apologia is a mere "senti-

[29] See Kaske's review, p. 189 ff.   [30] Robertson, p. 457.

[31] *Op. cit.*, p. 472.

[32] D. W. Robertson, Jr., "Chaucerian Tragedy", *E.L.H.*, XIX (1952), pp. 1-37.

[33] Robertson, p. 479.

[34] Robertson does show some appreciation of Charlotte d'Evelyn's attack on the above article in "Pandarus a Devil?", *P.M.L.A.*, LXXI (1956), pp. 275-9, for he now declares: "Pandarus is neither a devil nor a man, but an element in

mental statement",[35] and Troilus's ingenuous offering of his own sisters represents savage irony. Criseyde's honour is but "the honor of appearances",[36] a remarkable failure to appreciate the skilful semantic development of this ambiguous word *honour* throughout the poem. Her "Who yaf me drynke?"[37] marks no sudden response to external stimulus but calculated self-will. "Ultimately, her love is a self-love that seeks the favor of Fortune".[38] Chaucer's magnanimous, valorous, "worthy" Troilus is another narcissist: "The pleasure he finds in Criseyde's bed has become the center of his universe, a center that actually rests within himself".[39] A somewhat Freudian interpretation for a devoted anti-modernist! Robertson's hierarchical probing continues, and Troilus's noble apostrophe to Criseyde's house, the "shryne, of which the seynt is oute",[40] is reduced to a pun on "queynt", to an "empty inverted church of Troilus' love".[41] Criseyde's defence of her love for Troilus, which she declares was based not on his "estat roial, Ne veyn delit" but only on "moral vertu, grounded upon trouthe",[42] is taken as mere "elevated doctrine" perverted into "so much idle talk".[43]

In adversity Troilus becomes the

> "aimlessly drifting megalopolitan man" of the modern philosophers, the frustrated, neurotic, and maladjusted hero of modern fiction, an existentialist for whom Being itself, which he has concentrated in his own person, becomes dubious. He is hypersensitive, sentimental, a romantic hopelessly involved in a lost cause.[44]

This, like narcissism of the hero and heroine, is a strange characterisation from one who wishes to view Chaucer only through the eyes of the *Glossa Ordinaria* and fourteenth-century aesthetics.

a poem" (p. 479). But he cites neither Miss d'Evelyn's article nor the *Middle English Dictionary* entry, s.v. *devel* 6c (Part D3, p. 1054), which confirms her philological predictions.

[35] Robertson, p. 489.   [36] *Op. cit.*, p. 484.

[37] *Troilus and Criseyde*, II, 651, *The Works of Geoffrey Chaucer*, ed. F. N. Robinson, 2nd edn., London, 1957.

[38] Robertson, p. 486.   [39] *Op. cit.*, p. 493.

[40] *Troilus and Criseyde*, V, 553.   [41] Robertson, p. 500.

[42] *Troilus and Criseyde*, IV, 1672.   [43] Robertson, p. 496.

[44] *Op. cit.*, p. 497.

How was this stumbling and defective hero ever granted the anagnorisis of the Epilogue, the cosmic irony and self-revelation which came in the eighth sphere? Yet this opinion does not prevent Robertson from setting the ten final stanzas, some of them ambivalent and some humorous, in the scales against the whole remaining poem, in which youthful love is seen in all its glory and in the agony of its inevitable end, where pagan and worldly dust and ashes in Book v long precede Chaucer's search for Christian consolation in the complex Epilogue. With all this distortion of character and action it is significant that Diomede alone gains approval: "He takes Criseyde by the 'reyne', and for a short time the little filly will be his. . . . Like Polonius or Iago, Diomede is a man true to himself".[45]

Though the foregoing summary condemns Robertson in his own words, a formal statement on a few of his methodological flaws seems desirable:

(1) If one confronts moderns with their philological blindness, one should provide some kind of contemporary evidence from the time being reinterpreted. With the notable exception of the Letter to Can Grande ascribed to Dante,[46] the authenticity of which is still being questioned, there is no contemporary evidence for consciously contrived religious allegory of secular poetry. Nor is Dante, of course, writing a secular poem such as *Troilus and Criseyde*. Robertson does provide many statements from the early Fathers about exegesis of scripture, and others which show how medieval exegetes moralised classical works like Ovid, the Physiologus, and the tales in the *Gesta Romanorum*, to save them for their own brand of modernity. The best bridge to a conscious Chaucerian scriptural allegory which he can adduce is a few passages which demonstrate that Chaucer joked about such exegesis, and some transparent glossing in "The Parson's Tale". The method which pretends to be medieval, in short, provides no genuine medieval evidence for secular poems centring on patristic exegesis.

(2) Because of his antagonism to the scholars' "conspiracy", Robertson neglects almost every writer who might disagree with

[45] *Ibid.*
[46] See *A Translation of the Latin Works of Dante Alighieri*, London, 1904, p. 343 ff. (Epistle X).

him. There is no confrontation, no use of the giants on whose shoulders we rest. The perverse view is offered as fresh discovery. Thus, writing on heroic love,[47] he fails to mention John Livingston Lowes' famous article,[48] which would have demonstrated that the malady in Chaucer and in the courtly love tradition was deadly serious to medical men from Galen to Robert Burton. He cites the physicians but only to show how ugly a thing love is; he seems unaware how strange physicians are as bedfellows to theologians. The whole problem of courtly love is never confronted with the systematic body of evidence which Sidney Painter provided from noblewomen, courtiers, clerics, and life itself.[49]

(3) Except for the useful chapter on iconography the entire book is an extended use of the genetic fallacy. Since allegorical treatment in the times of St Paul and St Augustine primarily served the purpose of scriptural exegesis and moral intent, it must be the same in Chaucer's time. Though anything like conventional use of sources is eschewed as philological folly, the study equates throughout the source with its product. *Glossa Ordinaria*, *Piers Plowman*, Andreas, *Charrette*, *Troilus*, and the *Canterbury Tales* all become a charitable doctrine about gardens.

(4) Some selection tightening the unity of a book is a legitimate endeavour. The study of allegory and patristics can be of high value in revealing a poem we have long read with our eye on other elements. What is the difference between selection for emphasis and thoroughgoing reductionism? Selection is innocuous, if labelled for what it is. Sometimes, as when Farnham shows us the continuity of medieval tragedy in Elizabethan times, we are greatly enlightened;[50] at other times, as with a dissertation on Anglo-Saxon fishhooks in *Beowulf*, we are saved by the gift of sleep. In contrast, the reductionist claims that his part is the whole, that his new salient is the road to the riddle which has baffled centuries of the blind. Thus one commentator finds a vegetation deity in every medieval poem worth noting, another

---

[47] Robertson, p. 458.

[48] "The Loveres Maladye of Hereos", *Modern Philology*, XI (1913-14), pp. 491-546.

[49] *French Chivalry: Chivalric Ideas and Practices in France*, Baltimore, 1940.

[50] W. Farnham, *The Medieval Heritage of Elizabethan Tragedy*, Oxford, 1956.

discovers that *Hamlet* and *Little Red Riding Hood* are all Oedipal, yet another rescues *Boris Godunov* for Marxist-Leninism or makes Andreas, *Lancelot*, and *Troilus* into equally tedious exempla. If we really want to ascertain what allegorically-minded monks could do to a secular poem when they wished to increase its spiritual potential we have only to look at the *Queste del Saint Graal* and the *Perlesvaus*, as well as at Malory, who does his best to reinstate Lancelot as a Grail knight, and to diminish the role of his son Galahad. As John Lawlor has remarked, when Langland wants his words to bear a second meaning, "he is careful to point out the true gloss"; in the main he lets the literal sense bear the central meaning.[51] And as Kaske further observes, the burlesque elements in *Aucassin* and *Gawain* and "Sir Thopas" lose their point if what they are burlesquing is already ironic, already full of double vision.[52] Robertson throws out the baby with the bath; the reduction is complete.

It may be our Hegelian and Freudian commitments which lead us to take irony and paradox as double vision and multivalence, as evidence of our own complex and frustrating sets of values and disvaluations. Robertson would set against this the clear hierarchy of medieval values and a plain antiphrastic irony which merely says the opposite of what it means, with some help from exegetical obliquity. Yet it is certain that Robertson is himself full of paradoxes which, unless he is more malicious than we think, are unconscious and uncontrolled. Let us look at some of them.

We have already seen how he provides an apparatus of irony with nothing to be ironic about. Rebuking us for applying our prejudices to the Middle Ages, he commends that period for applying its own to Scripture and the classics. While putting humour into Andreas, more than ever was there, he carefully extracts it from Chaucer, who has some reputation for being a wit. His essay on *Troilus*, for instance, ignores the prankish reverse moral of v, 1772-85, in which a poem about woman's fickleness and man's fidelity suddenly turns into a warning about wicked men. Whatever this passage may mean, it certainly asks us to pause in our weighing of the complex envoy and epilogue which is imminent. Robertson's Middle Ages had no "tensions",

[51] *Piers Plowman: An Essay in Criticism*, London, 1962, pp. 249-58, 261.
[52] See Kaske, p. 189 ff.

yet medieval Latin poetry is the showplace of paradox and serious wit, Christian dualism always threatens to become Manicheanism, and the struggles of Lancelot's valour with love and of Gawain's courtesy with chastity are as tense as any struggle in Faulkner or Hemingway.[53] Robertson does not, in Augustinian fashion, confine himself to the dark passages of Scripture in need of moral and doctrinal explication; rather he seems to make dark the clear passages of Chaucer and Chrétien.

His predilection for puzzle-solving makes him succumb, through that branch of the lust of the eyes known as curiosity, to the second of his own favourite Triple Temptations: the puzzle syndrome used by Irving Babbitt to be called the lust for knowledge, a sin of conventional literary historians. Perhaps these peerings beneath the surfaces also are allied to the lust of the flesh, an undue preoccupation with the obscene. The saint of Troilus's shrine is a mere tabooed word. The "soft, red lips" of Chaucer's Prioress and her Ovidian brooch place her directly among the daughters of Venus, an interpretation which would have shocked equally Sister Mary Madeleva[54] and Professor Lowes,[55] and which critically cancels out the gentle and throttled increase in satire marking the opening set of portraits in the "General Prologue". Chaucer's Monk, whose passions for rich clothes, administration, and hunting do not suffice to condemn him, becomes a lecher also, following ambiguous meanings of *priking* and *venerie*, and *hunting for the hare*.[56] One wonders what Robertson would do to the first line of *The Faerie Queene*.

But of course the shock is ours, not that of Chaucer's contemporaries. Since medieval obscenity is hierarchical, says Robertson, it brought no blush to any maiden's countenance. We agree; any study of grotesque sculpture or wood-carving demonstrates the point, settled long ago. The attitudes of Puritanism and Jansenism towards art are fairly well-known; there is a genuine danger in transposing these to the Middle Ages. We owe a great debt to Robertson for his 118 illustrations, re-

---

[53] On medieval "polarities" see Kaske, pp. 185-8.

[54] Sister Mary Madeleva, *Chaucer's Nuns and Other Essays*, New York, 1925.

[55] J. L. Lowes, "Simple and Coy: A Note on Fourteenth Century Poetic Diction", *Anglia*, XXXIII (1910), pp. 440-51.

[56] "General Prologue", A 166, 191.

produced with the skill the Princeton University Press has lavished on Michelangelo, Ghiberti, and the Dome. But surely the medieval hierarchy is violated in some fashion when almost half of the illustrations involve an obscenity (I count at least 48 examples, but being unskilled in eye I may have missed some suggestion, which has deprived me of delectation without consent). This raises a scholarly problem about balance and emphasis. I am afraid I shall never be able to look at a bagpipe again without blushing.

There is a final paradox. Each historical scholar hopes that he may by his own special insights and searchings achieve a better view of the past than his fellows. He may legitimately emphasise *contrast* between epochs or *continuity* from one epoch to another. Since Robertson charges our epoch with being Hegelian, romantic, and therefore subjective, we are in grave danger of choosing the second course, and finding more equation between the Middle Ages and our own age than we should. But in choosing the way of contrast Robertson has not avoided subjectivity. The Middle Ages becomes an Eden, where sensual passages in poetry and sensual representations in art are made morally acceptable parts of the hierarchy, didactically justified allegories. There is some insight here, though it is doubtful whether the Master Architect approved all the designs on the choir-boys' misericords. No doubt the Edenic medieval man might escape peril, but the medievalist who dwells on these matters too closely may be accused not only of the lust of flesh and eyes but also of that arrogance which is the pride of life.

One delusion of modern critics is that humanists distrust allegory, and that we, being humanists, must do the same. Robertson rightly cites Petrarch, Ficino, Erasmus, and Spenser against the position.[57] He might have dipped deeper into the mediocre and cited a preface (1526) to the *Roman de la Rose* which identifies de Lorris' Rose with sapience, grace, "la glorieuse vierge Marie", and "le souverain bien infiny et la gloire d'éternelle béatitude".[58] As late as the eighteenth century we find Dr Johnson complaining that critics

[57] Robertson, p. 286.
[58] *Critical Prefaces of the French Renaissance*, ed. B. Weinberg, Evanston, Ill., 1950, pp. 61-3.

discover in every passage some remote allusion, some artful allegory, or some occult intimation which no other reader ever suspected . . . but of all that engages the attention of others, they are totally insensible, while they pry into worlds of conjecture, and amuse themselves with phantoms in the clouds.[59]

One does not have to wait for Dr Johnson to find the practice both attested and condemned. In that delightful humanistic satire, the *Epistolae Obscurorum Virorum*, Friar Conrad Dollenkopf writes to Mag. Ortwin Gratius of his remarkable new discoveries in the use of the fourfold method. He can expound all the fables of Ovid "naturally, literally, historically, and spiritually", and "this is more than the secular poets can do". Mavors means "mares vorans", a "man-eater"; the Nine Muses are the Seven Choirs of Angels; Mercury or "mercatorum curius" is "the god of merchants, and curious concerning them". For Christian allegory of the kind favoured by Robertson, Friar Dollenkopf cites Thomas of Wales as authority. Diana is the Blessed Virgin, Jupiter's return after his amour with Callisto is recorded in the words of Matthew xii: "I will return to my house from whence I came out". Cadmus seeking his sister is Christ seeking the Church, and Actaeon beholding Diana well illustrates Robertson's "hierarchical" principle: "Thou wast bare and full of confusion, and I passed by and saw thee" (Ezekiel). "All this, and much more have I learned out of that book. If you were but with me you should behold marvellous things. And this is the way in which we ought to study Poetry".[60] Robertson's anti-humanistic model is plain.

Let me emphasise again that I have nothing against allegory, irony, epochal contrast, still less against the use of patristic scholarship. All of these have been long needed in the study of medieval literature, and much activity of the last fifteen or twenty years has been of high value. It is merely that we prefer St Augustine or Philo Judaeus to Friar Dollenkopf. Robertson's way of dealing with patristic influence on a secular literature does not

<hr />

[59] *Rambler*, No. 176, quoted by B. H. Bronson, *In Search of Chaucer*, Toronto, 1960, p. 9.

[60] Ed. and tr. F. G. Stokes, London, 1925, pp. 342-5 (Epistle I, p. 28).

seem to be a necessary and sufficient one. Conceivably, by arousing controversy, by appealing to the jigsawpuzzle and off-colour instincts of our students, by forcing startling paradoxes and making a tract for our own non-Babbitean times, he has awakened interest in patristic exegesis to a degree which conventional scholarship could never have achieved. The young need new slings annually to slay the Goliath of modern scholarship with his armoury of bibliographies. But the lure is dangerous, since novelty soon wears off, and the result may be either dull retracing of the central clichés or desertion of the field, both results equally unfortunate. We will have to give our students this book, with its amazing ingenuity and its equally amazing erudition, its audacious scope and its prejudices. Perhaps we may warn them against its claims of infallibility with a wise counsel from a much profounder theologian than either Robertson or myself, Nicolas Berdyaev:

> When a time revolts against eternity, the only thing to set against it is genuine eternity itself, and not some other time which has already roused, and not without reason, a violent reaction against itself.[61]

There is more than one way of looking at charity. Let us be charitable enough to say that Robertson's is one way.

[61] *The Russian Revolution*, Ann Arbor, Mich., 1961, p. 88.

James G. Southworth

CHAUCER'S PROSODY: A PLEA FOR
A RELIABLE TEXT[1]

The publication of Robinson's revised edition of *The Works of Geoffrey Chaucer* (1957), of Donaldson's *Chaucer's Poetry* (1958), and of Baugh's *Chaucer's Major Poetry* (1963) has made available to the teacher-scholar a great and convenient mass of textual and critical material. It would be difficult to overvalue the contributions of each of the above editors. They have given the teacher-scholar everything he needs *except* reliable texts of the poems; and by reliable texts I mean those based on a faithful reproduction of the spelling and punctuation of the manuscripts selected by the editor. The editor should not, as these editors have done, assume a certain prosodic base and then alter the texts to fit the base. Only faithfully reproduced texts permit the reader to discuss the possible nature of Chaucer's prosody – a prosody unlikely to be antagonistic to the speech rhythms of his day or to be isolated from the English tradition preceding, running concurrently with, or immediately following him.

The reason for the present unsatisfactory texts does not, of course, stem from the carelessness or incompetence of the editors, but from a nineteenth-century conception, or misconception, of editorial policy. Editor after editor has striven for the archetype – the original of Chaucer's poems, an archetype with a definite metrical basis. Since no manuscript poem in Chaucer's hand exists, and his poetry has been transmitted to us by scribes whose texts differ from one another in spelling, scribal marks, and even important readings of the texts themselves,

---

[1] [Reprinted, with revisions, from *College English*, XXVI (1964), pp. 173-9. Original title, "Chaucer: A Plea for a Reliable Text".]

editors have vainly sought the ideal original. Furthermore, they have accepted as their patterns for Chaucer's prosody, forms which have no proved basis of fact. They have not only added final -*e*'s where none exist in the manuscripts, but have frequently inserted words in their basic text or made transpositions. Such alterations, while making possible an iambic reading of the text, often ruin the rhythm which Chaucer could well have had in mind. Above all, they have ignored the presence of an important punctuation mark – the *punctus elevatus* (:') – in the best manuscripts.

The majority of teachers still accept the iambic theory and pronounce the final -*e*'s because the edited texts print them. What, I wonder, would these same teachers do with the evidence offered by facsimile texts of Additional 5140 (*Canterbury Tales*), or Harley 2392 (*Troilus and Criseyde*), or Bodleian Fairfax 16 (Minor Poems) where the final -*e*'s, whether in rhyme or within the line, are not so frequent? I am afraid they accept the edited texts as they find them and assume the infallibility of the editors. In truth, most editors have shown themselves to be less than infallible in the preparation of their texts by not taking fully into consideration the work done on Chaucer's language in recent years; in particular, they have tended to ignore the fact that final unaccented -*e* was in the process of disappearing from London English during the second half of the fourteenth century.

The iambic theory began to harden into scholarly dogma as a result of the work of Francis James Child.[2] When Child formulated his hypothesis that Chaucer wrote iambic decasyllables, he did so partly on the basis of a statement by Tyrwhitt that *Troilus* and "The Knight's Tale" were "juvenile productions"[3] and that Chaucer's model was, therefore, the Italian *endecasyllabo*. Moreover, Child assumed two things: (1) that final -*e* was *just beginning* to disappear, and (2) that the Italian *endecasyllabo* was a verse made up of regular iambic feet ending with an unaccented syllable. He made it abundantly clear that he thought he was capturing

[2] F. J. Child, "Observations on the Language of Chaucer", *Memoirs of the American Academy*, N.S., VIII (1863), p. 445 ff.; rearranged and abridged by A. J. Ellis, *Early English Pronunciation*, Early English Text Society, 1867, I, pp. 342-97.

[3] Thomas Tyrwhitt, "An Essay on the Language and Versification of Chaucer", in his edition of the *Canterbury Tales*, 5 vols., 1775-8; frequently reprinted.

Chaucer's speech rhythms, "puerile" though they seemed to his ear.[4]

As Child was aware, no Chaucer poem in manuscript could be scanned as iambic decasyllables without considerable emendation. The metrical game was now on in all seriousness and with a determined search for the truth. Unfortunately, as Saintsbury has remarked: "a so-called 'critical' text, with its pickings from this manuscript and that, or its reconstruction of a single one according to manufactured rules, may to some extent restore prosodic system, but will always be subject to the doubt whether it in the least resembles what the poet wrote".[5] He also castigated the German tendency to classify everything. This tendency reached the height of absurdity in Ten Brink's *Chaucers Sprache und Verskunst* (1884), where he laid down the rule that every line in Chaucer which did not scan as a regular iambic line (no anapaestic substitutions allowed) should be emended. Fortunately, few scholars any longer heed Ten Brink.

Modern scholars, perhaps less optimistic that the archetype is achievable, have still let themselves be influenced by the un-supported and improbable iambic theory. I say "improbable" advisedly. Since no manuscript poem of Chaucer invariably scans as iambic, especially if we heed the scribe's punctuation marks (/ or ⸴ or ·), Chaucer's scribes – as well as his followers – must have been tone-deaf. The likelihood of this being true is extremely slight.

I have pointed out elsewhere that "the greater the alteration of the poetic tradition of any country the slower will be the acceptance of the poetry causing the alteration".[6] In our day we have seen the struggle of Robinson, Frost, Eliot, Auden, Spender, Roethke, and Nemerov to establish themselves. In music it is the same. When a musician like Schönberg or Webern consciously breaks with tradition his reception is slow indeed. That Hoccleve,

---

[4] J. Payne, in his essay on "The use of final -*e* in Early English, and especially in Chaucer's *Canterbury Tales*" (*Essays on Chaucer*, Part II, Chaucer Society, 1874, p. 139), "hopes to receive the thanks of Professor Child for disposing of thousands of cases of final -*e* at the end of the verse, which he agrees with him in considering as a 'puerile' sound".

[5] G. Saintsbury, *A History of English Prosody*, 3 vols., London, 1906-10, I, p. 222.

[6] J. G. Southworth, *Verses of Cadence*, Oxford, 1954, p. 49.

Chaucer's pupil, and Lydgate, who acknowledged Chaucer as his master, failed to understand Chaucer's prosody is incredible. In approaching Chaucer, scholars are too apt to look back to Chaucer from known metrical bases rather than towards Chaucer from the possible influences on him, and his modification of those influences. It was the "scholars" and not the poets in the eighteenth century who thought Chaucer's prosodic base was metrical (see Preface to Urry's edition).[7]

It is now pertinent to consider briefly the effect on an understanding of Chaucer's prosody of scholarly work done in recent years. Of first importance, as I have said, is the bringing forward of the terminal date for the loss of final -e in Chaucer's English.[8] My own investigation of the Middle English lyrics based on known Latin metrical models supports a date as early as 1350, or an even earlier one. But the second half of the fourteenth century will do, because the acceptance of this date seriously disturbs the underpinning of the whole iambic theory.

It has been popular among some medieval scholars who know little about the history of English prosody to say that Chaucer, even though final -e had largely gone out during his day, consciously strove for a certain archaism. Yet there is no record of any poet, popular in his day, who did not attempt to use the current speech rhythms. It is difficult to believe that at the court of Richard II, the most sophisticated court in Europe at the time, a poet would have been rewarded for *not* using a heightened version of the speech of his day. Think of those remarkable passages of sprightly dialogue between Criseyde and Pandarus, or Troilus and Pandarus, and of those tender passages between Criseyde and

---

[7] According to T. Thomas, in his Preface to John Urry's edition of Chaucer (1721), "He [Urry] found it was the opinion of some learned Men that *Chaucer*'s Verses originally consisted of an equal number of Feet; and he himself was perswaded that *Chaucer* made them exact Metre, and therefore he proposed in this Edition to restore him (to use his own Expression) *to his feet again*"; see Caroline Spurgeon, *Five Hundred Years of Chaucer Criticism and Allusion, 1357-1900*, Cambridge, 1925, I, p. 357.

[8] See R. Jordan, *Handbuch der mittelenglischen Grammatik*, Heidelberg, 1934, p. 131; M. Schlauch, *The English Language in Modern Times*, Warszawa, 1959, p. 8; *cf.* S. Moore (rev. A. H. Marckwardt), *Historical Outlines of English Sounds and Inflections*, Ann Arbor, 1960, p. 63: "In Chaucer's time the final *e* was beginning to be lost. . . . In Chaucer's time the final *e* was still pronounced, but not universally".

Troilus being read with a pronunciation that had disappeared forty years earlier. Or think of the Reeve, a northern man, pronouncing the final -e that had disappeared in his dialect probably not later than 1300 or thereabouts.

George Puttenham in *The Art of English Poesie* (1589) said of "the speach wherein the Poet or maker writeth": "This part in our maker or Poet must be heedyly looked unto, that it be naturall, pure, and the most usuall of all his countrey: and for the same purpose rather that which is spoken in the kings Court, or in the good townes and Cities within the land". Puttenham found the language of the universities as unsuitable, because of its verbal affectations, as that of the "craftes man or carter, or other of the inferiour sort". But the poet "shall follow generally the better brought up sort . . . ye shall therefore take the usuall speach of the Court, and that of London and the shires lying about London within *LX.* myles, and not much above".[9] This, according to Saintsbury, is just what Chaucer did. Chaucer performed a great service to poetry by "selecting and . . . creating a poetic diction suitable for the forms which he practised and taught. Perfectly easy, and so perfectly capable of dignity or passion; supporting and supported by the prosodic framework which it filled".[10]

Other factors combine to render the iambic theory untenable; these have been demonstrated by Margaret Schlauch, Margery Morgan, Dorothy Everett, and others.[11] Miss Schlauch, for example, has not only pointed out Chaucer's use of colloquial speech but has demonstrated his use of the *cursus* or *cadence*.[12] But

[9] Puttenham, *The Arte of English Poesie* (1589), ed. E. Arber, London, 1869, pp. 156-7.

[10] Saintsbury, p. 290.

[11] Three studies by Margaret Schlauch: "Chaucer's Prose Rhythms", *P.M.L.A.*, LXV (1950), p. 568; "Chaucer's Colloquial English: Its Structural Traits", *P.M.L.A.*, LXVII (1952), p. 1103; "The Art of Chaucer's Prose", *Chaucer and Chaucerians*, ed. D. S. Brewer, London, 1966, pp. 140-63; Margery Morgan, "A Treatise on Cadence", *Modern Language Review*, XLVII (1952), p. 156; Dorothy Everett, "Chaucer's 'Good Ear' ", *Review of English Studies*, XXIII (1947), p. 201.

[12] *Cursus* is defined by one medieval teacher of the epistolary style (*dictamen*) as "the artificial placement of speech units to achieve a running-on of sounds pleasing to the auditors' ears" (Schlauch, *P.M.L.A.*, LXV, p. 572). For Chaucer *cadence* could have meant much the same thing, *i.e.* "prose rhythm systematically worked out" (*op. cit.*, p. 578).

though she found abundant use of the *cursus* in his prose, she stopped short of his poetry, in the belief that the prosodic basis had been firmly established by other scholars. In my own independent study of the *cursus*, before learning of Miss Schlauch's article and not being bound by unsubstantiated hypotheses of prosody, I had found that *An A B C* was an example of Chaucer's "verses of cadence".[13]

What is true of Chaucer's prose – that he used the natural speech rhythms of his day – is equally true of his verse. Most medievalists are willing to recognise that Chaucer's predecessors and followers wrote, not in regular metre, but in rhythms or phrasal units. They are much less willing to recognise that Chaucer himself achieved the finest effects of which this type of prosody is possible in the *Canterbury Tales*. After him, all is decline, but a slow decline. A metrical prosody in the form of iambic decasyllabic verse did not reach England until the experiments of Wyatt and Surrey, probably on the Italian models of Petrarch's sonnets. Today, after four centuries of poetry making abundant use of a decasyllabic line of five alternating stresses, in which a tension is set up between the natural speech rhythms and a metrical pattern, our ears are accustomed to rhythms that must have seemed very strange to the men of the sixteenth century. These are rhythms which Chaucer could nowhere have heard, not even in Dante. It is impossible for us, accustomed as we are to the iambic decasyllable, to realise the difficulty of naturalising this line in English. To blend speech rhythms with a metrical pattern is difficult. A glance at some of Wyatt's attempts in his sonnets illustrates the difficulty. In the following lines from the *Arundel Harington MS of Tudor Poetry*[14] and *Tottel's Miscellany*[15] a sensitive ear will hear Wyatt struggling against the rhythms of the earlier poetry:

A.H. (No. 110) Because I have the still kepte fro lyes and
          blame
T.M. (No. 48) Because I still kept thee fro lyes, and blame

[13] J. G. Southworth, *The Prosody of Chaucer*, Oxford, 1962, pp. 29-30.
[14] *The Arundel Harington Manuscript of Tudor Poetry*, 2 vols., ed. Ruth Hughey, Columbus, Ohio, 1960, I, pp. 152-3.
[15] *Tottel's Miscellany (1557-1587)*, 2 vols., ed. H. E. Rollins, Cambridge, Mass., 1928, I, pp. 37-8.

A.H.	and to my poure alwaies have the honowred
T.M.	And to my power alwayes thee honoured,
A.H.	unkind tongue right well hast thou me rendrid
T.M.	Unkind tongue, to yll hast thou me rendred,
A.H. (No. 112)	thweene rock and rock and eke myne enemye alas
T.M. (No. 50)	Twene rocke, and rocke: and eke my fo (alas)
A.H.	Wreathid with errour and eke with ignoraunce
T.M.	Wrethed with errour, and wyth ignorance.

The first editor of Tottel did what modern editors of Chaucer have done – removed evidences of the struggle towards a metrical prosody. To think that Chaucer, any more than Wyatt, could spring in full metrical maturity from the head of Apollo is fanciful.

Of no less importance to the prosodist is the discovery by Peter Clemoes of the probable significance of the punctuation marks in the best manuscripts.[16] Three marks are commonly used in Chaucerian manuscripts before 1415: the *punctus elevatus* (⁚), the *virgula* (/), and the high point (·). The first of these, the *punctus elevatus*, signified a rise in the voice, and is still used in the *Liber Usualis*, edited by the Benedictines of Solesmes, with this function. In other words, it is an intonational mark of ecclesiastical origin signifying what modern linguists term a double-bar juncture (//), a raising of the voice at a pause. Hundreds of lines in the manuscripts of the *Canterbury Tales* scan easily as iambic if one disregards this mark; few completely so if one regards it. Hengwrt 154 and Additional 5140 (from different "families" of manuscripts of the *Canterbury Tales*) employ this mark in identical ways, and in a subtler fashion than does the Ellesmere. Fortunately, editors are beginning to recognise the significance of the *punctus elevatus*, and are now more willing to preserve it.[17]

In Chaucer's line there is no evidence of tensions between a fixed metrical pattern and a normal speech rhythm. A satisfactory

[16] Peter Clemoes, *Liturgical Influence on Punctuation in Late Old English and Early Middle English Manuscripts*, Cambridge, 1952.

[17] *E.g.* G. L. Brook and R. F. Leslie in their edition of Laȝamon's *Brut*, Early English Text Society, 1963.

resolution of these tensions demands a struggle. The early Shakespeare, for example, was handicapped by the conflict between natural speech and the metrical patterns. In the early plays the metrical pattern dominates the speech pattern. The change came gradually, first in the speeches of Richard in *Richard III* and then in the speeches of the Bastard in *King John*, and of Hotspur in *Henry IV*. By the time of *Julius Caesar*, he is the master; he can now modulate the speech rhythms with the metrical pattern. A rhythmical analysis, for example, of the balcony scenes in *Romeo and Juliet* is simple; not so that of the "Tomorrow, and tomorrow" speech in *Macbeth*. In the late nineteenth century in America the metrical pattern dominated the speech rhythm. The metrical revolution in American poetry is the result of poets striving to modulate speech rhythms with the metrical patterns.

Our ears have become so thoroughly accustomed to the five-beat line that, regardless of the system we think Chaucer used, we tend to hear five beats in his lines; and yet Spenser thought of them as four-beat lines, as his February Eclogue will show. Chaucer's lines vary from 8 to 10 syllables and have a definite medial pause. If we are to hear them as four-stressed lines, we cannot think of the foot as the unit, but of the phrase.[18] Not only is it possible to read the "Prologue" to the *Canterbury Tales* with four stresses, but also the following lines from the Harley 2392 copy of *Troilus*, although from habit it is all too easy to hear them as five-stressed:

1:      3 In lovyng/how his auntres fell
        5 My purpos is/or that I parte fro the
        9 Thou cruel wiht/that sorwist ever in peyne
       11 to helpe loverys/as I can to pleyne
       18 So far am I/fro his helpe/in darknesse

IV: 1232 allas/how nyh we were bothe dede
    1308 than I may ride ayen/on half a morwe
    1377 for ay with gold/men may the herte/grave
    1392 towards the court/to do the wreche/pace
    1481 forwhy/the grekes all/han it sworn

[18] *Cf.* John Lawlor, *Piers Plowman: An Essay in Criticism*, London, 1962, p. 191, who finds that the unit of metrical organisation in *Piers Plowman* is "the phrase, whole and indivisible".

v: 388 and ris now up/with oute any mor spech
     401 and trews lestyn/al this mene while
     403 to Sarpedon/non hens but a myle
     404 and thus thou shalt/the tyme weel bigile
     410 for treuli/of oo thyng trust me

Since Root[19] recognises the importance of Harley 2392, we cannot lightly dismiss its readings. Inasmuch, too, as it is probably the most carefully pointed manuscript of *Troilus* it is of great value to the prosodist. In the first 50 lines of this manuscript there are at least 15 lines that do not scan as iambic. How can any scholar believe that a scribe would be so careless, and in this belief emend the text for the purpose of restoring Chaucer to his feet again?

Lest the reader think I am merely setting up a straw man to knock down, let me illustrate the editorial method in one of the most recent student texts. The editor states that his text of *Troilus and Criseyde* is basically that of MS Corpus Christi, Cambridge, with occasional readings from Campsall and St John's College, Cambridge, MSS. "Basically" and "occasional" are dangerous words which obscure the facts. The truth is that if we take one spelling from one manuscript, another from another, and so on, we can construct an iambic text. In the first 200 lines of *Troilus*, the editor emends his text some 16 times in order to make it "regular". The same editor has used the Ellesmere MS as his basic text for the *Canterbury Tales*. But what has he done to it to make it fit his theory that Chaucer's verse was iambic? Of the 53 editorial alterations in the "General Prologue" to the *Canterbury Tales*, over 35 are made for the purpose of regularising the metre. Some of the changes can be supported by readings from Hengwrt, but most of them cannot. He adds final -*e* to the rhyme-word when neither Ellesmere nor Hengwrt have one;[20] he omits words which would destroy the iambic metre; he adds or removes final -*e*'s within the verse to regularise the lines; he alters spellings and even the word order.[21] Is it likely that the scribe of one of our best manuscripts made so many errors in copying 858 verses? If an

[19] *The Book of Troilus and Criseyde*, ed. R. K. Root, Princeton, 1926, p. lvii.
[20] "General Prologue", A 251, 599.
[21] *Op. cit.*, A 516, 686.

editor were to attempt to regularise the metre by using Hengwrt, he would find as many scribal deviations from the iambic in that manuscript as in Ellesmere. If he were to use Additional 5140, he would go iambically insane. Yet all of the manuscripts of *Troilus*, of the *Canterbury Tales*, and of the Minor Poems read well enough without emendation if attention is paid to the medial mark; in other words, if each line is read as two (or occasionally three) phrasal units.

What then should the editor of Chaucer do? Certainly he should not try to give us a normalised version. As early as 1838 Guest was aware of the importance of the scribal mark in Chaucer manuscripts and believed that "no edition of Chaucer or his contemporaries can be perfect without it".[22] With this I heartily agree. Again, both the editor and his readers should follow the advice of H. Frank Heath (one of the editors of the Globe edition): "they [the readers] will, I trust, be willing to assume for Chaucer a development in technique similar to that of Shakespeare and some other poets. They will also . . . resist the temptation of setting down these 'freely' constructed lines either to the poet's bad ear or (when all the MS authorities agree) to the copyist's careless hand, but will look for an explanation in the survival of that rhythmic but non-syllabic system of verse which still lived on in England down to Chaucer's day. . . . These native measures must have echoed in the young poet's ear when he first began to write".[23]

For the Minor Poems, few scholars would disagree with the choice of Bodleian Fairfax 16.

For *Troilus*, the Campsall is a favourite among scholars, but from the point of view of Chaucer's prosody it has little value. It was made as a presentation copy for Henry v and the scribal marks were, except in a few instances, omitted. Campsall, St John's, and Corpus Christi fail to make regular use of such marks. Harley 2392, because the scribal mark is carefully used throughout and the manuscript is (according to Root) the best representative of the alpha-text, would be excellent for the student. The fact that this manuscript lacks the predestination-freewill stanzas may indi-

[22] E. Guest, *A History of English Rhythms*, 2 vols., London, 1838, I, p. 153.
[23] *The Works of Geoffrey Chaucer*, ed. H. Frank Heath, London, 1899, p. xxxiii.

cate that the scribe used an unrevised text closer to the period of composition. The text is not so "smooth", even from the point of view of a rhythmical prosody, as some of the others, and it quite possibly represents an earlier version. But whichever manuscript is used, it should be one with scribal marks.

For the *Canterbury Tales*, the problem is relatively simple: for the undergraduate, the Hengwrt MS; and for the graduate student, the Hengwrt and Additional 5140. I suggest Additional 5140 because, although the scribal marks are identical with those of the Hengwrt, the text is, I should think, an earlier version. Certainly it belongs to a different family of manuscripts.

One scholar has questioned the advisability of including the scribal marks in a student edition because of their difficulty for the student. My own experience in using a transcript of "The Pardoner's Tale" from the Hengwrt MS is that the student reads it with greater ease than he does a modern overpunctuated text. He captures readily in the easy movement of the speech rhythms the differences in tone of the various portions of the tale. Chaucer's music, rightly apprehended, is superb. A straightjacketed iambic reading obscures its variety.

III. ASPECTS OF CHAUCER'S ART

Dorothy Everett

SOME REFLEXIONS
ON CHAUCER'S "ART POETICAL"[1]

The third book of Chaucer's *House of Fame* opens with the poet's
plea to Apollo to guide him in what he is about to write, a plea
that echoes Dante's at the beginning of the *Paradiso*: but, instead
of continuing as Dante does, Chaucer adds:

> Nat that I wilne, for maistrye,
> Here art poetical be shewed.[2]

I am not going to consider in detail what precisely Chaucer meant
by "art poetical"; I shall assume that, in this context, the expression, like the word "craft", which seems to be used as a synonym a
few lines later, implies knowledge of how to write poetry (or skill
in writing it) according to established rules. This is, I think, in
line with what many medieval writers understood by "art".[3]

Chaucer's statement in the *House of Fame* that he does not wish
to manifest such knowledge or skill reminds one of other passages
in which he, or sometimes one of his characters, disclaims any
power as a writer or speaker but that of plain speech. More than

---

[1] [Given as the Sir Israel Gollancz Memorial Lecture on 15 Nov. 1950.
Published in the *Proceedings of the British Academy*, XXXVI (1950), pp. 132-54.]

[2] *House of Fame*, 1094-5, *The Works of Geoffrey Chaucer*, ed. F. N. Robinson,
Cambridge, Mass., 1933.

[3] Several medieval definitions of art are given by E. de Bruyne, *Etudes
d'esthétique médiévale*, 1946, II, p. 371 ff. He sums up as follows: "le Moyen-
Âge ... distingue nettement le théoricien (artifex theorice) de celui que nous
appelons le créateur (artifex practice). Le premier parle de l'art, le second
agit par art. Mais chez l'un comme chez l'autre, la dignité de l'art vient de sa
participation à un savoir organisé. Le Moyen-Âge ne s'imagine pas un
artiste qui 'ignore' les règles de son métier" (p. 374).

once what is specifically disclaimed is a knowledge of the
"colours" of rhetoric.[4] "Thyng that I speke, it moot be bare and
pleyn", says the Franklin, and adds, "Colours ne knowe I none".
It can therefore, I think, be assumed that, to Chaucer, "art poetical"
could mean, more particularly, knowledge of poetic art (or, as we
might call it, technique) as set out in such medieval treatises as
Geoffroi de Vinsauf's *Nova Poetria* (which Chaucer certainly knew)
and the *Ars versificatoria* of Matthieu de Vendôme—treatises in
which certain parts of the old doctrine of *rhetorica* are applied to
poetry. Whatever be the reason for Chaucer's disclaimers – and it
should be remarked that they usually occur in works which are by
no means devoid of poetic art in the sense in which I am thinking
of it – they suggest a consciousness on his part, perhaps even an
acute consciousness, of the kind of thing they disclaim.

   The effect which the teaching of the so-called rhetoricians
(Geoffroi de Vinsauf, Matthieu de Vendôme, and the rest) had
on Chaucer's writing has been discussed by a number of scholars,
notably by the late Professor Manly.[5] Attention has been drawn
to Chaucer's artificial beginnings, his use of some of the means
of amplification described in the treatises, and his frequent introduction of certain rhetorical tropes and figures. The tendency in
several of these discussions has been to consider such features in
Chaucer's poetry more or less in isolation, and to look upon them
as mere ornaments, appendages to something which could have

[4] See *Canterbury Tales*, Franklin's Prologue, F 716-27, "The Squire's Tale",
F 34-41, 102-8. The eagle in the *House of Fame* (853 ff.) is proud of his power
to explain things simply. Pandarus deliberately eschews "subtyl art" (*Troilus
and Criseyde*, II, 255 ff.).
[5] See J. M. Manly, "Chaucer and the Rhetoricians", *Proceedings of the
British Academy*, XII (1926); T. Naunin, *Der Einfluss der mittelalterlichen Rhetorik
auf Chaucers Dichtung*, 1930; F. E. Teager, "Chaucer's Eagle and the Rhetorical
Colors", *P.M.L.A.*, XLVII (1932); M. P. Hamilton, "Notes on Chaucer and
the Rhetoricians", *op. cit.* The following also deal, in various ways, with the
relations between Chaucer's writings and rhetorical teaching: R. C. Goffin,
"Chaucer and 'Reason' ", *Modern Language Review*, XXI (1926) and "Chaucer
and Elocution", *Medium Aevum*, IV (1935); C. S. Baldwin, "Cicero on Parnas-
sus", *P.M.L.A.*, XLII (1927) and *Medieval Rhetoric and Poetic*, New York,
1928; B. S. Harrison, "Medieval Rhetoric in the *Book of the Duchess*", *P.M.L.A.*,
XLIX (1934) and "The Rhetorical Inconsistency of Chaucer's Franklin",
Studies in Philology, XXXII (1935); J. W. H. Atkins, *English Literary Criticism:
The Medieval Phase*, Cambridge, 1943.

existed without them,[6] and which, it is sometimes implied, would have been the better for their absence. This attitude is natural enough, for as one reads the late twelfth and early thirteenth century Arts of Poetry which have been mainly considered in relation to Chaucer, they do suggest a purely mechanical conception of poetry. But, to understand fully the influence which these treatises had on medieval poets, I think it is necessary to keep in mind the purpose for which they were written. Several of them were school-books, written either by schoolmasters, or for them.[7] They were intended for use in teaching boys who had already received instruction in *grammatica*, that is (to paraphrase one of the well-known definitions) who had been taught how to interpret authors (including poets) and how to write and speak correctly.[8] The treatises of the so-called rhetoricians seem to have been designed to carry this elementary study farther by directing attention to certain aspects of poetical composition not already considered, including the use of rhetorical tropes and "colours". It is likely that, as in the earlier study of *grammatica*, a boy was expected to learn both by analysis and by composition (of course in Latin).[9] Inevitably, those so trained (which means, I suppose,

[6] An exception is G. Plessow's discussion of "The Manciple's Tale" (*Des Haushalters Erzählung*, Berlin and Leipzig, 1929), in which he shows that the tale is largely built up by means of rhetorical devices (see especially p. 17 ff., p. 126 ff.).

It is not, of course, to be denied that some of Chaucer's rhetorical devices are mere "appendages". Many of those in "The Man of Law's Tale", for instance, are obviously so. This tale, indeed, appears to be an experiment in the application of rhetorical ornament to a simple story. If the experiment is not, on the whole, to the taste of the modern reader, yet it has to be granted that the best thing in the tale, the simile beginning "Have ye nat seyn somtyme a pale face . . ." (645-51), is, equally with the apostrophes and *exempla*, a rhetorical ornament.

[7] Matthieu de Vendôme taught grammar at Orléans. Évrard the German, whose *Laborintus* was written as a guide to the teacher of grammar and poetry, mentions Geoffroi de Vinsauf's *Nova Poetria* and Matthieu de Vendôme's *Ars versificatoria* in his list of authors suitable for boys to study (see *Laborintus*, 665 ff., in *Les Arts Poétiques du XIIe et du XIIIe Siècle*, ed. E. Faral). Évrard himself probably taught at Bremen (see Faral, pp. 38-9).

[8] "Grammatica est scientia interpretandi poetas atque historicos et recte scribendi loquendique" (Rabanus Maurus, *De institutione clericorum*, III, 18).

[9] The practice in England at the time when Chaucer was educated can only be conjectured. John of Salisbury's famous description of the teaching of

the majority of educated men) would come to think of poetry largely in terms of the statements and descriptions they had been taught, and, if a man were himself a poet, he would, both consciously and unconsciously, apply what he had learnt to his own writing.[10] That this resulted in some excessively ornate verse, we know: but it has of late years been recognised that there were also other, quite different, results, of more fundamental importance for literature. Professor Vinaver has claimed that it was from the study of *rhetorica* (at least partly as presented in treatises of the kind I have mentioned) that medieval French writers of romance learnt how to organise their stories so as to express a particular point of view; and he has shown that the form of, for instance, the *Suite du Merlin* is the result of using the device of *digressio* to explain the story. Writing of the general significance of the study of rhetoric in the earlier Middle Ages, Professor Vinaver says:

> The discipline which in the later Middle Ages was to be largely reduced to mere stylistic ornamentation had not at that time lost its original composing function. In a number of important works embodying the doctrine of the rhetoricians from Quintilian onwards the term *colores rhetoricae* refers, as in Cicero, not so much to formal elaboration as to the "treatment of the matter" from the speaker's or writer's point of view.[11]

Bernard shows how authors were studied at Chartres in the twelfth century. He refers to composition in prose and verse (*Metalogicon*, ed. Webb, i, xxiv). Gervais of Melkley, who must have written his *Ars versificaria* in the early years of the thirteenth century, also speaks of composition (see résumé by Faral, *op. cit.*, p. 328 ff.; on Gervais of Melkley, see Faral, p. 34 ff.). For an early fourteenth-century reference to the practice of composition in England, see A. F. Leach, *The Schools of Medieval England*, pp. 180-1. The Oxford statute to which Leach refers suggests that composition must have been practised by intending schoolmasters as well as by boys learning grammar, and the statutes made for St Alban's Grammar School (1309) also indicate that it was practised by older pupils (see Leach, p. 186).

[10] The unconscious application of rhetorical rules is recognised by Gervais of Melkley, who (according to Faral, p. 328), speaks of "un sens naturel, d'où vient que, même sans penser à la théorie, le génie des écrivains applique les règles d'instinct et fait spontanément des trouvailles heureuses".

[11] See *The Works of Sir Thomas Malory*, ed. E. Vinaver, i, xlviii-lxvii. For Professor Vinaver's discussion of the *Suite du Merlin*, see his introduction to *Le Roman de Balain*, ed. M. D. Legge, especially p. xii ff. Reference is made

Professor Vinaver then goes on to show that there is "a significant agreement in this respect" between Quintilian and certain medieval writers, even as late as John of Salisbury.

There is one point in this passage to which I would object – the assumption that it was no longer possible to regard rhetoric in this way in the later Middle Ages. I believe that, for a number of English poets of the late fourteenth century, *rhetorica* still had some of its old "composing function". In particular, I think that it can be shown that Chaucer dealt with certain problems of presentation and organisation in ways which are traceable, though certainly not always directly, to rhetorical teaching.[12]

I shall begin with a simple example, the opening stanza of the *Parlement of Foules*. The first line, "The lyf so short, the craft so long to lerne", has often been remarked on as an instance of one of the artificial ways of beginning a poem – the beginning with a *sententia* – and there are several other rhetorical devices in the stanza. But what is interesting is the way the devices are used. Chaucer's subject in the *Parlement* was to be love, a subject

here to Professor Vinaver because his statements appear most relevant to the present discussion: but it is not possible to write on the influence of rhetoric on medieval literature without being indebted to the work of H. Brinkmann (in *Zu Wesen und Form mittelalterlicher Dichtung*, 1928) and of E. R. Curtius (in *Europäische Literatur und lateinisches Mittelalter*, 1948, and in many articles).

[12] I am assuming that Chaucer was trained in *grammatica* and *rhetorica* (or perhaps "poetria") in his youth. In fact, of course, we know nothing about his education except what can be deduced from his works. His service in the household of the Countess of Ulster need not, I take it, preclude his having been so trained, either previous to it or during it (possibly by a *grammaticus* especially hired for him and other youths in her service). His earliest extant works (or what are generally taken to be such), the *A B C* and the *Book of the Duchess*, reveal the influence of rhetorical teaching; and his knowledge of the standard medieval school-reader, the *Liber Catonianus*, is some slight indication that he had received instruction in grammar. For information about this book and Chaucer's knowledge of it, see R. A. Pratt, "Chaucer's Claudian", *Speculum*, XXII (1947), *A Memoir of Karl Young*, p. 45 ff. (privately printed, New Haven, 1946), and "The Importance of Manuscripts for the Study of Medieval Education as Revealed by the Learning of Chaucer", *Progress of Medieval and Renaissance Studies*, Bulletin No. 20 (1949). It may be worth recalling that a copy of the *Liber Catonianus* was left in 1358 by William Ravenstone, a former master, to the Almonry School of St Paul's Cathedral, the school which, it is held, Chaucer is most likely to have attended (see E. Rickert, *Chaucer's World*, New York and London, 1948, p. 123 and n. 51).

familiar enough in the courtly poetry of his day. His problem
was to introduce it so as immediately to arrest the attention of his
hearers or readers.[13] What he does is to take the well-known
sententia "Ars longa, vita brevis" and use it as a circumlocutory
description of his subject. Its form, that of a *contentio* (two contrasted phrases, here applied to the same thing) is arresting, and
Chaucer emphasises it by adding a second circumlocution in the
same form:

> Th'assay so hard, so sharp the conquerynge.

The third line repeats the pattern with a difference, the phrase
"the dredful joye" itself containing a contrast, and being ampli-
fied by a descriptive phrase, "alwey that slit so yerne". Then
comes the point to which Chaucer has been leading – "Al this
mene I by love". Having thus given great stress to the idea of
love, and at the same time provided some indication of the kind
of love he is going to write of, Chaucer amplifies the idea by
another descriptive phrase suggesting love's mysterious power
and something of his own attitude towards it:

> Al this mene I by love, that my felynge
> Astonyeth with his wonderful werkynge
> So sore, iwis, that whan I on hym thynke,
> Nat wot I wel wher that I flete or synke.

This analysis, I hope, makes it clear that the rhetorical devices
used here are not, as it were, appended to the fabric of the
stanza; they are themselves the fabric. The problem of how to
present the subject effectively has been solved entirely by rhetorical methods.

---

[13] The importance of engaging the hearer's attention and goodwill at the
beginning of a speech is stressed by Quintilian and the writer of *Ad Herennium*.
See Quintilian on the *exordium* (principium): "Causa principii nulla alia est,
quam ut auditorem, quo sit nobis in ceteris partibus accommodatior,
praeparemus" (*Institutio Oratoria*, IV, i, 5); see also *Ad Herennium* (ed. F.
Marx, p. 4): "Exordiorum duo sunt genera: principium, quod Graece
prohemium appellatur, et insinuatio. . . . Principium est, cum statim auditoris
animum nobis idoneum reddimus ad audiendum. Id ita sumitur, ut attentos,
ut dociles, ut benivolos auditores habere possimus". While most of the
twelfth- and thirteenth-century rhetoricians are interested in ways of beginning, they do not consider why an author should take special pains with this
part of his work.

It may be objected that the *Parlement* is a comparatively early work, written when Chaucer was most under the influence of the rhetoricians. In answer to this, I would suggest that the opening of the "Prologue" to the *Canterbury Tales*, though more complex, is organised on lines which are not dissimilar. To present the idea of spring which, as it revivifies all things, fires men with the desire to go on pilgrimage, Chaucer once again begins with several circumlocutory descriptive phrases (each, it may incidentally be noted, displaying some "colour" of rhetoric):

> Whan that Aprill with his shoures soote
> The droghte of March hath perced to the roote . . .
> Whan Zephirus eek with his sweete breeth
> Inspired hath in every holt and heeth
> The tendre croppes, and the yonge sonne
> Hath in the Ram his halve cours yronne . . .

Finally he comes to his point:

> Thanne longen folk to goon on pilgrimages.

From *Troilus and Criseyde* one other example may be quoted which is not, like these two, from the beginning of a work. Chaucer has told how Troilus was struck "atte fulle" by the god of love, and he wishes us to see his case in wider perspective. We are to understand that, for all his pride, Troilus could not hope to escape love. It was his destiny, as it is every man's. Chaucer begins with the apostrophe:

> O blynde world, O blynde entencioun!
> How often falleth al the effect contraire
> Of surquidrie and foul presumpcioun;
> For kaught is proud, and kaught is debonaire.
> This Troilus is clomben on the staire,
> And litel weneth that he moot descenden;
> But alday faileth thing that fooles wenden.[14]

---

[14] *Troilus and Criseyde*, I, 211 ff. The apostrophe and the reference to Troilus's ignorance of his fate are in Boccaccio's *Il Filostrato* (I, st. 25), but not the metaphor of Troilus climbing the stair, nor the *sententia* with which Chaucer's stanza ends. The following three stanzas (ll. 218-38) have no parallel in *Il Filostrato*.

The *sentencia* which forms the last line of this stanza is followed by
the comparison of Troilus to "proude Bayard", kept in check by
the whip, and this in turn by an apostrophe to "worthi folkes alle"
to take example from Troilus not to scorn love, "For may no man
fordon the lawe of kynde".

I have chosen to illustrate the rhetorical presentation of an
idea, but Chaucer uses similar methods for other purposes, for
the presentation of an argument, for instance, as when the old
hag in "The Wife of Bath's Tale" discourses to her husband on the
true nature of "gentillesse" and the virtues of poverty, or when
Pluto and Proserpyne, in "The Merchant's Tale", dispute about
January's predicament.[15] Most of all he uses these methods in
description; but instances of descriptions rhetorically presented
are so common in his work at all periods that there is no need
for me to "sermoun of it more".

To catch the hearer's or the reader's attention and fix it on an
idea is one thing; it is a different matter to ensure that his mind
will retain that idea for just as long as the poet wishes. In the
early *Book of the Duchess*, Chaucer employs, for this end, a means
which, in our day, Mr T. S. Eliot has found effective – that of
verbal repetition.[16] The opening lines of the poem, in which the
poet complains that he cannot sleep, contain a succession of
phrases expressing the main idea, "withoute slep", "I may nat

[15] See "The Wife of Bath's Tale", D 1109-1206 (1177-1206 provide a
particularly good example of rhetorical presentation) and "The Merchant's
Tale", E 2237 ff., especially Proserpyne's reply (2264-2304). The argument
by which Pandarus persuades Troilus to tell him who it is he loves (*Troilus*, I,
624-714) is another example. Comparison of this passage with *Il Filostrato*, II,
sts. 10-13 shows that, while most of the main points of the argument were
taken by Chaucer from the earlier poem, he added almost all the rhetorical
amplification. The odd thing is that Pandarus's argument, for all its rhetorical
devices, does not sound less "natural" than Pandaro's, but rather more so.
Boccaccio's passage is perhaps too straightforward to be quite convincing as
the speech of one friend to another at a time when both are under the stress of
emotion.

[16] See Helen Gardner, *The Art of T. S. Eliot*, London, 1949, p. 51 ff. As
Miss Gardner points out, however, the meaning of Mr Eliot's repeated words
does not remain constant, as with Chaucer; "it is deepened or expanded by
each fresh use". In aim and effect Mr Eliot's use is rather nearer to the *Pearl*
poet's practice of ringing the changes on the various meanings of some of
his refrain words (*cortaysye*, *ryȝt*, for instance), though close analysis would
reveal some interesting differences between them.

slepe", "defaute of slep", the last two of which occur more than once. This might be thought accidental, but further examination of the poem shows that it is not. There is an echo of these phrases a little later when Chaucer is about to relate how he took a book to "drive the night away"; and, when he has finished reading about Ceys and Alcyone, and is telling how this story gave him the idea of praying to the god of sleep for help,[17] his lines echo and re-echo with phrases containing the words "sleep" or "sleeping", in the following order: "defaute of slep", "For I ne myghte, for bote ne bale, Slepe", "goddes of slepyng", "goddes that koude make Men to slepe", "defaute of slepynge", "make me slepe", "make me slepe a lyte", "to slepe softe", "make me slepe sone". These all occur in about forty lines; they culminate, some ten lines farther on, in the statement:

> Such a lust anoon me took
> To slepe, that ryght upon my book
> Y fil aslepe.

Other parts of the *Book of the Duchess* show a similar, though usually less frequent and less effective, repetition of what one may call a key-word or key-phrase. In the passage describing the hunt, the words "hunt", "hunting", "huntes" (hunters), "hunten" recur, and a little later the changes are rung on the words "floury", "floures". It would, I think, be possible to show that in the first part of the description of the poet's dream, almost every paragraph has its own key-word or phrase, and though the practice is less marked later, there are still signs of it, for example in ll. 617-54, where the word "fals", first introduced in the phrase "fals Fortune", appears again and again.

This kind of verbal repetition is not confined to Chaucer's early work. There is a more restrained and more subtle use of it in "The Prioress's Tale". The word "litel", several times repeated in the opening stanzas ("A litel scole", "A litel clergeon", "This litel child, his litel book lernynge"), is caught up from time to time, later in the tale, in the phrases "this litel child", "hir litel child", "My litel child". The reiteration of this word is doubly effective, as recalling the boy martyr who "so yong and tendre was of age", and as a reminder of the teller of the tale, with whose

[17] *Book of the Duchess,* 221 ff.

nature it is so perfectly in keeping. With the line, "He Alma redemptoris herde synge", a second *motif* is introduced, which is reflected by the repetition, at intervals throughout the rest of the tale, both of the word "synge" (or "song") and of some part of the phrase "O Alma redemptoris mater". The two combine in a triumphant line when the martyred child is lying on his bier before the high altar:

> Yet spak this child, whan spreynd was hooly water,
> And song O Alma redemptoris mater.[18]

The opening sections of the *Book of the Duchess* also provide the first hints for another use of repetition. The repeated word "slepe", besides sounding the key-note of a passage, serves as a link between one paragraph and another some distance from it. This use of repetition, as a device to link different parts of a work, is also to be found in Chaucer's later poems. An instance of it in the *Canterbury Tales*, the echo in the Merchant's Prologue of the last line of the Clerk's Envoy, is well known: but it is, I think, worth while to look at it again. The Clerk has followed up his tale of Griselda with the warning that "Grisilde is deed and eek hire pacience", and then, addressing wives, he ironically bids them "sharply taak on yow the governaille". He concludes:

---

[18] There are also in "The Prioress's Tale" some slight traces of stanza linking by repetition, notably in 1838-9, but see also 1691-2, 1726-7, 1866-7.

A study of the various kinds of verbal repetition in Chaucer's works (both those which are recognised by the rhetoricians and those which are not), and of their effects, might give interesting results. Even when the practice is technically the same, the results are often different. For instance, the repetition noted in the *Book of the Duchess* and "The Prioress's Tale" makes its appeal to the emotions, but the repetition in "The Wife of Bath's Tale" of the words *gentillesse, gentil, gent(e)rye* (D 1109-76) and of the word *poverte* (1177-1206) helps to drive home the arguments, that is, its appeal is to the intellect. In the latter part of this argument Chaucer is using the rhetorical device of *repetitio* (the repetition of the first word of a clause), which he also frequently employs elsewhere, again with varying effects. Compare, for instance, the repetition in "The Manciple's Tale", H 318 ff. with that in "The Knight's Tale", A 2918 ff. or with that of the words "Thou seist" ("seistow") in "The Wife of Bath's Prologue". (It may incidentally be remarked that "The Manciple's Tale", 318 ff. exemplifies the difficulty of making clear-cut distinctions between some of the rhetoricians' terms. Naunin, *op. cit.*, p. 45, calls the figure here used *repetitio*, while Plessow labels it *conduplicatio*. In fact, Geoffroi's definition of either term could cover it.)

Be ay of chiere as light as leef on lynde,   [waille.
And lat hym [the husband] care, and wepe, and wrynge, and

This is too much for the Merchant, who bursts out,

> Wepyng and waylyng, care and oother sorwe
> I knowe ynogh . . .

and he explains that he has a wife, "the worste that may be", to
whom he has been wedded just two months. Here the Merchant's
repetition of the Clerk's words acts as a mechanical link between
two tales: but it does much more than this. It reveals at once the
overcharged heart of the Merchant and so prepares us for the
bitter tone of the tale that follows.

A rather different effect is produced by the same device in the
Parlement of Foules. In Chaucer's account of the *Somnium Scipionis*,
Africanus tells Scipio that

> what man, lered other lewed,
> That lovede commune profyt, wel ithewed,
> He shulde into a blysful place wende,
> There as joye is that last withouten ende.

The words "blysful place" are again used by Africanus at the end
of the dream, and are kept in mind during the course of it by the
phrases "hevene blisse" and "that ful of blysse is". When
Chaucer has ceased his reading, which has given him a hint of
celestial bliss, he falls asleep and is himself led by Africanus to
a gate which we shall presently know to be the entrance to the
garden of love. The first inscription he reads over the gate runs,

> Thorgh me men gon into that blysful place
> Of hertes hele and dedly woundes cure.

So, at the moment of entering the garden of love, we are made
to recall the other "blysful place".[19]

One more instance, from "The Merchant's Tale". Chaucer tells
us that the young wife May is so moved by pity for the squire
Damyan that she decides to grant him her grace. "Whom that

---

[19] Another slight verbal link between these two passages (compare 62
"welle of musik and melodye" and 129 "welle of grace") may or may not be
intentional.

this thyng displese, I rekke noght", she says to herself. This is
the prelude to her deception of her old husband and, at this point,
Chaucer slips in the words which he twice uses elsewhere in the
Canterbury Tales:

> Lo, pitee renneth soone in gentil herte!

The repetition reveals, as nothing else could, the gulf between
May's pity for Damyan, and the pity of Duke Thesus for the rival
lovers or of the innocent Canacee for the deserted falcon.[20]

It would be well to consider at this point how Chaucer's
practice in this matter of verbal repetition is related to the
teaching of the rhetoricians. They recognise, among the
"colours" of rhetoric, seven or eight varieties of verbal repetition,
minutely distinguished by such characteristics as the position of
the repeated words in the sentence (*repetitio, conversio, complexio*),
whether the repetition is of identical or similar sounds, either in
related forms or otherwise (*annominatio*), or of words with the
same sound but different meanings (a species of *traductio*). Some
of these rigidly defined varieties of repetition are to be found in
Chaucer's writings, but most of the instances I have just been
considering could not, I believe, be classified under any of the
types mentioned in the treatises. Moreover, the rhetoricians do
not as a rule make any suggestion as to how or why repetition
should be used. It is not possible, therefore, to claim that
Chaucer learnt the kind of practice which I have illustrated
directly from the precepts of the rhetoricians.[21] This, however, is

[20] See "The Merchant's Tale", E 1986, "The Knight's Tale," A 1761, "The
Squire's Tale", F 479. The line, as used of Canacee, comes after "The
Merchant's Tale" in our modern editions: but uncertainty about the chrono-
logy of the tales and about their order (particularly the order of those in
Groups E and F), combined with what can now be called the certainty that
Chaucer never finally arranged them, leaves it an open question whether
Chaucer wrote "The Merchant's Tale" before or after the Squire's, and how
he would ultimately have placed them in relation to one another.

[21] Some of Geoffroi de Vinsauf's own verses in *Nova Poetria*, especially
those composed to illustrate *gradatio* (1145 ff.) and *conduplicatio* (1169-72),
might have provided some suggestion for the kind of repetition found in
the *Book of the Duchess*, however.

An exception to the statement that the rhetoricians do not indicate why
repetition should be used is to be found in Geoffroi's definition of *conduplicatio*:
"*Conduplicatio* est quando motu irae vel indignationis idem conduplicamus

not what I am trying to show: but rather – to repeat what I said
earlier – that in certain problems of presentation or organisation
he used methods adapted from the teaching of the rhetoricians or
in some way traceable to its influence. Sometimes he combined a
number of devices actually described in the treatises known to us,
as he does at the beginning of the *Parlement of Foules* or of the
"General Prologue". Sometimes he adapted devices (that is, either
devices actually mentioned by the rhetoricians or others like them)
to special purposes which the rhetoricians themselves need not
have considered. Here his use of verbal repetition as a linking
device may possibly be included, though I think that even this is
likely to be an over-simplification of the facts. This particular use
of repetition is not confined to Chaucer; it appears elsewhere in
medieval poetry, particularly perhaps in Middle English alliterative poetry. There are traces of it in Laȝamon's *Brut* and the
alliterative *Morte Arthure*; and in *Purity* (*Cleanness*) the repetition
of part, or the whole, of the text of the homily helps to link the
several Biblical stories which illustrate it.[22] Chaucer may have

verbum" (*Summa de Coloribus Rhetoricis*, ed. Faral, p. 324). See also Geoffroi's
remarks under *interpretatio* (Faral, p. 325).

[22] In the story of Lear as told by Laȝamon the phrases "hauekes & hundes"
and "feowerti hired cnihtes" (or slight variations of them) provide a link
between some important stages of the story (see *The Brut*, ed. F. Madden,
3256-8, 3274-5, 3295-9, 3560-3).

Verbal repetition, though very common in the alliterative *Morte Arthure*,
is not generally used there as a linking device, at least in the way Chaucer uses
it. In 3523-78, however, it does act as a link between Sir Cradok's news of
Modred's treachery and Arthur's recital of the news to his council and it
is effective as suggesting Arthur's state of mind, his stunned horror at what
he has been told.

In *Purity*, the text which forms the theme of the whole poem, "Beati mundo
corde, quoniam ipsi Deum videbunt", is paraphrased in 27-28, and immediately after (29-30) the converse is stated:

> As so saytz, to þat syȝt seche schal he never
> Þat any unclannesse hatz on, auwhere abowte.

The second part of the text (Vulgate "Deum videbunt") is echoed in
varying forms throughout the poem, often in the transitional passages from
one part of the matter to another, but also elsewhere. At the end of the
parable of the man without a wedding garment, comes the phrase "Þenne
may þou se þy Savior" (176); the words "Ne never see hym with syȝt" (192)
come at the end of section II, and "þe syȝte of þe Soverayn" just after the

known in earlier or contemporary poetry something which gave
him a hint of the possibilities of repetition as a linking device,
and he may have been consciously influenced by that. In that
case his use of the device is traceable to the teaching of the
rhetoricians only in the widest possible sense – that a poet
trained in that teaching could hardly have failed to observe it and
to consider its value for purposes of presentation.

It is necessary to make a distinction between a slavish imitation
of the devices which the rhetoricians describe, and the adaptation
of these devices, or others like them, to individual ends, because
most of the examples of Chaucer's methods which I am going to
consider next may not seem to have any connexion with the Arts
of Poetry. All these examples have to do with a major problem of
organisation, the layout (or *dispositio*) of a poem as a whole, or of
a large part of it; and more than one critic has pointed out that
the rhetoricians have little to say about this.

For my first example I turn once again to the *Book of the Duchess*.
We have here the unusual advantage of knowing the occasion
for which it was written. We can say with certainty that, in the
poet's dream of the Black Knight who is grieving for the loss of
his dead lady, Chaucer figures the loss which John of Gaunt
suffered in the death of his wife Blanche. Before this dream
begins, however, there is a long introductory passage which
includes the story of Ceys and Alcyone. Chaucer gives a reason
for the inclusion of this story when he tells us that the reading of
it gave him the idea of praying to Morpheus for sleep. But there
is another, unstated reason, of much more significance for the
poem as a whole. The real point of the story for Chaucer was
that it told of a wife's grief for the loss of her husband, and thus
provided a parallel, with a difference, to the main theme of the
poem. (That Chaucer meant it to be so understood is clear from
his omission of the beautiful end of Ovid's story; for the trans-
formation of Ceys and Alcyone into birds, and their happy

story of the Flood (552), and so on (see 576, 595, 1055, 1112). The words
"clannesse","clene", and their opposites "unclannesse", "fylþe", representing
the first part of the text, also echo through the poem, and the two parts are
once more combined at the end:

> Ande clannes is his comfort, and coyntyse he lovyes,
> And þose þat seme arn and swete schyn se his face. (1809-10)

reunion, have no part in the parallel.)[23] To the medieval mind, accustomed to look behind appearances to the inner meaning, this story, and the dream of the Black Knight, could be two examples of the same theme – the loss of a loved one and the grief of the one who is left. Looked at in this way, Chaucer's organisation of this poem could, I think, be regarded as a special application of Geoffroi de Vinsauf's first means of amplification, *interpretatio*, of which he writes, "let the same thing be covered in many forms; be various and yet the same" ("multiplice forma dissimuletur idem; varius sis et tamen idem").[24]

There is an obvious similarity between the layout of the *Book of the Duchess* and that of the earlier part of the *Parlement of Foules*. In the *Parlement* the poet places side by side two visions, the one read in a book and concerned with the blissful place that awaits the righteous who work for common profit, the other concerned with that blissful place, which, to some, is the "wey to al good aventure", but brings others to the "mortal strokes of the spere" – that is, the garden of love. The two visions are linked, not merely verbally, but by the fact that Africanus is the guide to both.[25] But the similarity of this arrangement to that of the *Book of the Duchess* is only partial, for the two stories in the earlier poem are parallels, but the two visions in the *Parlement* are parallel only in form; in significance they present a contrast. This is never stated, for the contrast between heavenly and earthly bliss, which Chaucer makes explicitly at the end of *Troilus and Criseyde*, would be too weighty a matter for this much lighter poem. Yet I think it is just hinted

[23] It is for the same reason that the death of Alcyone is dismissed so abruptly (see *Book of the Duchess*, 212-17).

[24] I am not suggesting that Geoffroi de Vinsauf himself had anything like the organisation of the *Book of the Duchess* in mind when he used these words. In part of what he says about *interpretatio* in the *Nova Poetria* (ed. Faral, 220-5) he is almost certainly thinking only of verbal variation (*cf.* "Sub verbis aliis praesumpta resume; repone Pluribus in clausis unum"); and this seems to be all that is in his mind in the *Documentum de arte versificandi* (Faral, p. 277). Even so, a creative mind, occupied with problems of organisation, might have found in his words a hint for variation on a larger scale.

The parallelism between the story of Ceys and Alcyone and the theme of the poet's dream is pointed out by W. Clemen in *Der Junge Chaucer*, 1938, p. 39 ff., but his interpretation of it differs from mine.

[25] Chaucer twice draws attention to this connecting link; see ll. 96 ff., 106-8.

at in the lines at the end of the first vision where the poet tells us
that, on finishing his book, he went to bed

> Fulfyld of thought and busy hevynesse;
> For bothe I hadde thyng which that I nolde,
> And ek I nadde that thyng that I wolde.[26]

Later in this poem another contrast is suggested by the descriptions of the two goddesses, Venus and Nature. Chaucer
first describes Venus lying in a dark corner of the temple which,
he has told us, is filled with the sound of "sykes (sighs) hoote as
fyr . . . Whiche sikes were engendered with desyr". Then he
presents Nature, the deputy of that almighty Lord who knits the
discordant elements into a harmony. Nature sits, surrounded by
the birds, on a hill of flowers, and Chaucer remarks that her halls
and bowers were made of branches. Again no explicit contrast is
made; the two juxtaposed descriptions merely hint at the difference
between courtly love and the natural love of creature for creature
which will culminate in the unions of the lesser birds.

This method of presenting, in more or less parallel forms, two
things which are essentially to be contrasted cannot be directly
related to anything recommended by the rhetoricians, though
Matthieu de Vendôme's portraits of Helen and Beroe, which
present the antithesis of beauty and ugliness, could possibly have
provided some suggestion for it.[27] But it may well have been

[26] The significance of these lines is made clearer by reference to their
source in Boethius's *Consolation*. They echo a speech made by Philosophy in
the course of her discussion of true and false "blisfulnesse" (see *Boece*, III,
pr. 3).
On the similarity between *Parlement*, 50-70 and *Troilus*, v, 1807-20, and the
implied contrast in the *Parlement* between heavenly and earthly bliss, see
B. H. Bronson, "In Appreciation of Chaucer's *Parlement of Foules*", *University
of California Publications in English*, III (1935).

[27] See *Ars versificatoria*, ed. Faral, pp. 129-32. Faral (p. 77) remarks that
Matthieu treats these two portraits "en manière de pendants antithétiques"
and he notes other medieval examples of "opposed" descriptions. Nearly
related to these is the passage in *Sir Gawain and the Green Knight*, 943 ff., which
describes Morgan le Fay and the lady of the castle antithetically. What
Chaucer does in the *Parlement* is obviously much further removed from
Matthieu.
It is perhaps worth noting that Chaucer's presentation of the two visions
has a good deal in common with the presentation of ideas in the rhetorical

developed by Chaucer himself from his use of parallels in the *Book of the Duchess*. The more complex scheme was perhaps more after Chaucer's mind. Certainly he makes a masterly use of it in the *Canterbury Tales*, when the Miller "quits" the Knight's noble tale of the rivalry of Palamon and Arcite for Emelye with the low comedy of the rivalry of the two Oxford clerks for the carpenter's wife. Here, too, there is a verbal link, when the line spoken by the dying Arcite is applied to Nicholas in his neat chamber – "Allone, withouten any compaignye".

I turn next to some of Chaucer's tales, and I shall begin with "The Knight's Tale", the presentation of which has, perhaps, something in common with what I have been describing, though it is, of course, far more complex. But, before I can go "streght to my matere", I must digress a little to consider, though very sketchily, some of the ways in which parallels are used by other medieval story-tellers. Parallelism, of one kind or another, is, of course, a marked feature of medieval story-telling. In its simplest form, it consists in a repetition of the same incident with some variation in detail. This is what we often find in folk-tales, and in many medieval romances which are derived from them. There is an instance of it in Chaucer's "Man of Law's Tale" where, as in other versions of the Constance story known to us, the heroine is twice set adrift in an open boat. In this form the parallelism can have nothing to do with rhetorical teaching, though it witnesses, I suppose, to some primitive feeling for an ordered narrative. But this simple device was developed in various ways by story-tellers who had something of their own to express. One development has been explained by Professor Vinaver in his introduction to the French romance of *Balain*. In this romance, Balain has many and various adventures which appear to be quite unconnected with one another, but, as Professor Vinaver has shown, they are actually "parallels" in the sense that they all illustrate the same thing, the *mescheance* (ill fortune)

figure of thought known as *contentio*, of which Geoffroi de Vinsauf writes "quando res comparo, secum Contendunt positae rationes" (*Nova Poetria*, 1253-4). Chaucer uses *contentio* (both the figure of thought and the figure of words) rather frequently in the *Parlement*, and it seems possible that these figures, and the layout of the poem, reflect his state of mind at the time the poem was written.

which finally overwhelms Balain.[28] (It may be remarked, incidentally, that this seems to have something in common with Chaucer's method in the *Book of the Duchess*. To it, too, one could apply Geoffroi de Vinsauf's words, "multiplice forma dissimuletur idem".) This way of presenting a story does, as Professor Vinaver claims, render it coherent and emotionally satisfying: but it has the obvious disadvantage of leaving it shapeless. Yet, in parallelism itself there are the beginnings of design, as we can see from folk-tales; and this potentiality was also developed in medieval poetry. The Middle English romance of *Sir Gawain and the Green Knight* is an outstanding example of how, by means of parallel incidents and descriptions, a narrative can be fashioned into a comprehensive pattern. The poet of *Gawain* was not, however, content merely to produce a formal order. His interest was in knightly virtue, and particularly the virtue of "courtesy", as illustrated in the character of Gawain; and the incidents of the story have meaning and coherence because they throw light upon the various aspects of Gawain's "courtesy", just as Balain's many adventures are given meaning by the underlying theme of *mescheance*. The *Gawain*-poet has, in fact, seen how to use his parallels in two ways at once, so as to produce both an internal and an external order.

Chaucer never wrote anything quite like this, but his "Knight's Tale", though less completely patterned, is nevertheless an example of a narrative comprehensively organised for a particular end; and again the organisation largely depends on a skilful use of parallelism. In a recent article, to which I am very much indebted in what I shall say about this tale, Mr William Frost remarks that:

> Much of the beauty of the Knight's Tale . . . resides in a certain formal regularity of design. Thus the May-songs of Emelye and Arcite . . . come at two crucial points in the plot; while early May is also the time of the final contest that will make one hero happy and the other glorious. Thus the Tale begins with a wedding, a conquest and a funeral; and ends with a tournament, a funeral and a wedding.[29]

[28] See the introduction to *Le Roman de Balain*, especially p. xxv ff.

[29] See W. Frost, "An Interpretation of Chaucer's Knight's Tale", *Review of English Studies*, xxv (1949), pp. 289-304. That I am indebted to this article

These are, of course, relatively unimportant parts of the design, but they are interesting because they indicate how comprehensive the design is. At the centre of it, so to speak, there are the two knights, Arcite and Palamon, and, in order that our attention may not be distracted from them, Emelye's part in the action is diminished (as compared with that of Boccaccio's Emilia),[30] so that she is little more than the beautiful object of their desire.

Mr Frost has remarked on the "systematic and delicately balanced parallelism" of Chaucer's presentation of Arcite and Palamon, and on the fact that this parallelism intensifies the problem of who shall win Emily. It should also be noticed that it throws into relief the one point in which the heroes differ. Though Chaucer makes them similar in age, rank, and fortune,

for some fundamental ideas about "The Knight's Tale" is easily apparent: but I cannot accept Mr Frost's views completely. He appears to me to lay more stress on the *motif* of friendship than Chaucer does, and I do not agree that the "conflict between love and comradeship in the hearts of the two knights is the emotional focus of the story". As I understand the story, the "emotional focus" is their rivalry in love. The fact that they are kinsmen and sworn brothers adds poignancy to the situation, and their final reconciliation helps one to acquiesce in the solution: but these things appear to me to be subordinate in interest to the theme of rivalry in love.

Some of the expressions which Mr Frost uses of the tale seem unfortunate, as when he writes of its "theological" interest ("the theological interest attaching to the method by which a just providence fully stabilises a disintegrating human situation", p. 292) and of its teaching "a deep acceptance of Christian faith" (p. 302). Chaucer develops the wider issues of the story in the light of Boethian thought, as expounded in the *Consolation of Philosophy*, and its solution is in line with that thought. The general terms used by Mr Frost, while not actually misleading, do not adequately convey the conceptions that lie behind the tale. As for the term "tragic" (see pp. 299-301), I doubt whether the word, in any sense in which it is used in serious criticism today, or was understood in the Middle Ages, is properly applicable to this tale.

While it is not to be denied that the tale is sufficiently well suited to the Knight to arouse no questions in the reader's mind, it cannot safely be maintained that it is "an important function" of the tale "to present the mind and heart" of the Knight; for what little evidence we have suggests that it was written, substantially as it is, before Chaucer began the *Canterbury Tales*.

It may be noted that the "symmetry" of "The Knight's Tale" is again emphasised in C. Muscatine's article, "Form, Texture, and Meaning in Chaucer's 'Knight's Tale' ", *P.M.L.A.*, LXV (1950), which I did not see until after the delivery of this lecture.

[30] See *Teseida*, III, sts. 18-19, 28-31; IV, sts. 56-58, 61; V, sts. 77 ff. There is nothing in "The Knight's Tale" to correspond to any of these passages.

and in general individualises them little, he does differentiate them in the one point that matters for the story – their behaviour as lovers. Moreover, he remodels Boccaccio's account of their first sight of Emelye so that the impact of love immediately reveals this difference. In Chaucer's story it is Palamon who first sees Emelye, and it is only he who takes her to be the goddess Venus.[31] Arcite knows at once that she is a woman, and is quick to recognise that henceforth he and Palamon are rivals. It is he who casts aside the ties of friendship, declaring:

> Ech man for hymself: ther is noon oother.

The significance of this scene is well brought out by Mr Frost. It marks the beginning of the conflict and at the same time prepares the way for the resolving of it. For Arcite, who has shown himself to be what is now called a "realist" in love and in friendship, will pray to Mars for victory in the tournament, believing that thereby he will win Emelye: but Palamon will care nothing for victory and will simply beg Venus, "Yif me my love, thow blisful lady deere". So, when Mars and Venus are allowed to grant the two suppliants what they asked for, it follows that Arcite will be victorious, but must die before he can possess Emelye, and that Palamon will be defeated, but will win Emelye in the end. Chaucer leaves no loose end; even the broken friendship is repaired in the dying Arcite's generous words about Palamon. The conclusion is a neat and, one might almost say, logical result of the one difference in the two men who were in so many ways alike.

If this were all there is to the tale, I think one would object that it is too neat and logical to be just. Certainly one might feel this strongly in the case of Arcite, who cannot be thought to have fully deserved his cruel fate. But there is, of course, another aspect of Chaucer's tale. He inherited from Boccaccio's *Teseida* the conflict between Mars and Venus, of which the conflict between the two knights is a reflexion on the earthly plane; he also inherited the parallelism between Saturn's function, as arbiter between Mars and Venus, and Theseus's function, as arbiter between the knights. The parallelism between Saturn and

---

[31] Contrast *Teseida*, III, st. 13.

Theseus Chaucer developed farther. The story of Palamon and Arcite becomes in his hands an illustration of the power which destiny wields over man. This theme is emphasised at the beginning by the victims themselves. "Fortune hath yeven us this adversitee", says Arcite, of their imprisonment, "We moste endure it; this is the short and playn"; and a little later Palamon is railing at the "crueel goddes that governe This world with byndyng of youre word eterne". As they complain, they are the prisoners of Theseus, who at all times in the story has power of life and death over them. So, the control which the gods have over man is made manifest in the material world by the power of Theseus; he is (to quote Mr Frost again) the "executant of destiny" on earth, and in this respect, too, he parallels the functions of the planetary powers and, more particularly, of Saturn. But, according to the Boethian philosophy, which Chaucer is reflecting in this poem, the planetary powers are not the final arbiters. It is fittingly left to Theseus, who stands outside the conflict and can see a little more than the other human actors, to recall the "Firste Moevere", the "prince and cause of alle thyng", who, when he first made the fair chain of love, "Wel wiste he why, and what therof he mente". With this concluding speech Theseus removes the human conflict, and its apparently unjust resolving, to a yet more distant plane where earthly affairs, however they may seem to men, are part of an established order, a plan in which, though man cannot hope to understand it, he should acquiesce.

I have tried to show only the main features of the organisation of "The Knight's Tale", but there is much on a lesser scale which reveals similar methods. I will mention one instance only. It is well known that, in place of Boccaccio's diffuse account of the many champions who come to fight for Palamon and Arcite, Chaucer describes two champions only, Lygurge and Emetreus. Thereby his story obviously gains in brevity, neatness, and vividness. What is more important, it also gains in significance. The two champions stand as representatives of the two opposing forces in the coming tournament, and so, ultimately, as representatives of the two rival knights. The two descriptions, though entirely different in detail, are alike in manner, suggesting the same kind of parallelism as between Palamon and Arcite, between things similar yet dissimilar. In several ways this comparatively minor piece of reorganisation could be said to epitomise what Chaucer does in his tale as a whole.

It is a far cry from this finely ordered tale to the treatises of the rhetoricians, and I can produce no logical proof of a connexion between them. I can only hope that the various links which I have tried to establish between the Arts of Poetry and Chaucer's practice are sufficiently strong to support my feeling that this kind of order is the product of a genius which has known the discipline of a training in medieval rhetoric, or, more properly speaking, in the "art of poetry".

As my last examples I shall take three tales – the tales of the Pardoner, the Manciple, and the Nun's Priest – in which the methods of presentation are much more directly related to rhetorical teaching. Indeed, it can be said of all three, diverse as they are in subject and mood, that in them Chaucer used rhetorical methods more or less as the rhetoricians themselves intended. Manly remarked of "The Pardoner's Tale" that the story of the three rioters displays Chaucer's "advanced method" (by which he meant that the rhetorical influence in it is slight) and that "the long passages of rhetoric, placed between the opening twenty lines, . . . and the narrative itself, are thoroughly explained and justified by their function as part of the Pardoner's sermon".[32] This, I think, gives a false impression. "The Pardoner's Tale" does not consist of a more or less unadorned story plus some passages of rhetoric. On the contrary, the whole discourse which is known as the tale of the Pardoner is a closely integrated unity. In the opening twenty lines to which Manly refers, the Pardoner provides the setting for a story by describing a company of "yonge folk that haunteden folye". As he explains, these young folk spent their time whoring, playing at dice, eating and drinking excessively, and swearing oaths

so greet and so dampnable
That it is grisly for to heere hem swere.

The Pardoner then pauses to dilate upon some of these sins, in particular upon lechery, gluttony, gambling, and swearing. He uses for this purpose various means of amplification, apostrophe and *exemplum* being his favourites. When he has finished in-

[32] See "Chaucer and the Rhetoricians", p. 20.

veighing against the sins, he tells the terrible tale of the three rioters.[33] This is an impressive illustration, not only of his favourite theme, "Radix malorum est cupiditas", but also of what may befall those who commit the sins he has preached against, and he rounds it off with a final apostrophe against homicide, gluttony, hazardry, and swearing. The story and the tirade against the sins are so closely connected with one another that one can either regard the story as an *exemplum* illustrating the tirade, or one can consider the story as the central point and the dilations upon the sins as amplifications of it. Either way, the whole tale is organised according to rhetorical methods.

But this organisation is for a special purpose. By his words at the end of his Prologue.

> A moral tale yet I yow telle kan
> Which I am wont to preche . . .

the Pardoner has led the reader to expect something related to a sermon. What Chaucer gives him is not a sermon constructed according to the elaborate rules of the *artes praedicandi* (which would, in any case, have been unsuited to the Pardoner's usual audience, and his present one): but a tale so presented that it will create the illusion of a sermon. It has some of the regular features of a sermon. The theme is known, for the Pardoner has said that he has only one. His final apostrophe against the sins acts as a peroration, and is followed by a benediction.[34] In his dilations upon the sins of hazardry and swearing there is a slight suggestion of the "division" of the theme, so essential a part of the medieval sermon; for these are branches of avarice, as appears from a passage in the treatise on the seven deadly sins which forms part of "The Parson's Tale" – a passage which is actually echoed by the

[33] Actually, although Chaucer writes, "Thise riotoures thre of whiche I telle" (C 661), he has not previously mentioned them. This has led some critics to suspect that the tale of the three rioters was not originally connected with the preceding "homily on the sins of the tavern" (see Carleton Brown, *The Pardoner's Tale*, Oxford, 1935, for an exposition of this view). If Carleton Brown is right, and it is not a mere oversight that the three rioters are not mentioned in the opening lines of the tale, one can only marvel at the skill with which two originally distinct elements have been amalgamated and interrelated.

[34] See C 895-903, and 916-18.

Pardoner.[35] But, for the most part, the illusion depends upon the Pardoner's examples, especially the Scriptural ones at the beginning, and on his direct attacks upon the sins, or the sinner:

> O glotonye, ful of cursednesse!
> O cause first of oure confusioun!

and

> O dronke man, disfigured is thy face . . .

It depends, that is, on a few common rhetorical devices – devices fitting for a preacher and appropriate in the mouth of the Pardoner, who has told us that, as he preaches,

> Myne handes and my tonge goon so yerne
> That it is joye to se my bisynesse.

So the tale is shaped for its ultimate purpose, the completing of the portrait of the Pardoner: but that purpose is only fully achieved by the complex pattern of irony which Chaucer has woven into it. The Pardoner, who feels himself to be so much cleverer than his victims, delights in and confidently exploits the cheap irony of his preaching against his own vice:

> I preche of no thyng but for coveityse.
> Therfore my theme is yet, and evere was,
> Radix malorum est cupiditas.

He is not, however, as clever as he believes himself to be, for the Host is not gulled by him. But this is a small part of his self-deception; its full extent is revealed by his own sermon. In his tale of the three rioters, who went out to seek for death and – after they had given up the search – found it at one another's hands, there is an irony which cuts so much deeper than any the Pardoner shows himself to be conscious of, that we feel him, equally

---

[35] See "The Parson's Tale", *De Avaricia* (Robinson's edn., p. 301): "Now comth hasardrie with his apurtenaunces, as tables and rafles, of which comth deceite, false othes, chidynges and alle ravynes, blasphemynge and reneiynge of God, and hate of his neighebores, wast of goodes, mysspendynge of tyme, and somtyme manslaughtre". Compare with this passage, "The Pardoner's Tale", C 591-4. The tale of the three rioters gathers up most of the sins mentioned in the passages in "The Parson's Tale".

with them, to be the victim of it. He understands no more than they that the wages of sin is death.[36]

It is a descent from this tale to the Manciple's. Yet, in its method, "The Manciple's Tale" resembles the Pardoner's, and even more closely the Nun's Priest's, and I doubt whether it is any more dependent for its form on rhetorical devices than they are. When, therefore, it is condemned as being over-rhetorical, it would seem to be condemned for the wrong reason. The real difference between it and the other two tales is that, in it, Chaucer appears to have been interested in rhetorical devices only for their own sake; there is no motive for the amplification of the story of Phoebus and the crow.

In "The Nun's Priest's Tale" Chaucer uses almost every means of amplification known to the rhetoricians, *interpretatio*, *comparatio*, *prosopopeia*, apostrophe, digression, description; and he uses them precisely as the rhetoricians intended, to amplify, or extend, the little tale of the cock and the fox. It may be objected that this is a different case altogether, that here Chaucer is ridiculing the rhetoricians and is using their own methods to show them up. He is, of course, amusing himself at their expense; this would be clear if there were no echoes of Geoffroi's *Nova Poetria*[37] and no allusion to his famous apostrophe on the death of Richard I:

> O Gaufred, deere maister soverayn . . .
> Why ne hadde I now thy sentence and thy loore,
> The Friday for to chide, as diden ye?

But, when this mockery is quoted (as it sometimes is) to prove that Chaucer saw the folly of applying rhetorical methods to poetry, it should be remembered that, if he is here attacking rhetorical methods, he is at the same time attacking much of his own most serious poetry. The apostrophe, "O destinee, that

[36] I am indebted to Miss M. M. Lascelles for some suggestions about Chaucer's handling of "The Pardoner's Tale" and "The Nun's Priest's Tale", but she is not responsible for any statement made here or any opinion expressed.

[37] On these echoes, see Marie P. Hamilton, "Notes on Chaucer and the Rhetoricians", *P.M.L.A.*, XLVII (1932), K. Young, "Chaucer and Geoffrey de Vinsauf", *Modern Philology*, XLI (1944), and a brief note by R. A. Pratt, "The Classical Lamentations in the 'Nun's Priest's Tale' ", *Modern Language Notes*, LXIV (1949).

mayst nat been eschewed!" is not in itself more ridiculous than
some of Troilus's bitter outcries against Fortune. The joke lies
in the incongruity between the high-sounding line and the
farmyard birds to whose fate it refers:

> O destinee, that mayst nat been eschewed!
> Allas, that Chauntecleer fleigh fro the bemes!
> Allas, his wyf ne roghte nat of dremes!

The joke is a better one if it is recognised that fine apostrophes
and tragic *exempla* have their proper functions. It is the best joke
of all for those who, like Chaucer and presumably his readers, had
been taught the rhetorical doctrine of the three styles, and knew
that the only fitting style for the farmyard was the *stylus humilis*.[38]

I would ask you to consider for a moment what would happen
to "The Nun's Priest's Tale" if all traces of rhetorical amplification
were to be removed from it. (This means the delightful descriptions of the cock and the hens as well as Chauntecleer's examples
of prophetic dreams, the apostrophes, asides, and so on.) There
would be nothing left but the bare bones of the story, something
utterly different in kind from the subtly humorous poem which
Chaucer created for a quick-witted and sophisticated audience.
It is inconceivable that Chaucer should not have been aware
of the extent to which the structure of his story, and all that gave
it its special quality, depended on rhetorical methods. Chaucer
often makes fun of things for which he had a serious regard, and
particularly in "The Nun's Priest's Tale" he mockingly alludes to
many things in which he elsewhere shows deep interest – the
significance of dreams, for example, and the question of predestination and free will. So it seems to me likely that if, as we
read "The Nun's Priest's Tale", we laugh too heartily and un-
thinkingly at the rhetoricians, there is a danger that Chaucer may
be laughing at us.

[38] On the doctrine of the three styles see Faral, p. 86 ff., and, for a more
recent discussion, de Bruyne, *Etudes d'esthétique médiévale*, II, p. 41 ff.

A. C. Cawley

CHAUCER'S VALENTINE:
THE *PARLEMENT OF FOULES*

One of the most satisfying interpretations of the *Parlement of Foules* sees it as "a variety of apparently contradictory thoughts and attitudes about love (concretely or dramatically described for the most part), which puzzles the poet, and yet brings him delight".[1] This statement of the theme of the *Parlement* is representative of studies which have viewed the poem as a coherent whole, but without forcing it into either a "serious" or a "comic" mould.[2]

The following study of the *Parlement* is in general agreement with earlier interpretations that identify its theme as "the comic, contradictory variety of men's attitudes towards love".[3] But it parts company with many of them in suggesting that the garden in the poem is something more than a "good park",[4] a "joyous garden of love",[5] or an emblem "of Nature's plenitude".[6] The

[1] *The Parlement of Foulys*, ed. D. S. Brewer, London and Edinburgh, 1960, p. 14. Quotations are taken from this edition, with modernisation of some letter-forms.

[2] *E.g.* B. H. Bronson, "In Appreciation of Chaucer's *Parlement of Foules*", *University of California Publications in English*, III (1935), pp. 193-224; Dorothy Everett, *Essays on Middle English Literature*, London, 1955, pp. 97-114; C. O. McDonald, "An Interpretation of Chaucer's *Parlement of Foules*", *Speculum*, XXX (1955), pp. 444-57; J. A. W. Bennett, *The Parlement of Foules: An Interpretation*, Oxford, 1957; C. Muscatine, *Chaucer and the French Tradition*, Berkeley, 1957, pp. 115-23; W. Clemen, *Chaucer's Early Poetry*, London, 1963, pp. 122-69.

[3] Muscatine, p. 116.

[4] *The Parlement of Foulys*, p. 41.

[5] R. W. Frank, *P.M.L.A.*, LXXI (1956), p. 535.

[6] Bennett, p. 60.

garden is taken in this study to be a symbol of the world,[7] but much of it – and not simply the temple of Venus and its threshold – is seen as a picture of the world in a fallen state. The effect of this less optimistic way of looking at the dream garden is to complicate it and deepen its ambiguity,[8] and to sharpen the features distinguishing it from the celestial paradise of the *Somnium Scipionis*.[9]

It is further suggested that there is more than one time-scheme in the *Parlement*, and that the time-schemes are so arranged as to emphasise the worldly aspects of the garden and to strengthen the contrast between the celestial paradise of Scipio and the earthly paradise of Nature.

The study concludes by considering the ambiguous, demi-paradise of the garden in relation to Chaucer's experience of reading the *Somnium*, probably for the first time, just before he wrote the *Parlement of Foules*.

I

In the *Parlement* there is a progression from heavenly paradise to earthly garden, from garden to the brazen temple of Venus in its green meadow, from temple up to the hill of flowers where Nature has her arbour, and from there into the everyday world where the summer sun drives away the long black nights of

[7] *Cf.* D. S. Brewer, *Chaucer*, London, 1953, p. 80.

[8] Bronson, "In Appreciation . . ." (p. 197 ff.), B. F. Huppé and D. W. Robertson (pp. 115-17), as well as A. C. Spearing (p. 128), comment on the ambiguities of the garden, but they do not find any discordant elements until the dreamer comes to the environs of the temple of Venus. However, Bennett (p. 79) is aware of a "sense of ambivalence and indeterminacy" which "tinges even these six joyous stanzas [ll. 169-210]". See Bibliography and footnote 38.

[9] The *Dream of Scipio*, preserved during the Middle Ages by Macrobius (*c*. A.D. 400), who wrote a commentary on it, is part of Book VI of Cicero's *De Re Publica* (ed. C. W. Keyes, Loeb Classical Library, 1928). The *Commentary* of Macrobius (translated into English by W. H. Stahl, New York, 1952) "elucidates at length and with an unexpected air of intelligent charm such topics as the mystical significance of numbers, the after-life of the virtuous and the influence of the spheres. . . . It provided the best available source from which a knowledge of the Neoplatonic philosophy could be gained" (R. R. Bolgar, *The Classical Heritage and its Beneficiaries*, Cambridge, 1954, p. 44).

winter. This progression is expressed in a sequence of different scenes and moods – a sequence which includes the gravity of the celestial episode from the *Somnium Scipionis*, the flawed loveliness of the garden, the sinister splendour of Venus' temple beside the unspoilt beauty of Nature's dwelling, the courtly sentiments of the noble suitors in conflict with the comic "vilainye" of the humble suitors, and finally the joyous roundel of the small birds singing in unison.

Some of the main contrasts in the poem are between the heavenly and earthly paradises, between the joys and sorrows of love, between lawful and unlawful love, and between two kinds of lawful love – the courtly and uncourtly.

Each pair of contrasts is contrived with an amazing amount of significant detail. First it will be seen that several features of the heavenly paradise, which is denied to "lykerous folk"[10] and granted only to those who love and work for the common good, are reflected in the earthly garden. The abode of immortal spirits in the *Somnium* is a "blysful place" (Chaucer uses this phrase twice, in lines 48 and 83);[11] so too is the garden which the dreamer is invited to enter by the words written in large gold letters on one side of the gate:

> Thorw me men gon in to that blysful place
> Of hertis hele . . .[12]

Again, the celestial paradise of Scipio's dream is a place

> There as joye is that last withoutyn ende,[13]

while of the earthly paradise it is said:

> Yit was there joye more a thousentfold
> Than man can telle.[14]

The heavenly spheres are the "welle . . . of musik and melodye" and "cause of armonye":[15] but the birds in the garden are hardly less tuneful:

[10] *The Parlement of Foulys*, 79.
[11] *Cf.* "hevene blisse" (72) and "that place deere, That ful of blysse is" (76-7).
[12] *The Parlement of Foulys*, 127-8.
[13] *Op. cit.*, 49.   [14] *Op. cit.*, 208-9.   [15] *Op. cit.*, 62-3.

> On every bow the bryddis herde I synge
> With voys of aungel in here armonye.[16]

A man's love of the "comoun profyt"[17] – his passport to heaven – is echoed, ironically, in the cuckoo's concern for the "comun spede",[18] by which he means his own interests or, at most, the sectional interests of his own kind. The grace of God,[19] which Africanus prays may bring Scipio to the "blysful place" of heaven, is paralleled (with the use again of "blisful" and of the same rhyme-words) by the personal grace which Nature hopes will be the lot of every mating bird:

> And ho so may at this tyme have his grace,
> In blisful tyme he cam into this place.[20]

In addition to these echoes of the heavenly paradise, the garden in the *Parlement* has several of the characteristic features of the medieval earthly paradise – flowers and blossoming trees, streams, bird-song, breeze, and the temperate climate of eternal spring-time.[21] And yet, despite all these remembrances of paradise, this is an earthly paradise with a difference; it is Eden *after* the fall, and its original innocence is marred by death, sterility, and sorrow.

A warning note is struck by the two contrasting inscriptions which the dreamer sees over the gate leading to the garden. These inscriptions, one written in gold and the other in black, apparently describe the "swet and byttyrnesse"[22] of love; they may also be intended to oppose natural or procreative love and artificial or courtly love.[23] But, in doing this, they manage to convey both the worldly and otherworldly aspects of the garden.

---

[16] *Op. cit.*, 190-1.   [17] *Op. cit.*, 47, 75.

[18] *Op. cit.*, 507.   [19] *Op. cit.*, 83-4.   [20] *Op. cit.*, 412-13.

[21] For an account of the medieval earthly paradise see H. R. Patch, *The Other World*, Cambridge, Mass., 1950, and E. R. Curtius, *European Literature and the Latin Middle Ages*, tr. W. R. Trask, New York, 1953, p. 195. The beauty of Chaucer's garden owes something to de Lorris' garden of love and de Meun's paradisal park in the *Roman de la Rose*, with direct borrowings from the *Teseida*; see R. A. Pratt, "Chaucer's Use of the *Teseida*", *P.M.L.A.*, LXII (1947), pp. 605-6.

[22] *The Parlement of Foulys*, 161.

[23] See Macdonald Emslie, *Essays in Criticism*, v (1955), p. 2.

In particular, apart from their possible erotic meanings, the "welle of grace"[24] and barren trees[25] have religious overtones. The "welle of grace" may correspond to Jeun de Meun's "fontaine de vie",[26] which symbolises the source of everlasting life. Certainly, "welle of grace" is a familiar formula for describing Christ; it also echoes God's "grace" in l. 84 and stands in contrast to the "harde grace"[27] of this world. The trees that never "shal freut ne levys bere"[28] are reminiscent of the Dry Tree, which ceased to bear leaves when Christ was crucified[29] but which, according to the prophecy, one day "schall wexen grene and bere bothe fruyt and leves".[30]

It will be noticed that certain of the black verses contrast, not with the gold verses on the gate but with some of the loveliest features of the garden itself. Thus the barren trees[31] are a depressing complement to the "treis clad with levys that ay shal laste".[32] Again, the "sorweful were There as the fisch in prysoun is al drye"[33] contrasts less directly with the "welle of grace"[34] than with the

> colde welle-stremys, nothyng dede,
> That swemyn ful of smale fischis lighte,
> With fynnys rede and skalis sylvyr-bryghte.[35]

[24] *The Parlement of Foulys*, 129.   [25] *Op. cit.*, 137.

[26] *Roman de la Rose*, 20521, ed. E. Langlois, 5 vols., Paris, 1914-24; tr. into English verse by H. W. Robbins, New York, 1962.

[27] *The Parlement of Foulys*, 65.   [28] *Op. cit.*, 137.

[29] The words in black letters – "the mortal strokis of the spere" (135) – may recall the spear which pierced Christ's side.

[30] *Mandeville's Travels*, ed. P. Hamelius, Early English Text Society, 1919, p. 45, l. 7. According to the *Travels*, the Dry Tree grew on the hill of Mambre, near Hebron where Adam was created and where Adam and Eve returned to live after their expulsion from Paradise. For the history of the Dry Tree in medieval legend see *Kyng Alisaunder*, ed. G. V. Smithers, Early English Text Society, 1957, II, pp. 146-7.

[31] *The Parlement of Foulys*, 137.

[32] *Op. cit.*, 173.   [33] *Op. cit.*, 138-9.   [34] *Op. cit.*, 129.

[35] *Op. cit.*, 187-9. Chaucer's allusions to "fisch" (139) and "fischis" (188) seem to be details of his own invention (see Pratt, *P.M.L.A.*, LXII, p. 606) and not to have been suggested either by the "ideal landscape" convention or by the *Teseida*. The word "fish", in addition to its other associations with fertility, may be an astrological reference to February, when the sun enters the sign Pisces, which is the Exaltation of Venus (see "The Squire's Tale",

Inside the garden the leafy trees[36] are made by man the instruments of building and destroying, peace and war, life and death. The oak is used for building, the fir-tree for shipmasts, the olive for peace; but the elm is used for making coffins as well as pillars, the cypress for lamenting death, the yew for shooting, and the aspen for arrow-shafts. Although the listing of trees – each characterised by a word or phrase – is a convention in use from the *Aeneid* to *The Faerie Queene*, it is noteworthy that six of the thirteen characterising epithets used by Chaucer are not paralleled in earlier lists, and that four of these occur in two single lines.[37] It would seem, then, that Chaucer took some trouble to vary the conventional listing. The total impression made by the list of trees in the *Parlement* is that the "tree of life" in the Garden of Eden and the "tree of knowledge of good and evil" – "in the day that thou etest thereof thou shalt surely die" – have many descendants in Chaucer's garden.[38]

The corruption of the original innocence of this latter-day Eden is much more plainly to be seen as the dreamer approaches the temple of Venus, passing on his way the personified desires, sorrows and deceptions of love, by which its more agreeable aspects are outnumbered. Inside the temple there is nothing good to report: the place is heavy with desire,[39] noisy with sighs, embittered by jealousy, dark (in contrast to the "cler day" outside), its walls painted with stories of unlawful and tragic passion; and Venus herself lies "in a prive corner" on a bed of gold, "nakyd from the brest up to the hede".[40] Here, in the temple of

F 272-4 and "The Wife of Bath's Prologue", D 704). In view of the nearness of St Valentine's Day to Lent, it also seems possible that the fish is an allusion to lenten fare and so to the religious meaning of Lent.

[36] *The Parlement of Foulys*, 176 ff.

[37] *Op. cit.*, 177, 180. See R. K. Root, "Chaucer's Dares", *Modern Philology*, xv (1917), p. 21; also *The Parlement of Foulys*, p. 106.

[38] Bennett, p. 79, comments on the ambivalence of Chaucer's garden, with particular reference to the trees: "So in the midst of the forest, when our sense of its paradisal air is keenest, we do not entirely lose awareness of the human world".

[39] Priapus, the phallic god of gardens and fertility, is prominent, "with his septure in honde" (256); cf. "The Merchant's Tale", E 2034-6.

[40] *The Parlement of Foulys*, 269. The temple of Venus, which is taken from the *Teseida*, VII, 54 ff., is also described in the *House of Fame*, 119 ff. and in "The Knight's Tale", 1918 ff. As Brewer observes (p. 31), "The Venus

Venus, are the "brekeris of the lawe" and "lykerous folk" whose punishment has been described by Scipio.[41]

After gazing at this picture of sensual indulgence, with its pathetic detail of the "two yonge folk"[42] praying to Venus to help them,[43] it is a relief to leave the gloomy temple and return with the dreamer to the garden "sote and grene",[44] where

> sat a queene,
> That as of lyght the somer sunne shene
> Passith the sterre, right so over mesure
> She fayrere was than ony creature.[45]

This is the goddess Nature whom Chaucer borrowed mainly from the *De Planctu Naturae* of Alain de Lille.[46] Her dwelling is "in a launde, upon an hil of flouris",[47] which is opposed to the picture of Patience "upon an hil of sond"[48] at the entrance to the temple of Venus.[49] Nature's dwelling is made without artifice – "Of braunchis were here hallis and here bouris"[50] – in contrast to the brazen temple of Venus on its tall pillars of jasper. Nature herself is "ful of grace",[51] recalling the "welle of grace"[52] which is promised in letters of gold over the entrance to the garden. As the deputy of the almighty Lord she holds together the elements in harmonious unity;[53] she pleasurably incites her feathered creatures to choose their mates on St Valentine's Day; she rules over a hierarchical society symbolised by the birds of prey in the highest position, the worm-eating birds below them, and the waterfowls lowest of all, with the seed-eating birds in a special place of their own "on the grene".[54]

passage in the *Parlement* is clearly a moral allegory signifying selfish, lustful, illicit, disastrous love".

[41] *The Parlement of Foulys*, 78-9.   [42] *Op. cit.*, 278.

[43] This detail is added by Chaucer to his translation of Boccaccio's stanzas.

[44] *The Parlement of Foulys*, 296.   [45] *Op. cit.*, 298-301.

[46] Nature makes her entry into English literature with Chaucer. D. S. Brewer (*Modern Language Review*, LIII, p. 323) notes that Chaucer's most important modification of the love-vision was to make Nature the presiding deity in place of the god, or goddess, of love.

[47] *The Parlement of Foulys*, 302.   [48] *Op. cit.*, 243.

[49] Another detail added by Chaucer; *cf.* the "feld . . . of sond" (*House of Fame*, 486) in which the temple of Venus is situated.

[50] *The Parlement of Foulys*, 304.   [51] *Op. cit.*, 319.

[52] *Op. cit.*, 129.   [53] *Op. cit.*, 380-1.   [54] *Op. cit.*, 328.

The classes of birds that make up this motley crowd are a thinly disguised figure of the orders of medieval society, and of the variety of human types, good and bad, which are found in each social order. The birds of prey include not only the royal eagle but the goshawk who oppresses the smaller birds to satisfy his "outrageous ravyne".[55] Most of the lesser birds provide the opportunity for a sharp commentary on the baser passions and activities of mankind.[56] We see the "jelous swan",[57] the thieving chough and chattering pie,[58] the "false lapwynge, ful of trecherye",[59] the starling that betrays secrets, the cowardly kite, the lecherous sparrow who is the murderer of bees, the "onkynde" (unnaturally cruel) cuckoo, the wanton parrot, the drake destructive of its own kind, and the gluttonous cormorant. This picture of lechery, treachery, savagery, and murder would indeed be black if it were not relieved by the "tame rodok",[60] the nightingale that calls forth the new green leaves, the "wedded turtil, with hire herte trewe",[61] the peacock "with his aungelis federys bryghte",[62] the stork who is the avenger of adultery, and the wise raven.

In their courtship of the formel eagle her noble suitors claim what are, in effect, the good qualities of the lesser birds, and reject the bad.[63] The royal tercel, as described by Nature, is "wyse . . . trewe as stel",[64] like the raven and the turtle dove; and, unlike the magpie and starling, he is "secre".[65] When wooing the formel he protests that he will never be found "untrewe",[66] "avauntour",[67] or "unkynde".[68] The second tercel declares[69] that he will never be found "fals" (like the lapwing), "unkynde" (like the cuckoo), a "janglere" (like the magpie), or "gelous" (like the swan).

When we are speculating as to whether Chaucer's sympathies

[55] Op. cit., 336.

[56] T. P. Harrison, They Tell of Birds, Austin, Texas, 1956, p. 42: "In Chaucer generally, it may be observed, the despicable attributes of humanity most frequently suggest comparison with birds. Into this group fall twelve, or one-third, of the birds in the Parlement list".

[57] The Parlement of Foulys, 342.   [58] Op. cit., 345.
[59] Op. cit., 347.   [60] Op. cit., 349.   [61] Op. cit., 355.
[62] Op. cit., 356.   [63] Cf. Bennett, p. 164.
[64] The Parlement of Foulys, 395.   [65] Ibid.
[66] Op. cit., 428.   [67] Op. cit., 430.
[68] Op. cit., 434.   [69] Op. cit., 456 ff.

lie with the noble suitors or with their plebeian critics in the heated debate that follows, it is perhaps worth noticing that the spokesman for the worm-fowls is the cuckoo "evere onkynde",[70] and that the duck who attacks the gentle turtle suffers by association with "The drake, stroyere of his owene kynde".[71] As for the goose, who is the main spokesman for the water-fowls, he is presumably "wakyr"[72] but unavoidably goosish as well, despite his bold claim "Myn wit is sharp".[73]

The cuckoo, goose, and duck are not, however, the only spokesmen for the commonalty; the wedded turtle, "with hire herte trewe",[74] speaks in character by expressing her belief that a lover must serve his chosen lady, "straunge"[75] though she be, until the day he dies. The turtle is an avian equivalent of Dorigen in "The Franklin's Tale" – the happily married wife who, like her husband, is graced with all the qualities expected of a courtly lover.

In the end the newly-mated birds join in singing a roundel in honour of the goddess Nature. And, as they sing their joyful song, we realise that we are listening to the dawn chorus in the everyday world of seasonal change:

> Nowe welcome somor with thy sonne softe,
> That hast thes wintres wedres ovireshake,
> And drevyne away the longe nyghtes blake![76]

This is the happy ending to a poem which is Chaucer's own combination of a political philosopher's dream of heaven, an earthly love-vision and a *demande d'amour*.[77] It has unhappy elements and provides a remarkable number of contrasts, serious as well as comic, between varieties of human attitude and behaviour. Yet the dream garden, for all its imperfections, preserves many traces of its paradisal origin, and both good and bad

---

[70] *Op. cit.*, 358.
[71] *Op. cit.*, 360. It happily falls to the duck, by her use of the proverb "There been mo sterris, God wot, than a payre" (595), to recall the "sterry place" (43) from which Scipio looks down upon Carthage.
[72] *The Parlement of Foulys*, 358.
[73] *Op. cit.*, 565.   [74] *Op. cit.*, 355.
[75] *Op. cit.*, 584.   [76] *Op. cit.*, 680-2.
[77] See D. S. Brewer, "The Genre of the *Parlement of Foules*", *Modern Language Review*, LIII (1958), pp. 321-6.

are seen in perspective "against the backdrop of all eternity".[78]

2

There is more than one time-scheme in the *Parlement of Foules*: the duration of the poet's reading of the *Somnium* from morning to sunset and of his dream from sunset to sunrise on the following day;[79] the cosmic time of the *Somnium* episode; and the timelessness of the garden, side by side with its indications of annual and diurnal time.

The celestial episode from Cicero is given a grand vista of immortality and eternity; but the elder Scipio also finds it appropriate to do some cosmic measuring of time in terms of the great cycle of the Mundane Year,[80] upon the completion of which all the planets will return to their original positions, the end will become the beginning, and the slate of human deeds and misdeeds be wiped clean.[81] To this cosmic year corresponds the terrestrial year, the passing of which is marked by the anniversary of St Valentine's Day (14 February). There are several allusions to the completion of the yearly cycle,[82] when the birds assemble at Nature's bidding to choose their mates.

The garden is described as though it were timeless,[83] and yet this paradisal prerogative is denied by what actually happens in the dream garden. Thus there are two references to diurnal time – the setting of the sun[84] and the passing of a day from morning to

[78] A paraphrase of the Latin tag, borrowed from John Wain's short story *Master Richard*.

[79] W. W. Skeat (*The Works of Geoffrey Chaucer*, 1, pp. 509-10) notes that the narrator's references to the duration of his reading (see especially ll. 21, 85-8) suggest a date in summer for the composition of the poem. These references are to be distinguished from the timing of the Valentine's Day dream itself, which gives us a different scale of measurement – time within time.

[80] *The Parlement of Foulys*, 67 ff.

[81] For the idea of the Great Year in the Middle Ages see the references in A. Fowler, *Spenser and the Numbers of Time*, London, 1964, p. 40 n.

[82] *The Parlement of Foulys*, 23, 236, 321, 411, 647, 661, 664, 674.

[83] *Op. cit.*, 130, 209-10.

[84] *Op. cit.*, 266. Pratt (*P.M.L.A.*, LXII, p. 607) notes that l. 266 – "Tyl that the hote sunne gan to weste" – is a detail added by Chaucer to Boccaccio's description of the recumbent Venus. But whether this contradiction of the garden's timelessness is "gratuitous", as Pratt believes, is open to doubt.

sunset.[85] Far from being timeless, the garden is by no means exempt from the customary limitations of time.

All Chaucer's birds, except the royal tercel, are preoccupied with the subject of time. The royal eagle grandly asserts that he will never desist from serving the formel eagle:[86] but the second tercel protests that he has already served her longer than his rival and therefore has a better claim to be the successful suitor;[87] while the third tercel pooh-poohs the whole idea of length of service and declares that a man may love his mistress more ardently, and more to her liking, in half a year than another who has "servyd ful yoore".[88] This reduction by the third tercel eagle of the period of love's service to a bare six months brings us as near as any of the aristocratic birds allows himself to get to the goose who loves "no taryinge".[89] And finally we have the compromise suggested by the formel, and approved by Nature, that a trial period of one year should be observed.

All these varying attitudes to love and time are viewed against Nature's fixed cycle – the regular and predictable changes of day and year – just as these changes are in turn measured against the vast unfolding of the cosmic year. Thus the garden is seen once again to be paradisal and yet earthbound, timeless and yet subject to time. In such a garden it is not easy to forget that human love is "The dredful joye, alwey that slit so yerne",[90] in complete contrast to the heavenly joy "that last withoutyn ende".[91]

3

So far this study, by insisting on the earthly elements in the garden, has tended to stress the differences between the dreamer's garden and Scipio's heaven. It remains to consider how Chaucer first came to read the *Somnium Scipionis*, from which he extracted his essence of celestial joy for the *Parlement*; and then to bring together the "certeyn thing"[92] he had hoped to learn from the *Somnium* and the "sum thyng"[93] he still hopes to learn from his future reading.

Chaucer probably became aware of Macrobius and the *Dream*

---

[85] *The Parlement of Foulys*, 489-90.
[86] *Op. cit.*, 439-40.   [87] *Op. cit.*, 453-5.   [88] *Op. cit.*, 476.
[89] *Op. cit.*, 565.   [90] *Op. cit.*, 3.   [91] *Op. cit.*, 49.
[92] *Op. cit.*, 20.   [93] *Op. cit.*, 698.

of Scipio from his reading of the *Roman de la Rose*, where they are mentioned near the beginning of the poem and are followed by a dream of bird-song and garden. The *Somnium* was therefore associated in Chaucer's mind with the love-vision, especially as an introduction to it. He refers briefly to Scipio just before beginning his own dream in the *Book of the Duchess*[94] and before continuing the story of his dream in Book II of the *House of Fame*.[95] But it is doubtful whether Chaucer had read the *Somnium Scipionis* at the time of writing the *Book of the Duchess* or the *House of Fame*, in both of which he gives Scipio the title of king (an erroneous detail derived from the *Roman*, 10)[96] and believes (at least in the *Book of the Duchess*) that Macrobius was the author of the *Somnium*.[97] The evidence of the *Book of the Duchess* and the *House of Fame*, as far as it goes, definitely suggests that Chaucer read the *Somnium Scipionis* for the first time just before writing the *Parlement of Foules*, and that the *Parlement* is, among other things, a record of this experience.[98]

In view of the association of the *Somnium* with the love-vision Chaucer may very well have expected to find something in it about earthly love. The "certeyn thing"[99] he hoped to learn from his reading of Cicero's work presumably had something to do with love or, more particularly, with a dream involving lovers. He was disappointed, as we know from ll. 90-1:

[94] *Book of the Duchess*, 284-7, *The Works of Geoffrey Chaucer*, ed. F. N. Robinson, 2nd edn., London, 1957.

[95] *House of Fame*, 514.

[96] The *House of Fame* has "Scipion" (514) but "the kyng, Daun Scipio" (916). D. S. Fansler (*Chaucer and the Roman de la Rose*, New York, 1914, p. 38) believes that Chaucer "had surely ... read for himself Macrobius's commentary on the *Dream*" by the time he wrote the *House of Fame*; and yet, as Fansler points out, the reference to the *Somnium* in the *House of Fame*, 916-18, could very well have been taken straight from the *Roman de la Rose*, 19302-4.

[97] "The Nun's Priest's Tale", B 4314, also attributes the *Somnium* to Macrobius. But this is a special case since Chauntecleer's ignorance is not bound to have been shared by his maker; a special case, that is, unless we suppose that the same error in the *Book of the Duchess*, 285, was deliberately made by Chaucer as part of the simple narrator pose.

[98] *The Parlement of Foulys*, p. 41. The generally accepted order of composition – *Book of the Duchess* (c. 1369), *House of Fame* (c. 1380), *Parlement* (c. 1382) – is followed here. Chaucer was probably a man of nearly 40 when he wrote the *Parlement*.

[99] *The Parlement of Foulys*, 20.

For bothe I hadde thyng which that I nolde,
And ek I ne hadde that thyng that I wolde;

but he is resolved to go on reading in the hope that he will dream[1]
of "sum thyng" to make him "fare the bet",[2] *i.e.* fare the better,
"perhaps as a poet of love, but in any case as a poet".[3]

Although Chaucer's reading of the *Somnium* has so impressed
him that he later dreams of Africanus (the elder Scipio), we know
that Affrican's job is done when he has pushed the dreamer
through the garden gate. Earthly love – love of kind – influences
the dreamer's vision much more than the otherworldly love of the
Somnium. The very parallelism of the wording invites us to compare the respective parts played by Affrican and Cytherea in
determining the narrator's dream. His long reading of the
Somnium explains why Affrican appeared to him in his dream:

That made me to mete that he stod theere;[4]

but it is Cytherea, "thow blysful lady swete", who provided him
with the substance of his dream:

And madist me this swevene for to mete.[5]

Still, his reading of the *Somnium* was by no means wasted. It
put him in mind of another kind of love and another kind of
felicity which inevitably influenced the rest of his poem and gave
his earthly garden an extra dimension of meaning. Because
Chaucer had read the *Somnium Scipionis* the traditional love-vision
acquired a "backdrop of all eternity" and the garden of love
would never be quite the same again. Nor could Chaucer ever
again be single-minded about the courtly code after seeing it
from above in the distinguished company of Cicero, Boethius and
Dante, and from below in the plebeian company of the duck,
goose and cuckoo. But while his reading and his own experience
of life had made him more critical of the traditional garden, he was
not yet ready to reject it altogether. The spell of the garden was
still upon him, and in the *Parlement* he compensates handsomely
for his weakening allegiance.

[1] *Mete* (698) may mean either "meet" or "dream"; *cf. Parlement*, 115.
[2] *The Parlement of Foulys*, 698-9.
[3] P. V. D. Shelly, *The Living Chaucer*, Philadelphia, 1940, p. 77.
[4] *The Parlement of Foulys*, 108.   [5] *Op. cit.*, 115.

Chaucer owed some of the features of his paradisal-worldly antithesis to Jean de Meun. But, even as Jean de Meun complicates the courtly allegory of Guillaume de Lorris, so Chaucer complicates Jean's order of things by introducing Scipio and his world-denying morality which sees life in this world as "disseyvable, and ful of harde grace"[6] and as, indeed, "a maner deth".[7]

It was no doubt deliberate on Chaucer's part to keep his three protagonists – Affrican, Venus, and Nature – formally apart. Affrican disappears from the scene, in body if not in spirit, after shoving the dreamer through the gate. Nature, while having nothing to do with Venus directly, decides to respect the formel's wish to serve neither "Venus ne Cupide"[8] for a whole year. Here we have the spectacle of Nature allowing an act of self-denial which goes wholly against the purpose of St Valentine's Day. It would be hazardous to base on this slender point of evidence an inverted pyramid of argument designed to prove that Nature is cast in the role of arbiter between Affrican and Venus. Nature's decision may suggest that Venus and Cupid are subject to her, and that she approves of self-denial on special occasions. To go beyond this in attempting to bridge the gulf between Affrican and Venus would be to go further than Chaucer himself has gone. On the other hand, there is equally no warrant in the poem for deciding that the view of life in the *Somnium* has nothing at all in common with the worldly values of the garden. One critic has commented that the *contemptus mundi* of the *Somnium* leaves no room "either for love or for the appreciation of the beauty of this world as God's handiwork".[9] And yet love of the "comoun profyt"[10] *is* a kind of loving, and there *is* an appreciation of beauty in the description of the music of the spheres,[11] which are as much a part of God's handiwork as the garden is.

When it comes to harmonising human attitudes in conflict with each other, Chaucer is no philosopher or miracle-worker. The *Parlement* achieves coherence not through a reconciliation of irreconcilables but through a skilful juxtaposition of them, in which parallelism and contrast, aided by verbal echoes, bring the

[6] *Op. cit.*, 65.   [7] *Op. cit.*, 54.
[8] *Op. cit.*, 652.   [9] Clemen, p. 134.
[10] *The Parlement of Foulys*, 47.   [11] *Op. cit.*, 60 ff.

parts of the poem together into a complex whole that reflects some of the bewilderingly different kinds of love rather than solves any of love's problems.[12]

[12] See R. O. Payne, *The Key of Remembrance*, New Haven and London, 1963, pp. 139-46. I cannot accept Professor Payne's judgment of the *Parlement* as "contradictory rather than paradoxical, fragmentary rather than complex". I agree with him that "it leaves all [nearly all?] the basic questions about love and art unanswered" (p. 142). But he seems to assume that neither unity nor complexity can exist unless it is possible "to harmonize the various gospels" asserted in the poem. I do not share his assumption that harmony is a prerequisite of unity, and believe (in company with Professor Bronson and others) that the *Parlement* achieves a unity of its own – not by solving the problems it poses but by creating an ironic complex of conflicting attitudes towards love. I also believe that the poem, by purposeful design, begins seriously and ends joyfully in the manner of a medieval comedy.

Roger Sharrock

TROILUS AND CRISEYDE:
POEM OF CONTINGENCY[1]

The theoretical argument about the respective merits of practical
criticism and literary scholarship for the interpretation of works of
literature does not get us very far. Even the advocacy of a happy
compromise between the two is likely to win only paper victories.
Meanwhile the great bulk of modern criticism operates all along
the line between these extreme positions. Faced with a particular
poem, the critic must both relate it where necessary to its context
of thought and linguistic habit and attempt to judge it as a unique
creation; only the amount of scholarly elucidation necessary before
true criticism can begin will differ from work to work. On the
whole, though here one shrinks from generalisation, the ratio will
depend on the poem's degree of remoteness in time and the
consequently greater effort required to establish contact with
outmoded forms of sensibility. Remoteness from the mind of an
age cannot always, of course, be measured in purely chronological
terms: some nineteenth-century poems might seem more remote
imaginatively, and therefore more in need of this preliminary
effort of the historical imagination, than Donne's "The Good-
morrow" or Marvell's "To His Coy Mistress". But when one
goes really far back in literary history and considers medieval
literature, the ratio of historical explanation must increase
enormously. Complementarily, for the poetry of the present day
commentary on background is otiose unless the critic is playing
at being a sociologist. Mr Alvarez's comparative discussion of

[1] [Reprinted from *Essays in Criticism*, VIII (1958), pp. 123-37. Original title,
"Second Thoughts: C. S. Lewis on Chaucer's *Troilus*".]

Eliot and Yeats[2] illustrates this point: he is aided in this admirable exercise in pure criticism by the freedom of these poets' contemporaneity which enables him to dispense with less relevant matter on overt aims, origins, and summary of content. Even the private mythology of Yeats, about which so much fuss has been made, is profitably ignored. But it would only be fair to add that as well as contemporaneity (or near contemporaneity), the fact that we have all been working hard at our Eliot and Yeats for nearly a generation has also made possible the simplicity and seriousness of this approach.

On the other hand, if we look at that gallant but unsuccessful attempt to apply the spare, untrammelled method of critical attention to the text to medieval poems, Mr John Speirs' *Chaucer the Maker* (1951), I think we shall conclude that the reason for its failure is precisely that, when confronted with Chaucer, the critic is not able either to digest for himself or take for granted in his reader a knowledge of the fourteenth-century mind; thus much of his interpretation reads like the substituting of second-hand modern poems for this obscure and intractable material. And by an absence of knowledge I wish to indicate not the sort of gap that would necessarily be filled by more attention to sources, a study of Old French, and so on, but the doubt whether we can ever be so sure of the rightness of our responses to the nuances of humour or pathos in Chaucer, even when all the information about the Prioress's French pronunciation, convent education, etc. has been sifted.

But the labour of assimilation must be attempted. And it must be a genuine imaginative comprehension, not the digestion that is merely taking account in useless footnotes of this learned article and that unpublished thesis. Literary criticism of Chaucer necessarily marked time while scholarship was still revolutionising our knowledge of the principles governing fourteenth-century poetic and rhetoric. Chaucer was being transformed from a sort of medieval Browning (the connexion was first made, I think, by James Russell Lowell) into a poet of courtly art reared in a school of almost decadent sophistication. Now the revolution has taken place and is being consolidated. But no literary criticism has yet satisfactorily come to terms with it, neither the brilliant

[2] A. Alvarez, *The Shaping Spirit*, London, 1958, pp. 11-47.

ingenuity of Mr Raymond Preston's exposition[3] nor Dr D. S. Brewer's conscientious, more historical approach.[4] It is as if the hugeness of the medieval French and Latin tradition, sacred and secular, as represented, say, by the references in the notes to F. N. Robinson's edition, baulked the critic; however, it must be remembered that the scholarly revolution which has returned Chaucer to his medieval setting itself demands a critical judgment. The disinterested intelligence alone can give that, since the new view of Chaucer is based only partly on the presentation of newly discovered, incontrovertible facts, and much more on hypothesis and the purposive arrangement of the known facts.

C. S. Lewis's *The Allegory of Love* (1936) may seem a signal exception to almost everything I have said so far. It is a book which triumphantly makes just these vital connexions between the medieval mind and the literary work. It is remarkable as a history of sensibility, but the poems discussed are never treated primarily as the mere expression of different stages in the development of the courtly ideal; not, that is, when they are major poems. I wish to reconsider only those pages of the chapter on Chaucer devoted to *Troilus and Criseyde*. They have some title to be treated as an independent critical essay; and they seem to be specially revealing of both the virtues and the flaws of Lewis's method. The chapter has had an extraordinary influence in the universities for a generation; given such virtuoso persuasiveness of exposition, and such a convincing recreation of the drama of the three main characters, how many undergraduate essays have just written themselves?

But above all this, *Troilus and Criseyde* is the crucial work, the hinge on which the modern reorientation of our view of Chaucer has turned, and Lewis's critique has played a major part in giving currency to the new view. Given the older estimate of the artificiality and frigidity of love-allegory and dream-vision, it appeared as the poem of maturity in which Chaucer was seen to arrive for the first time at a direct interest in human psychology. It was, then, a stage before the consummation of the *Canterbury Tales*. On the new, sympathetic estimate of the courtly convention, however, it became the crown of his work, a finished poem

[3] Raymond Preston, *Chaucer*, London, 1952.
[4] D. S. Brewer, *Chaucer*, London, 1953.

bringing the greatest tact of dramatic portrayal to a fine tradition. For Lewis it is "the consummation, not the abandonment, of Chaucer's labours as a poet of courtly love. It is a wholly medieval poem". But he declares at the same time that "it speaks at once to our hearts, not because it is less medieval than the *Compleynt of Mars*, but because it deals with those elements in the medieval consciousness which survive in our own".[5]

Lewis's praise of *Troilus* and the distinction of his appreciation are part cause, part symptom, of a modern preoccupation with the poem that has been growing since the time of Kittredge; in the last fifty years the bulk of appreciative studies devoted to the poem has risen sharply.[6] It is well to remember how far *Troilus* was below the horizon of appreciation for the general reader in the whole period from Dryden to Ker; Scott could pass over it as "a long and somewhat dull poem". One thing we have found fascinating in it is the expression of a highly formalised way of thinking about human behaviour, this expression in turn being to a great extent extremely conventional: "heigh style", the lover's complaint, the "alba" or dawn-song of the lovers with its Provençal derivation: all this appeals to that element in modern taste which, having learnt in its catechism that good poetry is nurtured in a tradition, is ready to worship the most highly stylised conventions it can find, and to ask with Yeats

> How but in custom and in ceremony
> Are innocence and beauty born?

The poem has another claim to special favour in the twentieth century. It is the celebration of a love that goes wrong, not simply the story of an unhappy love or of unfaithfulness, but of a supreme happiness that turns sour:

> Fro wo to wele, and after out of joie.[7]

It is undeniable that some of the poem's peculiar attraction for the modern reader is due to this disenchantment; the love that is

---

[5] C. S. Lewis, *The Allegory of Love*, Oxford, 1936, p. 177.

[6] See A. C. Baugh, "Fifty Years of Chaucer Scholarship", *Speculum*, XXVI (1951), pp. 659-72; D. D. Griffith, *Bibliography of Chaucer* 1908-1953, Seattle, 1955; and the bibliographies in S. B. Meech, *Design in Chaucer's Troilus*, Syracuse, N.Y., 1959.

[7] *The Book of Troilus and Criseyde*, I, 4, ed. R. K. Root, Princeton, 1926.

treated so tenderly in the Third Book is remorselessly destroyed by
the progress of the fable, until when he sees the brooch, his love-
token, worn by his rival Diomede, Troilus can say

> Who shal now trowe on any othes mo?[8]

The simplicity of disillusion here, a simplicity of profound shock,
is, not surprisingly, close to the poetry of disillusion Shakespeare
developed out of his reading of Chaucer in *Troilus and Cressida*:

> Nothing at all, unless that this were she.[9]

It is the idea that spiritual maturity implies suffering and that a
mature understanding of human love must penetrate to the
canker at the heart of the rose, which has also assisted in the
rehabilitation of the "dark comedies". It fits in with the current
abuse by reviewers and others of the word "adult" as a critical
term.

Finally, like the dark comedies again, Chaucer's *Troilus* presents
the intriguing challenge of the problematic, that fatal Cleopatra
for both modern critics and sophisticated readers. The motives
governing Criseyde's conduct and prompting her fatal weakness
are now endlessly debated; with her charm and complexity she
comes to be seen as an enigmatic "character" demanding analysis.
Chaucer deliberately treats her later behaviour from the outside,
as if he were sure only of the bare outline of what passes with
Diomede in the Greek camp. By putting the kindest construction
possible on the reasons for her surrender, he leaves it open for
later readers to try their hand at further psychological analysis.
But this vagueness in presenting her state of mind in the Greek
camp, in contrast to the detailed treatment of her falling in love with
Troilus in the Second Book, is due to tenderness; he is not really
puzzled in the face of the enigmatic, but oppressed by his respon-
sibility as storyteller, like a Dumas coming out of his study
weeping because he has killed Porthos:

> And if I myghte excuse hire any wise,
> For she so sory was for hire untrouthe,
> Iwis, I wolde excuse hire yit for routhe.[10]

[8] *Op. cit.*, v, 1681.
[9] Shakespeare, *Troilus and Cressida*, v, ii, 132, ed. W. J. Craig, Oxford, 1924.
[10] *The Book of Troilus and Criseyde*, v, 1097-9.

Of course, however much *The Allegory of Love* may be held responsible for the growth of critical interest in *Troilus*, it can hardly be blamed for the existence of impure contemporary reasons for the poem's appeal – the modish preoccupation with the death of love, and an exaggeration of the enigmatical element in Criseyde beyond its merely typical femininity; though perhaps in the case of the latter the detail of Lewis's character study has provided an invitation to extend analysis on these lines. What I want to call in question in his interpretation of the meaning of the poem are (1) his emphasis on the importance of the courtly love code, and (2) his omission of any serious consideration of the concluding stanzas and their implication. The emphasis and the omission are closely related, though it is convenient to consider them separately. They make it possible for Lewis to conclude: "Thus *Troilus* is what Chaucer meant it to be – a great poem in praise of love." They make it possible for him to ignore that whole side of Chaucer's purpose which would seem rather to make it a great poem about human frailty and exposedness, tender in recognition of the limited human goodness of passionate love, as of other limited human ends, but agonisingly aware of the limitation:

> And whan that he was slayn in this manere,
> His lighte goost ful blisfully is went
> Up to the holughnesse of the eighte spere,
> In convers letyng everich element.
> And ther he saugh, with ful avysement,
> The erratik sterres, herkening armonye
> With sownes ful of hevenyssh melodie.
>
> And down from thennes faste he gan avyse
> This litel spot of erthe, that with the se
> Enbraced is, and fully gan despise
> This wrecched world, and held al vanite
> To respect of the pleyn felicite
> That is in hevene above . . . [11]
>
> O yonge fresshe folkes, he or she,
> In which that love up groweth with youre age,

[11] *Op. cit.*, v, 1807-19.

> Repeyreth hom fro worldly vanyte,
> And of youre herte up casteth the visage
> To thilke God that after his ymage
> Yow made, and thynketh al nys but a faire
> This world, that passeth soone as floures faire.[12]

This is *not* a conventional medieval palinode like the Retraction to the *Canterbury Tales*. It is in line with the Boethian echoes and intimations scattered throughout the poem, especially the close paraphrase in Troilus's speech on predestination in the Fourth Book, and the solemn astrological technicality with which, in the Third, the rainy weather is described that maroons Criseyde in Pandarus's house and thus brings about the union of the lovers:

> But execut was al bisyde hire leve
> The goddes wil, for which she moste bleve.
>
> The bente moone with hire hornes pale,
> Saturne, and Jove in Cancro joyned were . . .[13]

(Perhaps in this passage Chaucer is recalling and alluding to the storm that unites the lovers in the *Aeneid*, where again in an atmosphere of cosmic foreboding the human actors are the playthings of divine forces:

> prima et Tellus et pronuba Iuno
> dant signum; fulsere ignes et conscius aether
> conubiis, summoque ulularunt vertice nymphae.
> ille dies primus leti primusque malorum
> causa fuit.)[14]

In so far as Troilus and Criseyde make themselves dependent on frail human instruments for the superhuman happiness envisaged by romantic love ("of my wele or wo The welle and roote") they are bound to be disappointed. Simply to say this would be to add little to what has already been pointed out by Bertram Joseph[15] and Dorothy Everett,[16] but the importance of

---

[12] *Op. cit.*, v, 1835-41.   [13] *Op. cit.*, III, 622-5.

[14] *Aeneid*, IV, 166-70, ed. A. S. Pease, Cambridge, Mass., 1935.

[15] "Troilus and Criseyde", *Essays and Studies*, VII (1954), pp. 42-61.

[16] "Troilus and Criseyde", *Essays on Middle English Literature*, London, 1955, pp. 115-38.

the note of fate is not simply in providing a Christian and doctrinal criticism of courtly love; nor is it only structural and aimed at an effective reversal of fortune as dramatic climax to the poem: this is, of course, inherent in the fable. It reflects back on the whole treatment of the lovers and Pandarus: the colloquial naturalness of the interchanges, the proximity to the sublime of the ludicrous and frustrating, the continuous stress on the sheer vulnerableness of Troilus and Criseyde, whether to suffering or to love, are all aspects of a general sense of human limitation, which is given philosophic expression in the Boethian allusions:

> By which resoun men may wel yse
> That thilke thynges that in erthe falle,
> That by necessite they comen alle . . .
> And this suffiseth right ynough, certeyn,
> For to destroye oure fre chois every del.[17]

We are never allowed to forget the contingent, fortuitous character of ordinary life pressing upon the desires and projects of the lovers at every point. When Troilus waits hopelessly at the gate with Pandarus for Criseyde to return as she had promised, what he strains his eyes to think is her figure moving along the road turns out to be only a baggage cart; at nightfall he sees cattle being driven within the city walls before the gates are closed: ordinary life goes on without any regard for his sorrow. Similarly, when all has been said about the brutal decisiveness of "sodeyn Diomede" which makes him the predestined conqueror of the shrinking, fearful Criseyde, always in need of a protector, what remains most significant about their relationship is the fact that he is the first man she meets, her escort from Troy to the Grecian lines: he is simply what happens to her next, an extreme case of the law which prescribes a proportion of all human experience to be that which is not willed. Her degradation is not, as Lewis and other modern critics see it, the consequence of a special flaw in character ("slydinge of corage") meeting in the selective world of tragedy its special penalty, but the common human degradation of being responsible for one's worst moments as well as one's best. The element of traditional male cynicism which takes for granted the frailty of woman (like the Captain in

---

[17] *The Book of Troilus and Criseyde*, IV, 1048-50, 1058-9.

Strindberg's *The Father* telling how easily the bereaved girl on the pleasure-steamer found consolation) is tempered by Chaucer to this vista of universal human weakness. Kynaston's naïve reading of the problem in the preface to the manuscript version of his Latin translation will not do: "a beautifull & most coye lady, which being once overcome yields to the frailty of her sex".[18] The kind of proneness which Chaucer is revealing is the same, though now with a tragic outcome, that he has been dealing with throughout the poem: it is the quality which makes Troilus's roving eyes light on Criseyde rather than any other woman; it is in the mere human curiosity that brings Criseyde in the first place to listen to Pandarus pleading for his friend; and when she becomes Troilus's mistress it is what leaves her at the mercy of the engineered situation and the "smoky reyn" that prevents her from leaving Pandarus's house. It is not the result of a purely mechanical application of the Boethian conception of predestination and fortune to the narrative. (I use the term "Boethian", here and elsewhere, for convenience. More strictly, it is what Chaucer took out of the *De Consolatione*.) The point of view is all the time that of the suffering, exposed human beings, so that when at the end we are rushed to the cosmic vantage point of the eighth sphere to hear Troilus's ironic laughter and listen to the homiletic detachment of "O yonge fresshe folkes", the effect is one of startling revelation in spite of what has gone before.

In such a context, what Lewis says of Criseyde's surrender to Diomede seems too precisely intent on her individual case and unfairly positive: phrases like "such a woman", "women of her kind", recur, leading up to "Such a woman has no resistant virtues that should delay her complete degradation when once she is united with a degrading lover". Can criticism be so sure of a type and its behaviour? The horror into which Criseyde falls is that horror of the contingent that cuts across particular quirks of personality and lies in wait for all of us. To read the poem like this is to lift it on to a plane of more universal human interest than is allowed by individual character analysis in the manner of Bradley, and at the same time to remain faithful to the guides Chaucer gives us and to the view of human nature peculiar to the

---

[18] From Sir Francis Kynaston's commentary on his Latin verse translation of *Troilus and Criseyde* in Bodleian MS. Add. C. 287.

late Middle Ages, the period of the morality as well as of the allegory of love. When Humanum Genus is dying in *The Castle of Perseverance*, he asks the upstart who is taking over his property and pulling the very rings from his fingers what his name is, and the answer is "I wot nevere whoo".[19] This may helpfully be compared to the irruption of the cad Diomede (admirably discussed by Lewis) into the life of Criseyde, and so might the words of Miss Wade to Pet Meagles in the second chapter of *Little Dorrit*:

> . . . you may be sure that there are men and women already on their road who have their business to do with you, and who will do it. Of a certainty they will do it. They may be coming hundreds, thousands, of miles over the sea there; they may be close at hand now; they may be coming, for anything you know, or anything you can do to prevent it, from the vilest sweepings of this very town.

This last passage might indeed be a motto for the story of Criseyde; the acute pessimism behind the piety of the age which created the Dance of Death would certainly have understood the sentiment.

Of course, a student of poetry of Lewis's percipience has not been able to leave totally out of account the side of *Troilus* I have been describing. It is in the matter of balance – the final apportionment of our responses to the poem between the incidental splendours of erotic poetry in the tradition and this more chastening and sober vision of mortal life "under the mone", sympathising with, comprehending, and judging those splendours – that something goes wrong. The reason for the bias in Lewis's emphasis is not far to seek. It grows out of the whole historical survey of which his chapter on *Troilus* is a part. Also he is taking up the argument on *Troilus* where he had left it in an earlier study.[20] In this he is concerned with the medievalising process applied by Chaucer to the Italian poem, principally at two levels: the translation of the love story into terms of courtly romance and the introduction of "historical" matter relating to the tale of

---

[19] *The Castle of Perseverance*, 2969, in *Macro Plays*, ed. F. J. Furnivall and A. W. Pollard, Early English Text Society, 1904, p. 165.

[20] "What Chaucer really did to Il Filostrato", *Essays and Studies*, XVII (1932), pp. 56-75.

Troy which was more in keeping with the taste of the medieval reader. Now, though launched on a fuller appreciation of the poem, he is still chiefly interested in showing how Chaucer adapted his material with an eye to the French literary canons and the love-psychology dominant in his earlier poetry. His first purpose is to expound what a complete transmutation of his source in Boccaccio's *Il Filostrato* Chaucer had accomplished, and in so doing to expose the error of earlier critics who believed that Chaucer only found freedom for his realistic genius when he emancipated himself from the conventions of courtly poetry. Therefore pains are devoted to explaining the changes introduced into the story of Troilus's courtship to make it conform more closely to the pattern laid down in the *Roman de la Rose* (the slowness of the courtship, the perfect propriety of Criseyde in gradually and delicately favouring her lover under the impulsion of Pite and Bialacoil). But while fully aware of what Chaucer had done to *Il Filostrato*, Lewis does not give sufficient recognition to the fact that the original idyllic delightfulness of the love tradition has equally been transformed. His statement that "Chaucer turns a Renaissance story into a medieval story" is revealing, especially coming from one so highly conscious of the greater and lesser divides separating epochs of thought. For it is certain that there was a profound change in the art forms of the later Middle Ages. This can be seen by comparing the symbolism of the high Middle Ages or its Christian humanism (as in the sculptures of Chartres) with the pervading realism of northern Europe in the fourteenth and fifteenth centuries. There is the rise of bourgeois literary genres like the *fabliau*, and the daring exploitation of common life in the miracle plays and moralities; the use of humble and domestic detail in the treatment of sacred themes is variously exemplified in Flemish painting of the period. From the ordered, hierarchical art of early Gothic, the rhythmic discipline of which reflects the intellectual synthesis of contemporary theology, one has passed to an unabashed study of the dramatic and the emotional: the naturalistic treatment of the cold and poverty of the Holy Family in Nativity scenes, the Annunciation as a middle-class interior with a woman paying a visit, the outrageous pleasantries of the soldiers at the foot of the Cross in the Wakefield Crucifixion Play. As Erich Auerbach has said, the new movement is "a starkly creatural realism which does not shun but actually savors crass effects"; it is characterised by "ponderousness and somberness, dragging tempo, strongly charged coloration".[21]

The distinguishing features of this late medieval artistic culture have been monumentally charted in Huizinga's *The Waning of the Middle Ages*. Huizinga draws exclusively on Franco-Burgundian literature and art of the fourteenth and fifteenth centuries for his examples, and perhaps this is one reason why no one seems to have taken the trouble recently to see how the real liveliness of Chaucer's vision of human nature, its pathos and recognition of common human weakness under the levelling shadow of mortality, is more actively associated with the spirit of his own time than it is with those survivals from a past age, such as the dream-vision and the matter of the *Roman*, that came to him from the accident of his French literary education.

> He moot be deed, the kyng as shal a page;
> Som in his bed, som in the depe see,
> Som in the large feeld, as men may see;
> Ther helpeth noght, al goth that ilke weye.[22]

Here we catch the accent that found plastic expression in the Dance of Death: but the mark of creaturely realism is equally present in the wart on the Miller's nose and the "mormal" on the Cook's shin.

Thus it is that Chaucer is continually engaged in *Troilus* in introducing into his courtly story cold douches of the embarrassingly everyday. To be sure he developed the etiquette of the love-affair according to the canons of the *Roman*, as he had learnt from his French masters: but a part of the effect of this elaboration is to provide startling contrasts and juxtapositions. When Criseyde is too coy, too "dangerous" in disposition to take the letter proffered her by Pandarus as go-between, he prevails over her by a piece of horseplay, pushing the letter into her bosom. And at the supreme moment of the lovers when they are in bed together, creaturely realism does not allow them to be

[21] Erich Auerbach, *Mimesis: The Representation of Reality in Western Literature*, tr. W. R. Trask, Princeton, 1953, p. 247.
[22] "The Knight's Tale", A 3030-3, *The Works of Geoffrey Chaucer*, ed. F. N. Robinson, 2nd edn., London, 1957.

quite alone; the world is not blotted out as the myth of romantic passion would require: there is still Pandarus making obvious jokes and appearing with one of those humble "props" that recur so constantly in the art of the period:

> And bar the candel to the chymeneye.[23]

Lewis pleads a good deal about this passage; he wants at all costs to avoid the knowing leer, a degraded Pandarus; the goose in the *Parlement of Foules*, the Vekke, and Godfrey Gobelive are all invoked. It is perhaps sufficient to say that though Pandarus is not the salacious old man of Shakespeare's play, Shakespeare needed the hint of grotesque senility in passages like this on which to build his character. More important than defending Pandarus here as a serious exponent of the courtly code who yet sees "the hard or banal lineaments of the work-a-day world" is a realisation of how his presence affects the lovers; the shocking clash between their ecstasy and his prosing is another of those wry comments on the impingement upon the ideal of the banal and the work-a-day which furnish the substance of Chaucer's statement in *Troilus*.

Both Troilus and Criseyde let themselves be impelled by Pandarus, their minds made up and their affairs arranged, more than is proper for courtly lovers in the hands of the confidant. Though Criseyde says magnificently to Troilus in the Third Book,

> Ne hadde I or now, my swete herte deere,
> Ben yolde, iwys, I were now nat here,[24]

she allows herself to be pushed about by both Troilus and Pandarus in a fashion altogether too passive for the courtly *domina*, who should be mastering her lover by the bright influence of her eyes. If her love is genuinely, in Jeanroy's words, "le résultat d'une détermination librement prise",[25] her free decision is preceded by a veritable hounding from pillar to post and is followed by a wooing in which all the arrangements for her physical union with Troilus are left in Pandarus's hands. It does not make it any

---

23 *The Book of Troilus and Criseyde*, III, 1141.

24 *Op. cit.*, III, 1210-11.

25 A. Jeanroy, *La poésie lyrique des troubadours*, 2 vols., Paris, 1934, II, p. 97.

better from the point of view of ideal courtly love that there is a strong suspicion that she knows what may happen after Pandarus's dinner party:

> Nat list myn auctour fully to declare
> What that she thoughte whan he seyde so,
> That Troilus was out of towne yfare,
> As if he seyde soth therof or no . . .
> And seyde hym: "Em, syn I most on yow triste,
> Loke al be wel, for I do as yow liste."[26]

To note this is not to disparage the sincerity of the lovers or to deny the touching truth with which their relationship is depicted, but only to realise the dimension of tolerance and pity that their lack of will and self-knowledge inspires. When the darker part of the story is reached in the Fourth and Fifth Books, Lewis is prepared to recognise a poetry of a different kind, but he does this, strangely enough, by classifying it in such a way as to put it outside the range of poetry altogether:

> The end of *Troilus* is the great example in our literature of pathos pure and unrelieved . . . Chaucer spares us no detail of the prolonged and sickening process to despair: every fluctuation of gnawing hope, every fluctuation of the flattering imagination, is held up to our eyes without mercy. The thing is so painful that perhaps no one without reluctance reads it twice. In our cowardice we are tempted to call it sentimental. We turn with relief to the titanic passions and heroic deaths of tragedy. . . . But this, we feel, goes almost beyond the bounds of art; this is treason. Chaucer is letting the cat out of the bag.[27]

This defines admirably not just the effect of the final scenes of the poem, but the artistic direction of the whole; its purpose is indeed to let the cat out of the bag: that is the kind of tragic writing that Chaucer is aiming at throughout, wresting humour, pathos, and irony from the contradictions of the human search for happiness in a contingent world. It is the nature of such art to spare nothing. But immediately after this Lewis can again return

---

[26] *The Book of Troilus and Criseyde*, III, 575-8, 587-8.
[27] *The Allegory of Love*, pp. 195-6.

to the motive of fulfilled love and say that it is not a depressing poem. He speaks of the "purifying complexities of the real world" and of "the innocent snugness, as of a child's hiding-place", which the rain outside draws over the lovers. But in the poem the real world does not purify, it destroys; the hiding-place is brutally ransacked. The quest of courtly love from its source to the sea of modern love-marriage which is the thrilling theme of Lewis's book has in this chapter distorted the balance of his fine perceptions: he has ignored the fact that into its Chaucerian tributary there flowed another and a more powerful stream. The total effect of the resulting poem may not be depressing, but its hopefulness lies in a bizarre counterpointing of fleeting human love, the contingency of material life, and divine consolation.

Janette Richardson

HUNTER AND PREY:
FUNCTIONAL IMAGERY IN
"THE FRIAR'S TALE"[1]

Those scholars who have concerned themselves with Chaucer's
use of imagery have been interested primarily in relating the
poet's practices to the conventions of his age.[2] They have
demonstrated that he frequently followed the dictates of such
rhetoricians as Matthieu de Vendôme and Geoffroi de Vinsauf,
who regarded style, and hence imagery, principally as decoration;[3]
and they have pointed out that he often borrowed images directly
from his sources.[4] Valid and convincing as their arguments are,

---

[1] [Reprinted from *English Miscellany*, xii (1961), pp. 9-20.]

[2] For example, F. Klaeber, *Das Bild bei Chaucer*, Berlin, 1893, separates all
of Chaucer's metaphors and similes from their contexts, classifies them, and
suggests possible literary sources. The concern for Chaucer's relationship to
medieval rhetorical poetic has led a number of scholars to discussions which
have some connexion with imagery, but these studies are concerned primarily
with the poet's use of such formal devices as *descriptio, effictio, imago, similitudo,
translatio*, and *demonstratio*. Among these, Chaucer's handling of the portrait,
or *effictio*, has been thoroughly investigated, both for its conventional aspects
and for the poet's innovations. See J. M. Manly, "Chaucer and the Rhetoricians", *Proceedings of the British Academy*, xii (1926), pp. 95-113; M. P.
Hamilton, "Notes on Chaucer and the Rhetoricians", *P.M.L.A.*, xlvii
(1932), pp. 403-9; L. A. Haselmayer, "The Portraits in Chaucer's Fabliaux",
Review of English Studies, xiv (1938), pp. 310-14; J. L. Lowes, *Geoffrey Chaucer*,
London, 1934, p. 160 ff. and 176 ff.; R. Baldwin, *The Unity of the Canterbury
Tales*, Copenhagen, 1955.

[3] See C. S. Baldwin, *Medieval Rhetoric and Poetic*, New York, 1928; E.
Faral, *Les Arts Poétiques du XIIe et du XIIIe Siècle*, Paris, 1924.

[4] For example, S. B. Meech, *Design in Chaucer's Troilus*, Syracuse, 1959,
cites numerous examples in *Troilus* from Boccaccio's *Filostrato*.

the story which the Friar of the *Canterbury Tales* tells to insult his professional rival, the Summoner, shows Chaucer transcending the traditional even as he adheres to its essential forms. Here imagery serves an organic function within the aesthetic whole of the individual work: the poet manipulates a cluster of images, commonplace and conventional though they be, so that instead of functioning as mere decoration they reinforce and deepen the comic irony both inherent and explicit within the framework of the story.

We do not know the immediate source of Chaucer's tale, but the numerous analogues suggest that the anecdote of the heartfelt curse was popular during his lifetime.[5] The effectiveness of these consistently brief versions depends entirely upon the irony implicit in a situation whereby a would-be victimiser becomes himself the victim of a devil. In its simplest outlines "The Friar's Tale" is no exception. An unscrupulous summoner sets out to extort money from a poor widow and on the way meets a stranger with whom he swears an oath of brotherhood. After his new friend has proclaimed himself to be a devil, the two encounter an enraged carter condemning his team of horses to hell, but when the summoner suggests that his friend should take the property thus given him, the other replies that he cannot do so because the curses are not sincere. Immediately thereafter, the summoner affronts the widow who is the object of his designs. She consigns him to the devil with utter sincerity, and the friend, who proves indeed to be what he had asserted, snatches his booty.

To this stark skeleton Chaucer adds the flesh of realistic characterisation, disclosed in part by typical portrait description but primarily by self-revealing speech and action, and he animates his creation with a subtle dramatic conflict between the protagonists which emerges through the ironic implications of the dialogue and gains intensity and comic force through varied levels of awareness. Furthermore, he builds a pattern of images which parallels the action of the tale and serves not only to reinforce the movement of the narrative but also to clarify the intention,

---

[5] See R. D. French, *A Chaucer Handbook*, New York, 1947, pp. 284-7; A. Taylor, "The Devil and the Advocate", *P.M.L.A.*, xxxvi (1921), pp. 35-59; W. F. Bryan and G. Dempster, *Sources and Analogues of Chaucer's Canterbury Tales*, Chicago, 1941, pp. 269-74.

foreshadow the outcome, and as a result of all these functions, tighten the artistic unity of the whole.

As used here, the term "image" refers both to those pictures evoked by description and to formal figures of speech. In respect to the latter, it is significant that all the metaphors and similes in the poem depict various kinds of hunters and their prey. Although these comparisons are dispersed economically throughout the first half of the tale, their interweaving lines gradually form a pattern. Obviously, this single consistent image is intended to serve some function. Even if its use were determined by mere appropriateness or decorum, the result would be a kind of thematic imagery which goes far beyond the decorative function advocated by the rhetoricians.

The first seventy-five lines of "The Friar's Tale" are devoted to a description of the crafty summoner and his money-loving employer, the archdeacon. Within this passage the summoner is first compared to a hare:

> For thogh this somonour *wood were as an hare*,
> To telle his harlotrye I wol nat spare.[6]

Because the expression "as mad as a March hare" is so common a proverbial saying,[7] it has become what George Orwell called a "dead" simile, and the significance of the comparison is not immediately discerned. However, it illustrates Chaucer's method of twisting the commonplace or traditional to suit his own purposes, for the subsequent narrative shows that he intends to associate with his central character both the idea of the hare as an animal preyed upon by men and birds alike and the idea of madness.

A few lines later the Friar says that the summoner had "bawdes

---

[6] "The Friar's Tale", D 1327-8. This and all subsequent quotations are from F. N. Robinson, *The Works of Geoffrey Chaucer*, 2nd edn., London, 1957; italics are my own. In l. 1327 I have changed the capitalisation of the word "somonour" to lower case because, as I have argued in "An Ambiguous Reference in Chaucer's 'Friar's Tale' ", *Archiv*, CXCVIII (1962), pp. 388-90, Chaucer intends the word to refer to the protagonist of the tale rather than to the Friar's rival, the pilgrim. In capitalising the name so that it designates the pilgrim, Robinson has departed from both the major manuscripts and the practice of previous editors.

[7] W. W. Skeat, *Early English Proverbs*, Oxford, 1910, p. 115.

redy to his hond, As any *hauk* to lure in Engelond"[8] and goes on
to add that he could spot a lecher better than any "*dogge* for the
bowe, That kan an *hurt deer* from an hool yknowe".[9] Then the
action of the narrative begins:

> And so bifel that ones on a day
> This somnour, *evere waityng on his pray*,
> Rood for to somne an old wydwe, a ribibe,
> Feynynge a cause, for he wolde brybe.[10]

By this point, the image cluster has begun to take significant
shape. The summoner is pictured as a hunter preying on his
victims, innocent and guilty alike, with the ruthlessness of the
hawk and the avidness of the dog after the wounded deer. The
concept thus established is reinforced with yet another simile:
"This somonour . . . was as ful of jangles, As ful of venym been
thise *waryangles*".[11] The summoner's talkativeness is the point of
immediate reference, but like the hawk, the waryangle (the
modern shrike) is also a bird of prey. And yet, paradoxically,
although the summoner is the predatory pursuer, he is simultaneously the "wood hare", the frequent victim of hunters and just
such birds as the hawk.

The ironic import of this double image foreshadows the events
which are about to occur, for while the summoner is in pursuit of
his victim, the widow, he becomes himself the objective of a far
more effective hunter, the devil. Considering that Chaucer's
comparison of the summoner to a shrike occurs after the devil has
been introduced, one may even venture the argument that it
deliberately points up the contrast between the powers of the two
hunters: although most varieties of shrike prey upon mere insects
which they impale upon thorns, the devil's victim is man himself.
The foreshadowing function of the double image is also reinforced by an allusion to Biblical history. In the midst of the
description which contains the figures of speech discussed above,
the narrator says that just as "Judas hadde purses smale, And was
a theef", so too is the summoner. Since, according to Dante at
least, Judas damned himself for money, Chaucer's fourteenth-
century audience, whose ears were thoroughly attuned to the

8 "The Friar's Tale", D 1339-40.　　9 *Op. cit.*, 1369-70.
10 *Op. cit.*, 1375-8.　　11 *Op. cit.*, 1407-8.

import of Biblical references, may well have expected a similar fate for the avaricious summoner.

Thus, the composite image which has just emerged allows us to realise the irony inherent in the tale, for it permits us to share from the beginning the poet's understanding of a situation which the character vitally concerned comprehends only at the last. While the summoner erroneously looks upon himself only as a hunter and acts in a manner naturally and logically suited to his role as he perceives it, we see him more accurately as both hunter and prey. Nor is Chaucer's use of the epithet "wood" accidental. For once the story is underway, the summoner reveals his heedlessness and stupidity – indeed, his madness – by completely disregarding the most obvious warnings of his impending fate. He entraps himself unwittingly.[12] His complete unscrupulousness, his greed, his hypocrisy, and, above all, his stupidity and his pride in his own supposed cleverness lead him to seal his own doom. He condemns himself; he attempts to deceive the arch-deceiver. In the subsequent events we can recognise the dramatic conflict between the two characters and can appreciate the full depth of the irony because we have been given an insight which allows us to view the action on two distinct levels.

The ironic complexity of the situation increases with the entrance of the devil. Through a traditional *effictio* Chaucer expands his basic image to include the second hunter tacitly demanded by the double role previously established for the summoner. Like the Knight's Yeoman in the "General Prologue", the fiend wears a green coat and carries a bow and "arwes brighte and kene",[13] and the summoner naturally assumes from this garb that the stranger is a yeoman. We, however, being as it were in the poet's confidence, can perceive the intricate irony of

[12] Some authoritative critics have based their interpretation of the tale upon the assumption that the summoner believes what the devil says about his true identity; they suggest that the summoner is so abject, his soul so hardened in crime, that he has no fear of pledging brotherhood with a fiend. See G. Dempster, "Dramatic Irony in Chaucer", *Stanford University Publications*, IV (1932), pp. 42-5; R. K. Root, *The Poetry of Chaucer*, New York, 1906, pp. 248-9. However, if the present argument be valid, Chaucer's intention is more subtle, more deeply ironic, and the discourse on the nature of devils is an integral portion of the narrative rather than a learned digression.

[13] "The Friar's Tale", D 1381.

this disastrous mistake of identity. Because green clothing is traditional for underworld spirits who walk the earth,[14] the stranger's very first appearance gives us a clue to his true nature. At the same time we realise that the summoner's assumption is correct, but in a way which he does not suspect, for the devil actually *is* a hunter – a hunter, moreover, who has just flushed his prey.

Considered thus, the irony of the situation is further deepened by the summoner's vain attempt to deceive the devil in precisely the same way that he himself is deceived. The unsuspecting victim lies about his profession, pretending to be a bailiff, for "He dorste nat, for verray filthe and shame, Seye that he was a somonour",[15] and the fiend replies, "Depardieux . . . deere broother, Thou art a bailly, and I am another".[16] This loaded statement contains three levels of meaning, only one of which, of course, is evident to the victim: in addition to its overt assertion, the line implies that the devil is no more a bailiff than is the summoner; even more subtle is the essential truth of his remark, for the duties he has come to perform *are* those of a bailiff – to administer justice and collect his lord's due, in this case the soul of this "false theef".

The summoner, however, cannot hide his own nature for long. When the devil offers to share his gold and silver if the summoner should happen to visit his shire, the latter immediately makes a pledge of brotherhood. Unknowingly, he allows his greed to lead him into what we recognise as a trap set for the "wood hare". Unaware of how transparent his interest is, he questions his new "brother" about the location of his home, but the double meaning of the devil's reply is apparent only to us:

> Brother . . . fer in the north contree,
> Where-as I hope som tyme I shal thee see.
> Er we departe, I shal thee so wel wisse
> That of myn hous ne shaltow nevere mysse.[17]

[14] R. M. Garrett, "The Lay of Sir Gawayne and the Green Knight", *J.E.G.P.*, XXIV (1925), p. 129; W. C. Curry, *The Ideal of Personal Beauty in the Middle Ages*, Baltimore, 1916, p. 50; J. R. Hulbert, "Sir Gawayn and the Grene Knyght", *Modern Philology*, XIII (1915), pp. 454-60; D. W. Robertson, Jr., "Why the Devil wears Green", *Modern Language Notes*, LXIX (1954), pp. 470-2.   [15] "The Friar's Tale", D 1393-4.
[16] *Op. cit.*, 1395-6.   [17] *Op. cit.*, 1413-16.

The summoner fails to realise the significance of the "north contree", which is associated with infernal regions in Biblical tradition and Germanic mythology, and his blindness to the devil's purpose prevents him from seeing that he has almost no chance, indeed, of missing the "hous". In fact, he now ensures the doom which we anticipate, for he falls for a trick which brings him to an open confession of his misdeeds. When he questions the infernal "bailiff" about his technique for gaining profit from his office, the latter describes exactly such unscrupulous practices as the summoner habitually uses. As a result the summoner forgets his assumed respectability and exclaims:

> Now certes . . . so fare I.
> I spare nat to taken, God it woot,
> But if it be to hevy or to hoot.
> What I may gete in conseil prively,
> No maner conscience of that have I.
> Nere myn extorcioun, I myghte nat lyven,
> Ne of swiche japes wol I nat be shryven.
> Stomak ne conscience ne knowe I noon;
> I shrewe thise shrifte-fadres everychoon.[18]

Thus the devil's appeal to the summoner's greed has produced precisely the desired effect: not only does the unsuspecting victim voluntarily swear an oath which binds him to his destiny and admit his own guilt, but he also abjures confession and penance, the one source of forgiveness which might even yet save his soul. In his delight at having found a boon companion who is apparently both rich and generous, he even cries out: "Wel be we met, by God and by Seint Jame!".[19] The comic irony of his exclamation is apparent to us for we know that if he understood the import of the encounter, he would hardly consider that the two of them were "wel met". On yet another level, however, the meeting, by God and by Seint Jame, *is* providential, for it gives the devil his opportunity to serve as "Goddes instrument"[20] in

[18] *Op. cit.*, 1434-42.
[19] *Op. cit.*, 1443. This ironic device of having a character express approval of an ungodly state of affairs by swearing "by God" (and, in this case, by one of the principal medieval saints, St James of Compostela) is most typical of Chaucer. See, for example, "The Shipman's Tale", B² 1338-47.
[20] "The Friar's Tale", D 1483.

ridding the world of an evil parasite, a function which he later explains to the heedless summoner.

Knowing the extent to which he can mislead his victim, the devil now begins to tell the truth outspokenly. Although he asserts that he is a "feend" whose "dwellyng is in helle" and indicates exactly what is to happen to his "brother deere", he does so in such a way that the summoner completely misses the point. Just before announcing his real identity, the devil begins "a litel for to smyle",[21] and because we have been able to watch the preceding events unfold on different levels, we realise that the summoner's initial hypocrisy regarding his own profession is now about to blind him to the openly stated truth. He notices the smile and assumes that his friend is lying, just as he has lied himself. The playful casualness of his reaction to the news indicates his fatal error:

"A!" quod this somonour, "benedicite! what sey ye?
I wende ye were a yeman trewely."[22]

Secure in his belief that he understands what is actually happening, he is willing to go along with what seems to him an amusing pretence. He asks several questions about hell and the nature of fiends, but he fails to catch the implications of the replies, which are full of Biblical and classical allusions. Take, for example, the devil's reference to Dante and Virgil:

For thou shalt, by thyn owene experience,
Konne in a chayer rede of this sentence
Bet than Virgile, while he was on lyve,
Or Dant also.[23]

The illiterate summoner apparently does not know that these two poets are authorities on conditions in hell any more than he grasps the significance of such open warnings as the devil's remark that "A lowsy jogelour kan deceyve thee, And pardee, yet kan I moore craft than he".[24] Even when his friend says "brother myn, thy wit is al to bare To understonde",[25] we may assume that the summoner thinks this statement merely an evasion of the question he has just asked. The fiend also asserts that he

[21] *Op. cit.*, 1446.
[23] *Op. cit.*, 1517-20.
[25] *Op. cit.*, 1480-1.
[22] *Op. cit.*, 1456-7.
[24] *Op. cit.*, 1467-8.

would ride to the world's end for a "preye"[26] and that devils will "swiche formes make" as best enable them "preyes for to take".[27] To the victim such metaphors are but part of an elaborate lie which his "brother" is facetiously attempting to make him believe: but we, on the contrary, are reminded of the basic image which has allowed us to savour the full irony of this conversation and to see it as a dramatic conflict of character.

When the unutterably dense but realistic summoner reaffirms his brotherhood with the "feend" he says:

> My trouthe wol I holde, as in this cas.
> For though thou were the devel Sathanas,
> My trouthe wol I holde to my brother,
> As I am sworn, and ech of us til oother,
> For to be trewe brother in this cas.[28]

His qualifying clause, "though thou were the devel Sathanas", both implies the mistrust which his own dishonesty has fostered and suggests his acceptance of his friend's supposed game. He even reasserts at this point his lie about his own identity ("I am a yeman, knowen is ful wyde"[29]) and thus vainly attempts to keep up a disguise which he would surely consider unnecessary if he truly believed that he had sworn brotherhood with the devil rather than with a congenial (and wealthy) hypocrite who is practising the summoner's own deceit. In similar fashion, his reaction when they meet the swearing carter reveals further his erroneous judgment of the devil's veracity. He says to himself, "Heere shal we have a pley"[30] and then proposes that the devil take the horses. With sly but useless cleverness, unaware of how tightly his blind assumptions have ensnared him in the net of his own sins, he intends to use the situation to expose his long-winded, lying friend. In his obliviousness, he is indeed the "wood hare" to which he was first compared.

Up to this point much of the humour in the tale has resulted from a parallelism between the positions and actions of the two characters. The official function of each is to summon sinners to answer for offences. When the two meet, each hides his identity

[26] *Op. cit.,* 1455.
[27] *Op. cit.,* 1471-2.
[28] *Op. cit.,* 1525-9.
[29] *Op. cit.,* 1524.
[30] *Op. cit.,* 1548.

under the same bailiff disguise; yet each later reveals his true nature, the summoner unconsciously, the devil artfully. In terms of the basic image each is a hunter who has found his prey, but the two victims, the summoner and the widow, remain unaware of the impending danger. The paradoxical image developed in the first hundred lines of the tale makes it possible for us to realise this parallelism as it unfolds and thus to appreciate the full measure of both the humour and the irony. In the final episode both hunters will descend simultaneously upon their prey, but only the stronger will emerge with the kill.

In this concluding scene, in which the summoner curses himself and so outrages the widow that she condemns him with heartfelt sincerity, the image of the "wood hare" gains an added implication. The original basis for the saying "mad as a March hare" was the observation that hares behave with erratic recklessness during the breeding season, traditionally the month of March.[31] So widely accepted was this idea at one time that the hare became a common symbol for lechery, and allegorical drawings frequently extolled the triumph of chastity by depicting a hare crushed beneath the feet of a maiden.[32] These associations of lechery and of heedlessness prompted by sex are ironically duplicated in the summoner, who excels in extorting money from accused adulterers. The introductory description has established the fact that he employs bawds to spy out potential victims, and in this concluding episode it is most apt that, by accusing the widow of sexual trespass, he provokes the curse which allows the devil to seize him:

> "Whan that thou madest thyn housbonde cokewold,
> I payde at hoom for thy correccioun."
> "Thou lixt!" quod she, "by my savacioun,
> Ne was I nevere er now, wydwe ne wyf,
> Somoned unto youre court in al my lyf;
> Ne nevere I nas but of my body trewe!
> Unto the devel blak and rough of hewe
> Yeve I thy body and my panne also!"[33]

[31] Skeat, *loc. cit.*

[32] Eug. Droulers, *Dictionnaire des Attributs, Allégories, Emblèmes et Symboles*, Turnhout, 1948, p. 129.   [33] "The Friar's Tale", D 1616-23.

Thus, the basic image gains further ironic intensity. Not only is the summoner both hunter and prey, but he is also vulnerable to destruction in the same manner as the "mad hare" and for ironically similar reasons. Moreover, although the figures are vastly different, virtue here triumphs over the "hare" even as it does in its graphic allegorical representations. With this added complexity, the organic relationship of the composite image to the overall structure is strengthened, even as the image, in turn, tightens the unity of the whole.[34]

When at the end of the tale the Friar points a moral for the benefit of the listeners, he uses the same hunter-prey image but diverts it from his characters to the pilgrims themselves. He warns them to take heed of the summoner's fate, for although this victim was guilty, "the temptour Sathanas", like the lion, "sit in his awayt alway To sle the innocent, if that he may".[35] But he adds, if they dispose their hearts to withstand the "feend", Christ will be their "champion and knyght". In this way the image of the human prey is extended to include a defender who blends, in typical medieval fashion, the chivalric tradition with the Christian,[36] and the shift in application of the image turns Chaucer's masterpiece of comic irony into an exemplum which is at once completely in keeping with the traditions of his age and yet artistically unique.[37]

[34] If one wishes to consider the tale in relation to its narrator and its position within the framework of the *Canterbury Tales* as a whole, the image of the "wood hare" has further ironic parallels. The Friar tells the story to insult the Summoner, yet he himself is reckless in matters related to sex ("General Prologue", A 212-13), is willing to take bribes instead of strictly adhering to his religious duties (221-32), and extorts money from poor widows (253-5). The Summoner also is lecherous (A 626, 663-5) and eager to accept bribes (649-57). Thus both resemble the protagonist, the "wood hare" of "The Friar's Tale".

[35] "The Friar's Tale", D 1657-8.

[36] Notable examples are the episode of the harrowing of hell in *Piers Plowman* and the section of the *Ancrene Wisse* usually entitled "The Love of Christ".

[37] Some of the imagery analysed here has been discussed by Earle Birney in his incisive article " 'After His Ymage': the Central Ironies of the 'Friar's Tale' ", *Mediaeval Studies*, XXI (1959), pp. 17-35.

Dorothy Bethurum Loomis

CHAUCER AND SHAKESPEARE

Comparisons are odorous
DOGBERRY

I

Chaucer's role in the sixteenth and early seventeenth centuries is a complex one. Of his popularity throughout this period there can be little doubt. The tide of praise that began to rise soon after his death had ebbed but little, and Miss Spurgeon's allusions tell the story in some detail. Scholars both before and after her survey was published have further documented Elizabethan borrowings from Chaucer, and the list need not be given again.[1] But by the third quarter of the sixteenth century it was a dubious popularity that he enjoyed. "Mismetred", as he had prayed he might not be, because of the linguistic changes of a hundred and fifty years he appeared even to his admirers to be a crude metrist, writing in antiquated diction, though Spenser and Sidney, as well as other poets, continued to award him a high measure of praise. We must add to the linguistic misunderstandings the fact that the Chaucerian canon had not been fixed, and that he was believed to be the author of the anti-Roman diatribes, *Jack Upland*, the *Pilgrim's Tale*, and the *Plowman's Tale*, and that consequently he was drawn into the Puritan camp and praised for a reforming zeal he did not possess. On the other hand, his bawdry offended austere moralists, who regarded him as trivial of mind, a menace to decent mores.[2] But by the end of the century when Speght

[1] Caroline Spurgeon, *Five Hundred Years of Chaucer Criticism and Allusion, 1357-1900*, Cambridge, 1925, Vol. I. There are references in following footnotes to relevant articles by N. Coghill, Muriel Bradbrook, and O. Bellmann.

[2] *Op. cit.*, pp. xix-xxi.

brought out his edition (1598), helped by Francis Beaumont the elder, and Francis Thynne published his "Animadversions" against Speght's edition, Chaucer was again much discussed, much admired, influential upon poets, dramatists, and critics.

The case for his influence on Shakespeare is hard to make. That Shakespeare read him and used him is indubitable, but his real influence is better judged by similarities in tone and situation between *Romeo and Juliet*, for example, and Book IV of *Troilus and Criseyde* than by verbal parallels here and there. These, as Professor Coghill has shown,[3] are most numerous in the plays that appeared between 1593 and 1597, and they never in themselves are very significant, except in the case of *A Midsummer-Night's Dream*.

Later, however, Shakespeare wrote *Troilus and Cressida* and at least a part of *The Two Noble Kinsmen*, both from Chaucer principally, however many other sources he used. Yet in spite of the degradation of Chaucer's story in *Troilus and Cressida* we cannot doubt that Shakespeare read it with appreciation, for his tribute to it is in the epithalamium of Act V of *The Merchant of Venice*:

> in such a night
> Troilus methinks mounted the Troyan walls,
> And sigh'd his soul toward the Grecian tents,
> Where Cressid lay that night.

It is also in the leave-taking of Romeo and Juliet. When he rewrote Chaucer's story in *Troilus and Cressida* he had other things in mind. It must be recognised, too, that the alchemy of a genius like Shakespeare's transmutes whatever it uses to another metal entirely, so that it is difficult to speak of "influence" in any normal sense. Leaving aside the history plays – and only some of these – one could hardly claim that any of his sources determined the quality of his work. Apparently he looked for a plot and a situation that evoked from him intellectual activity of a supreme kind, and he found his materials in the unlikeliest places. If we had to judge his taste by what he chose to rewrite, we would have to rate it very low. Senecan blood and madness, Italian stories of

[3] N. Coghill, "Shakespeare's Reading in Chaucer", *Elizabethan and Jacobean Studies Presented to F. P. Wilson*, Oxford, 1959, pp. 86-99.

CMA M

lust and murder, cheap accounts of sordid intrigue – all served
him equally. Shakespeare knew Ovid well and used him throughout his life, but as far as the plays go it would never be possible
to point to the same kind of Ovidian influence on him that we see
on Chaucer. The relation of *Romeo and Juliet* to Brooke's poem[4]
is about that of *Troilus and Criseyde* to Boccaccio's *Filostrato*. But
there is much more of Boccaccio in *Troilus* than of Brooke in
Romeo and Juliet, changed as Chaucer's story is, and perhaps the
reason is that Chaucer "appreciated" Boccaccio more than
Shakespeare did Brooke, that he drew his material from better
sources.

2

More profitable, perhaps, than retracing the details of Shakespeare's borrowings from Chaucer, except for his rewriting of
Troilus and Criseyde and "The Knight's Tale", is to note some of
the similarities and contrasts between the two writers.

There are similarities between Chaucer and Shakespeare,
though they are more superficial than essential. A curious
parallel in biography is that in the records we have of them, both
disappear from sight for about seven years, Chaucer from 1360,
when he was known to be in the household of Lionel, Earl of
Ulster, until 1367, when he received from Edward III a life pen-
sion of twenty marks and was referred to as the King's *dilectus
vallectus*;[5] Shakespeare from 1585, when he was still in Stratford,
until 1592, when he appears as the object of Greene's attack in the
Groatsworth of Wit as the "absolute *Johannes factotum*" of his
company. They were crucial years and cover almost the same
span in both poets; Chaucer was eighteen or nineteen in 1360 and
Shakespeare twenty-one in 1585. Surmise and gossip have filled
both lacunae. It is probable that Chaucer remained in the service
of Lionel for those years – they coincide almost exactly with
Lionel's absence in Ireland as the King's Lieutenant – but he may,
as one thin tradition has it,[6] have attended one of the Inns of

---

[4] Arthur Brooke's *The Tragicall Historye of Romeus and Juliet* (1562).

[5] See Martin M. Crow and Clair C. Olson, *Chaucer Life-Records*, Oxford,
1966, p. 123.

[6] Speght reported that Master Buckley, keeper of the records of the Inner
Temple in the sixteenth century, said that he had seen in them a note that

Court during this period. A somewhat better tradition reports that Shakespeare was a schoolmaster for a part of this time,[7] but he could not have attracted the attention he got from Greene as author and adapter of plays, actor, and general handyman in the theatre if he had not by 1592 served a considerable apprenticeship there.

Both Chaucer and Shakespeare must have had unusual personal charm, for both inspired devotion in their friends – in Chaucer's case Lydgate, Hoccleve, and Gower, to take merely the evidence of their writings; and Jonson, Drayton, Heminge, Condell, and Richard Burbage in Shakespeare's. Chaucer's whole successful career in the reign of three kings is evidence of his tact, and Shakespeare's biography yields similar proof of his graciousness.[8]

It is hard to compare their positions in society, for Chaucer was throughout his life attached to the court as a civil servant of some kind and wrote for an aristocratic audience, while Shakespeare followed a profession which in his early career caused him some shame,[9] though at times he also wrote at royal command and enjoyed the patronage of the Earl of Southampton. Both Chaucer and Shakespeare belonged to the upper middle class, and both were men of some wealth.[10]

More important than these scraps of biography is the nature of Chaucer's and of Shakespeare's art. Both wrote for the ear, not the eye, and both relied for their effects on aural reception on the part of accomplished audiences. For Chaucer the audience was narrow, the aristocratic circle attached to John of Gaunt or to Richard II and probably to a number of important men of affairs in England – Sir William Beauchamp, Sir Lewis Clifford, Sir

Chaucer had been fined two shillings for beating a Franciscan friar in Fleet Street. See Crow and Olson, *op. cit.*, p. 12, n. 5.

[7] Aubrey in his *Brief Lives* (ed. Oliver L. Dick, London, 1950, p. 276) tells us that he heard this from William Beeston, son of Christopher Beeston, with whom Shakespeare had acted for six years. See also Peter Alexander, *Shakespeare's Life and Art*, London, 1946, pp. 24-6.

[8] E. K. Chambers, *William Shakespeare*, Oxford, 1963, Appendix B, pp. 186-237.

[9] See Sonnets CX, CXI, CXII.

[10] Chaucer's income in the latter part of 1375, for example has been estimated at about five thousand pounds. For Shakespeare's financial success see Peter Alexander, *op. cit.*, p. 199.

William Neville, Sir Philip de Vache, and Sir Peter Bukton – as
well as literary figures, John Gower, Ralph Strode, Henry Scogan,
Thomas Usk. For Shakespeare the audience was the mixed
crowds of aristocracy, middle class, and lower class that frequented
the Globe Theatre, and in the latter part of his career the more
sophisticated audience of Blackfriars. Though Chaucer shows
some concern for the integrity of his text in his "Wordes unto
Adam, his owne Scriveyn", it must not be supposed he had readers
in mind. His plea that *Troilus and Criseyde* be not "mismetred",
"red wherso thow be, or elles songe",[11] shows that it is sound he
has in mind. Shakespeare showed even more than usual indifference to the printing of his plays, allowing the quartos to
appear full of errors that even Chaucer might have corrected,
indicating that his whole effort was directed to the realisation of
his effects in action and speech on the stage.[12] It is likely that the
silent reading which brings poetry to us now has much more of
imagined sound and beat in it than we customarily recognise; yet
there is a wide difference between our appreciation of *The Four
Quartets* and the communal hearing of *Troilus* that the illumination
of MS 61 of Corpus Christi College, Cambridge, so beautifully
shows us. There is similarly a wide difference between reading
Macbeth in solitude and as a part of an audience seeing and
hearing it played on the boards. Both poets in our usual experience
of them are remote from us now.

To this list of similarities can be added that both poets show a
hearty taste for bawdry which their dramatic use of it scarcely
conceals, and both are elusive, though in very different ways.

3

The contrasts between them are more striking. Chaucer among
English poets was conspicuously cosmopolitan. His diplomatic
missions took him to the courts of France and of Italy, and his
literary interests were equally continental. In his imitation of the

[11] *Troilus and Criseyde*, v, 1797, *The Works of Geoffrey Chaucer*, ed. F. N.
Robinson, 2nd edn., London, 1957.

[12] On this point see G. E. Bentley, *Shakespeare and His Theatre*, Lincoln,
Nebraska, 1964, Chap. I. It is possible, however, that in *Troilus and Cressida*
Shakespeare had readers in mind. For a recent controversy about the first
production of *Troilus* see an exchange of letters between Professors Coghill and
Alexander in the *Times Literary Supplement*, 19 Jan., 30 March, 20 April, 1967.

love-visions of Machaut, Deschamps, and Froissart in the early part of his career he brought to English audiences the sophistication of the gallic spirit. In his borrowings from Dante and from Petrarch and in his close study of Boccaccio he made the influence of Italy felt, at that time the most advanced culture of Europe. Furthermore, in translating the *Roman de la Rose* and Boethius's *Consolation of Philosophy* he made available for the English the two most influential books of the Middle Ages, vehicles for the currents of thought that had done most to shape Europe – Neoplatonism in Boethius and the vast and comprehensive study of sexual attraction in the *Roman*. Chaucer's boundaries were not those of the island on which he lived and were not entirely coterminous with Europe. The range of his interests is reflected in the great parade of pilgrims, with their own fictional characters which he created, where he shows his devotion to the goddess Natura and gives us, to paraphrase Dryden, Nature's plenty.

Shakespeare is a small-town man, faithful to Stratford all his life. His clowns illustrate this fact well enough. The naïve ones, unconscious butts of the sophisticated characters – Bottom, Dogberry, Costard – are rural and provincial: but even the clever ones such as Touchstone and Feste have no marks of London on them, and Touchstone's satire of both court and country serves to salt the pastoralism of the play rather than to prove his urban origin. Shakespeare's England is not the England of Drake's and Raleigh's voyages, the England that sent settlers to Jamestown in his own lifetime. It is an England safe behind the barrier of its surrounding waters which are "as a moat defensive to a house", protecting it "Against the envy of less happier lands".[13] And this famous speech Shakespeare gives to John of Gaunt, actually one of the most wide-ranging of feudal noblemen, whose envy of those less happier lands took him to Spain and almost made him King of Castile. France to Shakespeare is not the civiliser of Europe but the breeder of princes like the Dauphin in *Henry V*, and Italy is not the purveyor of humanism to all of Europe but the creator of foppish fashions and Machiavellian villains like Iago and Iachimo. To be sure, the plays have French, Italian, Sicilian, Danish settings, but in the comedies the settings are Arcadian really, and when anything recognisably

[13] *Richard II*, ii, i, 48-9, ed. W. J. Craig, Oxford, 1924.

characteristic of these lands appears, it is not laudatory. Shakespeare's travels may have taken him as far afield as Bristol[14] when
the plague closed the theatres in London, but all the definite
information we have is confined to his journeys between Stratford
and London. Shakespeare's indifference to the New World or
even to Europe does not mean that he devoted to his own
countrymen the close scrutiny that Jonson and Dekker did. His
subject was man, unaccommodated man and man in almost all his
adjustments to his position on this planet. His is the most
nearly universal canvas that European letters have ever produced,
his probings of what it is to be a human being the most searching
that art affords us.

   This difference is perhaps somewhat the result of the times and
of the conditions under which they lived, and these conditions
need emphasis. For Chaucer poetry was an avocation, an activity
that at least one critic claims never wholly engaged him.[15]   One
may search the *Life-Records* in vain for any references to Chaucer
as a poet. They show him as a busy civil servant going on diplomatic missions for the King, acting as Comptroller of the Customs
at the port of London (and writing the records in his own hand),
as Clerk of the King's Works in charge of building and repairs at
various royal residences, as Deputy Forester of the royal forest of
Petherton in Somerset, and representing Kent in Parliament. He
was attached in some capacity to the courts of Lionel, John of
Gaunt, Edward III, Richard II, and Henry IV all his life; and
though the audience these attachments provided for the reception
of his poetry must have been increasingly important to him, he
never was a professional poet. One is reminded that Dante gave
as much time to politics as to poetry, and that T. S. Eliot was a
confidential clerk and a successful business man.

   Shakespeare, though he became a considerable landholder and
took part in negotiations relating to real estate, was wholly
engaged in the theatre, as owner, producer, director, actor, and
dramatist. In his complete professionalism he is a contrast to
Marlowe or Ben Jonson, who were dramatists but not theatre men.
Perhaps no one else has ever known the theatre so well – Molière

---

[14] Chambers, *Shakespeare*, II, 313.

[15] See Paull Baum, *Chaucer: A Critical Appreciation*, Durham, N.C., 1958,
pp. 7-13.

comes nearest to it – and this intimate and detailed knowledge is what enables him to show man in action on the boards so convincingly that we sometimes confuse the stage of the Globe with that of the world it imitates, see the mirror as the nature that it reflects.

More significant than these contrasts, however, is the difference in literary form in Chaucer's and Shakespeare's work. Much has been made of the dramatic qualities in Chaucer's fiction, of his ability to create characters and to put them in action and to write sprightly dialogue. This is of course quite just, but yet in an important sense Chaucer is the least dramatic of writers of poetic fiction, and herein lies his sharpest contrast with Shakespeare. He does not achieve, or try to achieve, the complete lack of self-consciousness that is Shakespeare's supreme mark. As a writer he does not have the characterlessness, the "negative capability" that Keats attributed to Shakespeare. Most characteristically he tells his story through the mouthpiece of his naïve namesake whose comments on the events of the tale are a part of the story. We look in vain for Shakespeare's spokesman, however we wish to identify him with Berowne or Hamlet or Prospero; no *persona* appears to make an apology for Cressida or to comment on the folly of young love. (Rosalind comments on it, but she is involved in it.) The utter transparency with which the plays are projected allows everyone to find himself somewhere in Shakespeare, filling in the figure that refuses to appear; and we get heated controversy as to whether Shakespeare was a Roman Catholic, an Anglican, any sort of Christian, or an agnostic, a disbeliever. The extremes go from Bethel, who finds a figure of the Mass in the reports of the Delphic oracle in *The Winter's Tale*,[16] to Santayana's ambiguous comment on some lines in *Richard II*[17] that Shakespeare was faced with a choice of Christianity or nothing, and he chose nothing.[18] This is a point on which most people now hold decided opinions, but we could not be so sure, and so divided, if Shakespeare employed Chaucer's method. We may disagree on the extent to which Chaucer identified himself with orthodox

[16] S. L. Bethel, *The Winter's Tale: A Study*, London, 1947, pp. 83-4.

[17] *Richard II*, IV, i, 92-100.

[18] George Santayana, *Interpretations of Poetry and Religion*, New York, 1900, p. 152.

Christian teaching, and on the reach of his scepticism: but nobody claims that he was an agnostic, and very few claim that scepticism did not touch him at all.

In the end both Shakespeare and Chaucer remain elusive, Shakespeare by virtue of his very fecundity, and the success with which he drew clowns and wise men, villains and heroes; Chaucer because he manages to conceal himself behind his spokesman, because his position vis-à-vis his audience demanded detachment, and probably from a temperamental dislike for speaking out clear and plain. On some subjects, love, for instance, the only way Chaucer could maintain his position as a middle-class poet reading to an aristocratic audience was to refuse to wear the troubadour's robe and to assume a mask. Very likely the play between profession and a reality known to his audience made a rich humour. Whatever the reason, in spite of his surface accessibility it is hard to discover what Chaucer believed about anything. But Shakespeare wears no mask; he is not there at all.

Another fact makes Chaucer's fiction far from dramatic, and that is the extent to which it relies on description; and here we see how utterly unlike the two forms are. In a romance like "The Knight's Tale" the pageantry, as is to be expected, is built up by brilliant description, but even in the *fabliaux* where description might be held to a minimum it is important and necessary. The Friar's description of the Summoner at the beginning of his tale, for instance, with the list of the latter's abuses, is essential to the story; and the same is true of the Summoner's matchless picture of his friar in action. Chaucer is at his most brilliant in the portraits at the beginning of "The Miller's Tale" and "The Reeve's Tale", and we get the flavour of the action because of the careful characterisation of the *dramatis personae* – the "hende Nicholas"; Alison, "a prymerole, a piggesnye, For any lord to leggen in his bedde"; Absolon with curled hair that "strouted as a fanne large and brode"; the "hoote deynous Symkyn" and his wife "ful of hoker and bisemare". Most of Chaucer's portraits of people are in the tradition of the *effictio* of the medieval rhetoricians, though vivified and realistic beyond any medieval models: but in the legends retold from Ovid's *Heroides* in the *Legend of Good Women* he is content, usually, with a general characterisation of his heroines as faithful in love and of his villains as unfaithful. In the case of Hypermnestra he adds to Ovid's account a good astrological explanation for her gentleness and faithfulness; occasionally the typical Chaucerian touch is seen – "And Jason is as coy as is a mayde; He loketh pitously but nought he sayde" – but for the most part these are perfunctory performances bordering on satire. Yet even in the legends there are occasional vivid portrayals of action or scene. The most notable is the sea-fight in "Cleopatra";[19] the entertainment of Eneas in "Dido"[20] is also rich in detail. Almost everywhere else in Chaucer's fiction it can be held that description, usually leisurely, is the very heart of his power.

It may be said that drama needs none of this since character and scene are visible before us. That is true, and truer of Shakespeare's plays than of any others.[21] Where scenic atmosphere is important it is written into the lines, whether of the freezing ramparts of Elsinore or of the moon-drenched wood in *A Midsummer-Night's Dream*. And Shakespeare can sketch in a line or two a covered arbour in which Beatrice hides,[22] or even make the effect of the scene a moral test as in *The Tempest*, ii, i, 46-60. He could also dress his characters to secure something like the impression made by the vulgar black-and-white of Alison's shining dress or by Absolon's abundant hair. Hamlet's black cloak and Richard ii's gold not only appear but are commented on by other characters. Yet the absence of description and the resulting sharp impact of the play's action mark the drama as a form so different from Chaucer's longer fiction as to make a comparison of the two unprofitable. Chaucer must have read the story of Troilus's double sorrow in at least five instalments to his audience, and in the intervals the listeners could think of what had gone before. Romeo's and Juliet's short joy and its destruction is a "two hours' traffic of our stage".

[19] *Legend of Good Women*, 635-53.

[20] *Op. cit.*, 1100-24.

[21] Heywood's defence of the drama is apt here: "A description is only a shadow, received by the eare, but not perceived by the eye; lively portrature is meerely a forme seen by the eye, but can neither shew action, passion, motion, or any other gesture to moove the spirits of the beholder to admiration" (*An Apology for Actors*, Shakespeare Society Reprint, London, 1841, p. 20).

[2] *Much Ado*, iii, i, 7-9.

4

If we judge Chaucer's influence on Shakespeare by the latter's rewriting of *Troilus and Criseyde* and of "The Knight's Tale" we shall have to conclude that it was not fructifying, for in the Shakespearean canon *Troilus and Cressida* and *The Two Noble Kinsmen* occupy a low place. Why Shakespeare chose *Troilus and Criseyde* can perhaps be guessed. For one thing the Troy story was popular in Elizabethan England;[23] as Tatlock put it, "no traditional story was so popular in the Elizabethan Age as that of the siege of Troy and some of its episodes".[24] There was every reason for the Lord Chamberlain's Men to want Shakespeare to write a play on this subject. It must also have appealed to Shakespeare himself, because, even in Chaucer's poem, it illustrates one of his favourite themes – the corrupting influence of a world the lovers do not control – and it gave him the opportunity to underscore the idea. It allowed him, too, the exploration of what is honour, an equally congenial theme. Chaucer's poem is, of course, only one of several sources Shakespeare used;[25] from it he got the love story, with which he combined the story of the war to produce his relentless inversion of Chaucer's idealistic view of love. This he does, not from a complete rejection of the medieval code, though he does satirise it gently in the comedies, but from a strong conviction that such a love cannot flourish in the conflict of cultures which Troy and Greece exhibit, and that the corruption of the pragmatic and ruthless world of Achilles infects all it touches.

[23] Nicolas Grimoald (1519-62) wrote a comedy now lost, *Troilus ex Chaucero*, whether in Latin or in English we do not know; a new edition of Caxton's *The Recuyell of the Historyes of Troye* was issued in 1596; seven books of Chapman's translation of Homer appeared in 1598; Speght's edition of Chaucer, containing Henryson's *Testament of Cresseid*, came out in 1598; the Admiral's Men gave five performances of a play called *Troye* in 1599; Chettle and Dekker were at work on a play called *Troyless and Cresade* in 1599; the Admiral's Men played in 1599 four additional plays relating to the story of Troy. The legend of Brutus, known to all theatre-goers, put England solidly on the Trojan side of the conflict.

[24] J. S. P. Tatlock, "The Siege of Troy", *P.M.L.A.*, xxx (1915), p. 673.

[25] To the books listed in the above note should be added Lydgate's *Troy Book*. See Robert Presson, Shakespeare's *Troilus and Cressida and the Legends of Troy*, Madison, Wis., 1953.

But the values of the poem cannot be translated into drama, and in using Chaucer's masterpiece Shakespeare was taking the most intractable of materials. As Lawrence has pointed out,[26] the story is essentially undramatic and depends entirely on character. The poem gets its effect from Chaucer's leisurely pace which allows the characters to emerge and the plot to develop; and though Shakespeare also must concentrate on character, and though the play is much more complicated than the poem, it does not rest firmly on a well-managed plot, but becomes a sort of Shavian debate on love, lust, honour, and rule, with an ending so inconclusive as to disappoint all accustomed to Shakespeare's "dexterity and power". The epistle to the reader added to the quarto text by the printers, Bonian and Walley, praises the wit of the play. Wit it has, to be sure, but a wit that has turned sour, whether in the prurience of Pandarus, the sophisticated bawdry of Helen and Paris, the strained excess of Cressida's play with her uncle, or Thersites' scrofulous railing. It all reflects a society dominated by sexual relations which have no basic integrity – Paris and Helen first, the great cause of the war; Troilus and Cressida, whose moment of love is framed by Pandarus; Diomedes and Cressida, bullying lust and sycophantic willingness; Achilles and Polyxena; Achilles and Patroclus. The least corrupted are Troilus and Cressida in the beginning, but neither has the health of Shakespeare's other lovers.

Though there is little critical insight to be gained by it, a comparison of the play and the poem does show how incommensurable are romantic fiction and realistic drama. The play is more dependent on the poem than is usually admitted. Miss Bradbrook, however, has noted that each of Chaucer's five books is represented in one or two scenes in the play.[27] The situations do not need listing; every one is an inversion of Chaucer's values, none shrewder than the passing of the warriors across the stage in I, i, and Pandarus's failing to recognise Troilus at first. (Compare

---

[26] W. W. Lawrence, *Shakespeare's Problem Comedies*, New York, 1931, pp. 127-9.

[27] Muriel C. Bradbrook, "What Shakespeare did to Chaucer's *Troilus and Criseyde*", *Shakespeare Quarterly*, IX (1958), pp. 311-19. The Variorum *Troilus and Cressida*, ed. H. N. Hillebrand, Philadelphia, 1953, pp. 447-9, analyses the play's relation to Chaucer.

Troilus and Criseyde, 11, 610-51.) One interesting thing is to see
what Shakespeare makes of Chaucer's long descriptions. The
picture of Criseyde's woe when she hears that she is to be ex-
changed for Antenor is crucial to an understanding of both poem
and play. It is managed easily by Chaucer, from his omniscient
point of view, in forthright description:

> Hire ownded heer, that sonnyssh was of hewe,
> She rente, and ek hire fyngeres longe and smale
> She wrong ful ofte, and bad God on hire rewe,
> And with the deth to doon boote on hire bale.
> Hire hewe, whilom bright, that tho was pale,
> Bar witnesse of hire wo and hire constreynte.

> . . . with hire salte teris
> Hire brest, hire face, ybathed was ful wete.
> The myghty tresses of hire sonnysshe heeris,
> Unbroiden, hangen al aboute hire eeris.[28]

In the play Cressida herself must describe how the news affected
her:

Cressida: I'll go in and weep –
Pandarus: Do, do.
Cressida: Tear my bright hair, and scratch my praised cheeks,
            Crack my clear voice with sobs, and break my heart
            With sounding Troilus. I will not go from Troy.[29]

The first part of l. 110 is probably an echo of the *Testament of
Cresseid*; the rest is from Chaucer. But on Cressida's own lips the
threat sounds somehow too protesting. We never see her so
stained by grief. Another passage is a curious parallel of the
conventional *effictio* in Book v, 799-840, and describes only
Troilus.[30] In the play Ulysses speaks the lines and confuses the
critics. Shakespeare often through a report claims virtues for a
character whose actions scarcely justify what is being said.
Olivia's praise of Orsino, whom she dislikes, we may take to be
just:[31] but in the Ulysses passage it is doubtful whether Troilus

---

[28] *Troilus and Criseyde*, IV, 736-41, 814-17.
[29] Shakespeare, *Troilus and Cressida*, IV, ii, 112-16.
[30] *Op. cit.*, IV, v, 96-112.   [31] *Twelfth Night*, I, v, 279-83.

really was all that the lines claim, or whether, since Ulysses says this was told him by Aeneas some time ago, it points up the bad effects of love on Troilus. It almost seems to be Shakespeare's acknowledgment of failure in establishing Troilus's character.

Even had Shakespeare wished to reproduce the values of Chaucer's poem – and surely he did not – it is unlikely that they could have been copied in a play. In *Antony and Cleopatra* the movement is from fickleness to stability in love, with Cleopatra "marble-constant" after Antony's death. But it needs time, and lots of it, to sink Criseyde's defection in the tide of mutability that washes the world, so that she retains our pity to the end. Chaucer's blurring of time in Book v, his insistence on her slow yielding to Troilus in Books II and III cannot be translated into drama. There is little time in the play, though much talk of it; and the evocation of future time, the "fixing solution", as made by Troilus, Cressida, and Pandarus, establishes forever "As true as Troilus", "As false as Cressid", "let all pitiful goers-between be called to the world's end after my name; call them all Pandars".[32]

5

The *House of Fame* seems to have interested Ben Jonson more than any other of Chaucer's works, to the degree that Inigo Jones in designing the setting for *The Masque of Queens* "profest to follow that noble description made by Chaucer of the place".[33] Shakespeare, however, found "The Knight's Tale" most attractive, used it extensively in *A Midsummer-Night's Dream*, and later in his career collaborated with Fletcher in rewriting it in *The Two Noble Kinsmen*. Or so the title-page of the 1634 Quarto claims. There has been much debate about the degree of Shakespeare's collaboration, but until quite recently there was general agreement that Shakespeare wrote most of I; II, i; III, i, ii; IV, iii; V, i, iii, iv. In

[32] Shakespeare, *Troilus and Cressida*, III, ii, 189, 203, 208-10.
[33] See Herford and Simpson, *The Works of Ben Jonson*, Oxford, 1950, X, pp. 493-4. According to O. Bellmann ("Chaucers Einfluss auf das englische Drama", *Anglia*, XXV, 1902, pp. 1-85), of twenty-six borrowings from Chaucer by Jonson eight are from the *House of Fame*, five from *Troilus*, two from "The Man of Law's Tale", two from "The Physician's Tale", two from "The Nun's Priest's Tale", two from "The Squire's Tale", one from "The Reeve's Tale". The rest include the use of "The Canon's Yeoman's Tale" in *The Alchemist* and references to the Canterbury Pilgrims here and there.

1965 Paul Bertram made a strong claim for Shakespeare's authorship of the whole play.[34] His searching study, though it contains some telling evidence, does not carry full conviction. But certainly the play is a puzzling one, for if Shakespeare did not write the whole of it, it is far more difficult to divide the Shakespearean and non-Shakespearean parts than it is in the three *Henry VI* plays. The test of style, usually convincing, is not so here.

The Two Noble Kinsmen is a better articulated play than *Troilus and Cressida*, though by no means so serious, so concerned with moral issues. It has a sort of brilliance without being profound and without exhibiting the wit that the printers claimed for *Troilus and Cressida*. It is, perhaps, the absence of both the usual Shakespearean depth of thought and characterisation that has made scholars ready to believe the statement of the Quarto that Fletcher had some part in the play. But surely the shaping hand is Shakespeare's. Here the problem is quite different from that in *Troilus and Cressida*, where the dramatist's task was somehow to compensate for Chaucer's slow and sure development of his characters. "The Knight's Tale" is a romance of a very different sort, brilliant with all the trappings of chivalry, serious like the code it illustrates, and little concerned about realistic characterisation. Theseus emerges as the wise ruler; Emelye is not much more than the woman loved, as remote in her perfect beauty as the ladies that look out on tournaments in fourteenth-century ivories; Palamon and Arcite are little more than the contending lovers. Yet the excellence of "The Knight's Tale" is as inaccessible to drama as that of *Troilus and Criseyde*, for again the long descriptions that give character to the poem can have no place in the play. What Shakespeare has done is to create another kind of brilliance, that of gorgeous rhetoric, and to add a sub-plot which reverses the situation of the main plot by showing a woman infatuated by Palamon. He also adds the masque-like entertainment provided by the country dancers. Instead of being solely a picture of the

[34] *Shakespeare and The Two Noble Kinsmen*, New Brunswick, N.J., 1965. Bertram shows the eagerness of Victorian scholars to relieve Shakespeare of the onus of having written the more sensual scenes of the play; he argues for Shakespeare's sole authorship from Shakespearean spellings and echoes in the scenes attributed to Fletcher, from the evidence that the manuscript available to the printers was an authorial fair copy used as a prompt-book, and from what he regards as insufficient evidence for divided authorship.

aristocratic life of chivalry, *The Two Noble Kinsmen* has the characteristic Jacobean contrast of classes, with the aristocracy being rescued from serious danger by one of the lower classes, as in *Philaster, The Winter's Tale,* or *Cymbeline.* The play is a comedy, and the Jailer's Daughter recovers her sanity, though by such overstrained therapy as could not have cured Ophelia.

Even with the addition of the secondary action the play has a rather thin plot by comparison with most of Shakespeare's other plays. It does, however, show some of his usual skill in the management of situations. The first scene, in which Shakespeare combines the first episode of "The Knight's Tale" with the pleading of the ladies for Palamon and Arcite in the forest in Part ii of Chaucer's poem, is highly stylised and very effective. The entreaties of the three queens, supported by Hippolyta and Emilia, present the brilliant and unrealistic language and scene that pleased the Jacobean court, and the witness of the Quarto that the play was produced at Blackfriars "with great applause" indicates that Shakespeare knew how to write for a coterie audience. All the way through the play the emotions are heightened, the pageantry played up, though the latter never approaches the setting of the tournament in "The Knight's Tale"[35] or of the temples of Venus, Mars, and Diana.[36] The play is more exclusively centred on love than is the romance. Even in the first scene Theseus finally yields to the queens at Hippolyta's urging, not, as in the poem, from his own pity; and the occasion is not his return from Scythia after his wedding to Hippolyta, but the wedding procession itself. Shakespeare had already used the situation in *A Midsummer-Night's Dream,* but there Theseus, though eager for the marriage and impatient with delay, still is willing to allow ceremony its rites. The tension is heightened here, as throughout the play, and comes to a focus in the plight of the Jailer's Daughter. In all these scenes the maximum dramatic effect is secured.

The real weakness of Shakespeare's plot, as compared with the plot of Chaucer's story, is that the goddess Fortuna does not preside over the Jacobean tale and the planetary influences have lost their potency. Arcite's death in "The Knight's Tale" is the consequence of the celestial quarrel between Venus and Mars and the

[35] "The Knight's Tale", A 2483-536.
[36] *Op. cit.,* A 1881-2088.

yielding of Saturn to Venus' tears. In the play catastrophe comes simply because Arcite was riding a poorly trained horse. Ironically enough, it was the horse Emilia had given him. The flints of Athens' pavement "Cold as old *Saturne*, and like him possest With fire malevolent, darted a Sparke" that frightened the steed and made him fall with his whole weight on Arcite. It is too trivial a cause to evoke the Boethian comments of Theseus and Egeus, and indeed the play contains nothing so serious as this.

The changes in characterisation are largely in the direction of greater realism, but the resulting figures are quite unlike any others that Shakespeare was creating at the time when he contributed to the writing of this play. Emilia bears little resemblance to the heroines of the romances – Hermione, Imogen, or Miranda – changed though she is from Chaucer's passive figure. Where Chaucer's Emelye was reluctant to love either Palamon or Arcite, Emilia "must crie for both".[37] Palamon and Arcite, slightly differentiated in "The Knight's Tale", are greatly developed and their differences exploited in the play, though they remain suitors equal in their claim upon Emilia. In both the romance and the play Arcite is more philosophical, Palamon more impulsive. Shakespeare, however, enhances Arcite's generosity (as in III, i, iii, v) and maturity and makes him more aware of his tie to Palamon[38] than Palamon of his to Arcite. In all references to their kinship Arcite makes the first and strongest acknowledgment of it. At one point Palamon protests in a vivid line against Arcite's kindness to him: "be rough with me, and poure this oile out of your language". Palamon's impulsive confession to Theseus[39] is taken from Chaucer,[40] and his youthful plea, "Slay us both, but slay him first", is effective in both versions. Both Palamon and Arcite are transformed from medieval knights into sophisticated Jacobean courtiers. The language of the Jacobean lyrics is present in their speeches about Emilia (III, i, 4-11, for example). The recalling of their former love-affairs[41] (which offended the Victorians) marks them as contemporaries of Pharamond in

[37] *Two Noble Kinsmen*, IV, ii, 54, *The Shakespeare Apocrypha*, ed. C. F. Tucker Brooke, Oxford, 1908.

[38] *Op. cit.*, III, vi, 42-5.   [39] *Op. cit.*, III, vi, 172 ff.

[40] "The Knight's Tale", A 1714-41.

[41] *Two Noble Kinsmen*, III, iii, 36-54.

Philaster, and Palamon's prayer to Venus[42] is a far cry from the innocence of his namesake's plea in "The Knight's Tale", A 2221-60. Similarly, Arcite's address to Mars (especially v, i, 68-72) reveals an attitude to war that has no counterpart in Chaucer's poem. The character of Theseus is sacrificed to the exigencies of drama and theatre. The price Shakespeare paid for the vivid first scene with its antiphonal pleadings is that Theseus cannot behave as in Chaucer's story, where, as soon as he heard their complaint,

> This gentil duc doun from his courser sterte
> With herte pitous, whan he herde hem speke.
> Hym thoughte that his herte wolde breke.[43]

Pity and honour yield in the play to his eagerness to be married. Nor does he show the magnanimity of his prototype either in sparing the lives of Palamon and Arcite in the forest or in stating the terms of the tournament. And nowhere in the play does he express the ironic awareness of Chaucer's Theseus of young love's folly and his sympathy with it. It must be remembered that Shakespeare had already reproduced Chaucer's Theseus in *A Midsummer-Night's Dream*; this play had no place for so uncomplicated a character.

In the wide range of Shakespearean mood there is a place for *The Two Noble Kinsmen*, and we need not deny Shakespeare the play because it is on a different level from the late romances. Sensual it is, but no more so than Leontes' heated imagination and far less so than *Troilus and Cressida*. The difficult thing to accept is its intellectual shallowness. But its language is Shakespearean and the conduct of its action equally so. We can only say that Chaucer's romances with their outmoded cult of love moved him to a certain kind of debunking but in the case of *The Two Noble Kinsmen* did not prevent him from writing a good play.

6

Shakespeare and Chaucer meet in being the supreme masters of comedy in English literature. Again any comparison of their sense of the comic must stress the differences between drama and narrative, for both poets must surrender to the demands of form:

[42] *Op. cit.*, v, i, 83-135.   [43] "The Knight's Tale", A 952-4.

the effects of the *fabliaux* are impossible to drama, those of *Twelfth Night* or *The Winter's Tale* impossible to narrative. In fact, we must not speak of "comedy" in such a comparison without realising that the structure and conventions of the two forms are different.

These differences aside, Shakespeare and Chaucer share a liking for slapstick and great skill in a variety of styles used for comic effect. Shakespeare's virtuosity is the greater; there is nothing in Chaucer to match the elaborate arabesque of language in *Love's Labour's Lost* – the Gawain poet comes nearer to it – and there is not in Chaucer's stories the wide range of accents that Shakespeare's comic figures provide, even though there is obviously a difference between Theseus' ironic comment on the lovers in "The Knight's Tale" and the low-class obscenities of Alan and John in "The Reeve's Tale". Puns, Shakespeare's best-loved linguistic trick, are not very numerous in Chaucer, for the sixteenth-century obsession with words was not present in the fourteenth. Parody is rather more developed by Chaucer. To be sure, the lamentable comedy of Pyramus and Thisbe is a good example, but it is less subtle than the tale of Sir Thopas, and nowhere in the plays is there anything like the mock-heroic of "The Nun's Priest's Tale". Both poets depend on character contrast for humorous effect, Shakespeare more than Chaucer, for in the plays it is often the uncommented-on background of the comic action. It is the source also of much of the humour of *Troilus and Criseyde* and of the Prologue to the *Legend of Good Women*.

The greatest difference between the two poets is that Shakespeare is a romantic and Chaucer is not. This means largely that there is no pastoralism in Chaucer, no creation of an impossible world in which man's deep desires are realised. And that, in turn, means that there is in Chaucer much less dependence on myth, less evocation of primitivism in any form. The final scene in Shakespeare's typical romantic comedy, though it is never an actual wedding, is like a richly ceremonial wedding in which is created a new world to be inhabited by the brave and the young. Jack has his Jill and all shall go well. Chaucer's most elaborate picture of a wedding, that in "The Merchant's Tale", is so shot through with satire that the sacrament itself is mocked. The priest "made al [i.e. lust] siker ynogh with hoolynesse":[44] but certainly all does not go well. In the romances of Shakespeare's last period the daring goes even further, and what had been faintly hinted at in earlier comedies becomes actuality on the stage; the dead are restored to life in *Pericles* and *The Winter's Tale*. To be sure, something of the same thing happens in "The Clerk's Tale" and in "The Man of Law's Tale", but the latter is a saint's legend and Constance's return to her husband and to her father is effected by the intervention of Providence. Both tales, beneath their Christian exterior, draw more heavily upon myth than Chaucer ever does elsewhere. In the never-never land of Shakespeare's romantic comedies luck is on the side of the lovers, as it so rarely is in life and rarely enough in Chaucer's stories. When Chaucer's lover wins his girl it is by heavenly intervention, as in "The Knight's Tale", or by straight magic, as in "The Wife of Bath's Tale". The sense of man's lot being essentially a happy one is not to be found in his poems. Of course the romantic comedies are only one side of Shakespeare, but it is profitless to speak of his tragedies, for Chaucer wrote no tragedy except as the Monk understood the term. Shakespeare's pageant of comic figures exhibits a wider range than Chaucer's, perhaps because drama offered in Shakespeare's hands a means of bringing together almost every kind of human being. This variety in the same play is the very mark of his hand and has never been equalled in western literature. Even in the history plays the comic figures range from Pistol through Falstaff to Prince Hal and Hotspur, all but Hotspur being conscious humorists, and Hotspur affording to his audience the amused and affectionate delight his extravagant stance awakens. In the comedies themselves Shakespeare's comic vision includes the whole gallery of his characters – professional fools like Feste and Touchstone, natural ones like Costard and Dogberry, men in love like Orlando and Berowne, maidens in love like both Rosalinds, high and low, intelligent and stupid. Except for the contemptuous deflating of Pistol and of Parolles his treatment is inclined to be gentle, to laugh the aberrant like Beatrice and Benedict back into conformity and to send them away with his blessing.

The tone of plays technically listed as comedies varies as widely

[44] "The Merchant's Tale", E 1708.

as does the range of characters. The preface to the Quarto of *Troilus and Cressida* calls that play a comedy, a classification with which we find it hard to agree. But *All's Well That Ends Well* and *Measure for Measure* fit the structure of comedy, though in tone they are as far as possible from the evanescent mirth of *A Midsummer-Night's Dream*. In between are all combinations of laughter and anxiety.

Sometimes Shakespeare evokes from his audience an ambivalent attitude toward his comic characters. This is hard to assess because modern sensibility is much more liable to sentimentality than was that of the sixteenth century, and nothing calls for more delicate judgment than the definition of this attitude. I do not mean our view of the handsome but undistinguished young men with whom his romantic heroines typically fall in love, for we take the Orlandos and Orsinos at their lovers' valuation; it is part of the convention. But Don Armado and Shylock are in a different category, the former gaining dignity and evoking some pity in the last scene, and Shylock, in a few brief revelations, evoking pity also and a sense of man's inhumanity to man. There is little of this in Chaucer. Our attitude towards Pandarus comes nearest it.

Chaucer's sense of the comic, though his range is somewhat narrower, is more pervasive than Shakespeare's. Though Shakespeare produced no tragedy wholly without a comic figure, the basic action itself is entirely serious. Chaucer, on the other hand, produced few completely serious works – some of the short poems, *Anelida and Arcite*, and seven of the *Canterbury Tales*, three of which are saints' legends. Even the *Book of the Duchess* has many touches of humour in it, such as the gifts the dreamer promises Morpheus or the exchange of question and comment in ll. 1044 ff. This ability to treat even death with humour is paralleled in Juliet's last words to the apparently dead Romeo – "O churl! Drunk all, and left no friendly drop To help me after?" – though the tone of Chaucer's obtuse dreamer and of Juliet's desperate gaiety are far apart.

The pervasiveness of Chaucer's humour is notorious, so much so that critics from Matthew Arnold to Paull Baum have accused him of being unwilling to face the really serious issues of life.[45]

[45] For a summary of these views see R. S. Loomis, "Was Chaucer a

The accusation is unjust, I think, but the variety – and sometimes impropriety – of his wit and satire and ambiguity is almost boundless. There were few situations and few characters that seemed to him wholly admirable, and he salts the virtues of even those he seemed to admire with something like slight satire. The Prioress is the most obvious example. The Clerk, who comes off so well in his contest with the Wife of Bath, is made slightly ridiculous as he rides his thin nag towards Canterbury. The Squire, admirable son of his father that he was, amuses us in his over-devotion to the courtly ideal. Within the stories there is the same pervasive mirth. Theseus's comment on the two perfect lovers, the poet's refusal to keep a decorous grave tone at Arcite's funeral, the amusing extravagance of Palamon and Arcite in their outburst to Theseus in the wood (very like the contending lovers in the *Parlement*) – these instances break into the tone of a serious story, and in one case at least offer not merely variety but contradiction. In the Prologue to the *Legend of Good Women* the poet manages to squirm out of any genuine commitment to the vindication of women. Gavin Douglas, who excuses Chaucer for having blamed Aeneas for leaving Dido, says, "he was ever, God wait, wemenis frend". But was he? The legends of good women would not prove it (though they may prove that men are worse), for though the stories are unequivocal enough, the poet's own performance in the telling is too perfunctory to carry real conviction.

Some of Chaucer's humorous ambiguity has its origin in the rhetorical tradition in which he worked. Often the passages that strike us as misplaced humour are reactions against the rhetorical clichés.[46] And what is not much recognised is that paradox is of the essence of medieval verse, expressing itself in the prevailing fondness for oxymoron. When this figure is applied to love,[47] it

Laodicean?", *Essays and Studies in Honor of Carleton Brown*, New York, 1940, pp. 129-48.

[46] Carried to the point of mock-heroic the whole of "The Nun's Priest's Tale" is an illustration. The extended *occupatio* in the description of Arcite's funeral (A 2919-66) comes near humour. Chaucer's frequent claim that he will avoid prolixity and be brief is a reaction against the rhetoricians' teaching on how to elaborate a theme.

[47] See, for example, Metre v of Alanus de Insulis' *De Planctu Naturae*, ed. T. W. Wright, *The Anglo-Latin Satirical Poets and Epigrammatists of the Twelfth Century*, London, 1872, II, pp. 472-4.

expresses so admirably the double nature of the experience that it
lasts down to Romeo's mooning in Act I of *Romeo and Juliet*.
Even when paradox does not emerge as oxymoron in Chaucer's
poetry, it often underlies his attitudes.

Very revealing of both poets is their treatment of deception, an
inevitable feature of all comedy. It is at the heart of Shakespeare's
comedies and takes many forms, including actual disguise,
typically a woman masquerading as a man. Usually the comedies
work with self-deception, and the ending, the comic therapy, is
that the Orsinos, Angelos, Benedicts are made aware of their true
slant ("bias" is Shakespeare's word). In Chaucer's stories there
is deception, to be sure, but seldom are the self-deluded made
aware of their state. That is the heart of *his* comedy. January
refused the evidence of his own eyes and remained the fatuous
and lustful fool he had always been. The merchant of "The
Shipman's Tale", less deluded, is still much more merchant than
husband and allows his wife to fool him. (Neither wife nor Daun
John fool each other.) Among deluded husbands is Phebus in
"The Manciple's Tale" who in the end refused to believe the
crow. Absolon, it is true, is violently cured of his infatuation, but
he does not see himself as the ridiculous figure he is. The Canon's
Yeoman is the exception.

If we omit these deluded husbands and lovers there is not
much self-deception in Chaucer's world. The miller's wife in
"The Reeve's Tale", for example, is the object of mirth because
of the disproportion between her illegitimacy and her pretensions
to status, but she assumes her "hoker" quite consciously. Chaucer's
deceivers are conscious and intentional – the Friar, the Summoner,
the Pardoner, even the Merchant and the Man of Law; and the
victims upon whom they practise are not usually in the foreground
of the picture, as in Shakespeare they always are. The focus thus
shifted, Chaucer's sense of comedy emerges as more astringent
than Shakespeare's, his world of knaves and fools less amenable to
correction.

Basically Chaucer's comedy rests upon irony, and Pandarus is
its best example. The attitude of Pandarus, like that of his creator,
is a double one, involvement to the point of grief and danger in his
friend's plight,[48] and at the same time a sceptical realisation that

[48] See *Troilus and Criseyde*, II, 582; V, 624-7.

Criseyde is frail and fortune uncertain.[49] Pandarus took a chance
and it turned out disastrously. But to have refused to help the
lovers would have been to deny them their rich happiness. The
story is his tragedy as well as that of Troilus and Criseyde. He
trusted Criseyde more than he doubted her, and both she and
chance played him false. "Pitee renneth soone in gentil herte".
It was easily aroused in Pandarus and likewise in Chaucer, and
perhaps it is Chaucer's most characteristic attitude towards
humankind. But it does not exclude an irony that points up man's
inability to counter fortune and achieve stability.

Shakespeare's plays, whether comedies or tragedies, assert his
values positively. Chaucer, like any satirist, for the most part
asserts his negatively; that is, they form the unrealised norm
against which the aberrations of character and action are measured.
Yet certain key-words run through Chaucer's work, and even
though they may appear in an ironic context, as in "The Merchant's Tale", they represent the virtues he prized – *curteisye*,
gentilesse, *franchise*, *trouthe*. They define the medieval aristocratic
ideal, and Chaucer, both overtly in his shorter poems and by
implication in "The Clerk's Tale" and in "The Franklin's Tale",
widened their relevance to apply to other classes as well. Shakespeare's persistent concern with honour, true and specious,
justice, love, and loyalty set these qualities forth in Renaissance
terms. The courtly ideal has shifted somewhat; man's possibilities
are enlarged, both his virtues and his vices seen larger than life.
Neither Iago nor Lear could have inhabited Chaucer's world, nor
indeed was Chaucer capable of the supreme energy that created
Shakespeare's tragedies. If the two poets are at one it is in their
idea of "trouthe". The word as Chaucer uses it has several meanings – truth, promise, loyalty, troth, pledge, and perhaps in the
refrain of the *Balade de Bon Conseyl* ("trouthe thee shal delivere, it is
no drede") it has the meaning Langland gives it, God. In the
meaning loyalty, keeping one's promise, Shakespeare agrees with
Arveragus in "The Franklin's Tale": "Trouthe is the hyeste
thyng that man may kepe".[50] In Shakespeare it becomes the
supreme expression of love that does not alter when it alteration
finds. From Julia in *The Two Gentlemen of Verona* to Hermione in
The Winter's Tale his heroines assert it, Cordelia and Desdemona to

[49] *Op. cit.*, v, 505-8.   [50] "The Franklin's Tale", F 1479.

the edge of doom; and his heroes learn its value – Proteus, Lear, Othello, Leontes, Posthumus. It is the basis of the medieval code of honour, perhaps of any code of honour. Shakespeare deepens its meaning and presents it in its extreme form as that which makes man like a god; and different as Chaucer and Shakespeare are, in this point they are in agreement.

SELECT GENERAL BIBLIOGRAPHY

Except in Section xx, the order of names is chronological within the sections, which follow the course of D. S. Brewer's essay on "The Criticism of Chaucer in the Twentieth Century". Most of the items are the titles of books; periodical articles are listed in the Select Specialised Bibliographies.

I. GENERAL STUDIES

LEGOUIS, E. *Geoffrey Chaucer*, tr. L. Lailavoix. London, 1913; reprinted New York, 1961.

KITTREDGE, G. L. *Chaucer and his Poetry*. Cambridge, Mass., 1915.

ROOT, R. K. *The Poetry of Chaucer: A Guide to its Study and Appreciation.* New York, 1922.

MANLY, J. M. *Some New Light on Chaucer*. New York, 1926.

LÜDEKE, H. "Die Funktionen des Erzählers in Chaucers epischer Dichtung", *Studien zur englischen Philologie*, LXXII (1928), pp. 1-157.

DEMPSTER, G. "Dramatic Irony in Chaucer", *Stanford University Publications in Language and Literature*, IV (1932), pp. 245-346.

CHESTERTON, G. K. *Chaucer*. London, 1932.

LOWES, J. L. *Geoffrey Chaucer*. London, 1934.

PATCH, H. R. *On Rereading Chaucer*. Cambridge, Mass., 1939.

SHELLY, P. V. D. *The Living Chaucer*. Philadelphia, 1940.

BENNETT, H. S. *Chaucer and the Fifteenth Century*. Oxford, 1947.

COGHILL, N. *The Poet Chaucer*. London, 1949.

MADELEVA, SISTER MARY. *A Lost Language and other Essays on Chaucer.* New York, 1951.

MALONE, K. *Chapters on Chaucer*. Baltimore and London, 1951.

SPEIRS, J. *Chaucer the Maker*. London, 1951.

PRESTON, R. *Chaucer*. London and New York, 1952.

BREWER, D. S. *Chaucer*. London, 1953.

MUSCATINE, C. *Chaucer and the French Tradition: A Study in Style and Meaning*. Berkeley, 1957.

DONALDSON, E. T. (1958) *See Section X.*

BAUM, P. F. *Chaucer: A Critical Appreciation.* Durham, N.C., 1958.

BRONSON, B. H. *In Search of Chaucer.* Toronto, 1960.

ROBERTSON, D. W., Jr. *A Preface to Chaucer: Studies in Medieval Perspectives.* Princeton, 1962.

PAYNE, R. O. *The Key of Remembrance: A Study of Chaucer's Poetics.* New Haven and London, 1963.

II. TOPICS

a. *Love*

DODD, W. G. "Courtly Love in Chaucer and Gower", *Harvard Studies in English,* I (1913).

LEWIS, C. S. *The Allegory of Love.* Oxford, 1936.

ANDREW (ANDREAS CAPELLANUS). *De Arte Honeste Amandi,* tr. J. J. PARRY as *The Art of Courtly Love by Andreas Capellanus.* New York, 1941.

SLAUGHTER, E. E. *Virtue According to Love – in Chaucer.* New York, 1957.

BENTON, J. F. "The Court of Champagne as a Literary Centre", *Speculum,* XXXVI (1961), pp. 551-91.

b. *Allegory*

SMALLEY, BERYL. *The Study of the Bible in the Middle Ages.* 2nd edn., Oxford, 1952.

SEZNEC, J. J. *La Survivance des Dieux Antiques.* London, 1940. (English translation entitled *The Survival of the Pagan Gods.* New York, 1953.)

SPICQ, C. *Esquisse d'une Histoire de l'Exégèse Latine au Moyen Age.* Paris, 1944.

LUBAC, H. DE. *Exégèse Médiévale: Les Quatre Sens de l'Ecriture.* Paris, 1959.

BLOOMFIELD, M. W. "Symbolism in Medieval Literature", *Modern Philology,* LVI (1958), pp. 73-81.

BETHURUM, DOROTHY, ed. *Critical Approaches to Medieval Literature: Selected Papers from the English Institute, 1958-59.* New York, 1960. (The first three papers are on "Patristic Exegesis in the Criticism of Medieval Literature": the Opposition is by E. T. Donaldson, the Defence by R. E. Kaske, and the Summation by C. Donahue.)

ROBERTSON, D. W. (1962) *See Section I.*

HUPPÉ, B. F. and ROBERTSON, D. W. (1963) *See Section XV.*

KOONCE, B. G. (1966) *See Section XV.*

c. *Rhetoric*

MANLY, J. M. "Chaucer and the Rhetoricians", *Proceedings of the British Academy,* XII (1926), pp. 95-113.

NAUNIN, T. *Der Einfluss der mittelalterlichen Rhetorik auf Chaucers Dichtung.* Bonn Diss., 1930.

PAYNE, R. O. (1963) *See Section I.*

III. BIBLIOGRAPHIES AND BIBLIOGRAPHICAL STUDIES

HAMMOND, ELEANOR P. *Chaucer: A Bibliographical Manual.* New York, 1908; reprinted 1933.

WELLS, J. E. *A Manual of the Writings in Middle English* 1050-1400, and *Supplements I-IX.* New Haven, Conn., 1916-52.

BRUSENDORFF, A. *The Chaucer Tradition.* Oxford and Copenhagen, 1925.

BAUGH, A. C. "Fifty Years of Chaucer Scholarship", *Speculum*, XXVI (1951), pp. 659-72.

PURDY, R. R. "Chaucer Scholarship in England and America: A Review of Recent Trends", *Anglia*, LXX (1952), pp. 345-81.

GRIFFITH, D. D. *Bibliography of Chaucer 1908-1953.* Seattle, 1955.

ZESMER, D. M. and GREENFIELD, S. B. *Guide to English Literature.* New York, 1961.

BURROW, J. "A Short Guide to Chaucer Studies", *The Critical Survey: The Journal of the Critical Quarterly Society*, I (1963), pp. 107-10.

BATESON, F. W. *A Guide to English Literature.* London, 1965.

ACKERMAN, R. W. "Chaucer", in *The Medieval Literature of Western Europe: A Review of Research, Mainly 1930-1960*, ed. J. H. Fisher. New York and London, 1966, pp. 110-22.

CRAWFORD, W. R. *Bibliography of Chaucer 1954-63.* Seattle and London, 1967.
(Note also the bibliography with valuable commentary in the Chaucer chapter of *The Year's Work in English Studies*, London, 1919-.)

IV. LIFE AND TIMES

COULTON, G. G. *Chaucer and his England.* London, 1908.

CHUTE, MARCHETTE. *Geoffrey Chaucer of England.* New York, 1946.

RICKERT, E. *Chaucer's World*, ed. C. C. Olson and M. M. Crow. New York, 1948.

THRUPP, S. *The Merchant Class in Medieval London.* Ann Arbor and Toronto, 1948.

BREWER, D. S. *Chaucer in his Time.* London, 1963.

LOOMIS, R. S *A Mirror of Chaucer's World.* Princeton, 1965.

CROW, M. M. and OLSON, C. C. *Chaucer Life-Records.* Oxford, 1966.

HUSSEY, M. *Chaucer's World: A Pictorial Companion.* Cambridge, 1967.

V. INTELLECTUAL AND LITERARY TRADITIONS

FANSLER, D. S. *Chaucer and the Roman de la Rose.* New York, 1914.

CUMMINGS, H. M. *The Indebtedness of Chaucer's Works to the Italian Works of Boccaccio.* Cincinnati, O., 1916.

JEFFERSON, B. L. *Chaucer and the Consolation of Philosophy of Boethius.* Princeton, 1917.

CURRY, W. C. *Chaucer and the Mediaeval Sciences.* New York, 1926; rev. edn. 1960.

SHANNON, E. F. *Chaucer and the Roman Poets.* Cambridge, Mass., 1929.

PLIMPTON, G. A. *The Education of Chaucer.* Oxford, 1935.

BRADDY, H. *Chaucer and the French Poet Graunson.* Baton Rouge, La., 1947.

SCHAAR, C. *The Golden Mirror: Studies in Chaucer's Descriptive Technique and its Literary Background.* Lund, 1955.

HOFFMAN, R. L. *Ovid and the Canterbury Tales.* Philadelphia, Pa., and Oxford, 1967.

VI. SOURCES

BRYAN, W. F. and DEMPSTER, G., eds. *Sources and Analogues of Chaucer's Canterbury Tales.* Chicago, 1941.

PRATT, R. A. "Chaucer and *Le Roman de Troyle et de Criseida*", *Studies in Philology*, LIII (1956), pp. 509-39.

VII. LANGUAGE AND LITERARY-LINGUISTIC STUDIES

KLAEBER, F. *Das Bild bei Chaucer.* Berlin, 1893.

WILD, F. *Die sprachlichen Eigentumlichkeiten der wichtigeren Chaucer-Handschriften und die Sprache Chaucers.* Leipzig, 1915.

MERSAND, J. *Chaucer's Romance Vocabulary.* New York, 1937.

HÉRAUCOURT, W. *Die Wertwelt Chaucers.* Heidelberg, 1939.

KÖKERITZ, H. *A Guide to Chaucer's Pronunciation.* Stockholm and New Haven, Conn., 1954.

SCHAAR, C. *Some Types of Narrative in Chaucer's Poetry.* Lund, 1954.

MASUI, M., *The Structure of Chaucer's Rime Words: An Exploration into the Poetic Language of Chaucer.* Tokyo, 1964.

KERKHOF, J. *Studies in the Language of Geoffrey Chaucer.* Leiden, 1966.

VIII. CONCORDANCES ETC.

TATLOCK, J. S. P. and KENNEDY, A. G. *A Concordance to the Complete Works of Geoffrey Chaucer and to the Romaunt of the Rose.* Washington, D.C., 1927.

WHITING, B. J. *Chaucer's Use of Proverbs.* Cambridge, Mass., 1934.

MAGOUN, F. P. *A Chaucer Gazetteer.* Stockholm, 1961.

IX. METRE

SOUTHWORTH, J. G. *Verses of Cadence.* Oxford, 1954.

————*The Prosody of Chaucer and his followers.* Oxford, 1962.

BAUM, P. F. *Chaucer's Verse.* Durham, N.C., 1961.

X. EDITIONS

ROOT, R. K. *The Book of Troilus and Criseyde.* Princeton, 1926.

MANLY, J. M. *The Canterbury Tales.* New York, 1928.

ROBINSON, F. N. *The Works of Geoffrey Chaucer.* Cambridge, Mass., 1933; 2nd edn., London, 1957.

MANLY, J. M. and RICKERT, E. *The Text of the Canterbury Tales.* 8 vols., Chicago, 1940.

PRICE, D. J. *The Equatorie of the Planetis: with a linguistic analysis by R. M. Wilson.* Cambridge, 1955.

CAWLEY, A. C. *Geoffrey Chaucer: Canterbury Tales.* London, 1958.

DONALDSON, E. T. *Chaucer's Poetry: An Anthology for the Modern Reader.* New York, 1958.

BREWER, D. S. *The Parlement of Foulys.* London and Edinburgh, 1960.

BAUGH, A. C. *Chaucer's Major Poetry.* London, 1963.

SUTHERLAND, R. *The Romaunt of the Rose and Le Roman de la Rose.* Oxford, 1967.

XI. CANON AND CHRONOLOGY

SKEAT, W. W. *The Chaucer Canon.* Oxford, 1900.

TATLOCK, J. S. P. *The Development and Chronology of Chaucer's Works.* Chaucer Society, 2nd series, XXXVII, London, 1907.

SEATON, E. *Sir Richard Roos: Lancastrian Poet.* London, 1961.

XII. *THE CANTERBURY TALES*

LAWRENCE, W. W. *Chaucer and the Canterbury Tales.* London, 1950.

BALDWIN, R. *The Unity of the Canterbury Tales.* Anglistica V, Copenhagen, 1955.

LUMIANSKY, R. M. *Of Sondry Folk: The Dramatic Principle in the Canterbury Tales.* Austin, 1955.

RUGGIERS, P. G. *The Art of the Canterbury Tales.* Madison and Milwaukee, 1965.

CRAIK, T. W. *The Comic Tales of Chaucer.* London, 1964.

HUPPÉ, B. F. *A Reading of the Canterbury Tales.* New York, 1966.

XIII. COLLECTIONS OF ESSAYS

WAGENKNECHT, E., ed. *Chaucer: Modern Essays in Criticism.* New York, 1959.

SCHOECK, R. J. and TAYLOR, J., *Chaucer Criticism.* 2 vols., Notre Dame, Ind., 1960.

BREWER, D. S., ed. *Chaucer and Chaucerians: Critical Studies in Middle English Literature.* London and Edinburgh, 1966.

ROWLAND, BERYL, ed. *Companion to Chaucer Studies.* Toronto, New York, London, 1968.

XIV. *TROILUS AND CRISEYDE*

YOUNG, K. *The Origin and Development of the Story of Troilus and Criseyde.* Chaucer Society, 2nd series, XL, London, 1908.

KIRBY, T. A. *Chaucer's Troilus: A Study in Courtly Love.* Baton Rouge, La., 1940.

MEECH, S. B. *Design in Chaucer's Troilus.* Syracuse, N.Y., 1959.

XV. SHORTER POEMS

SYPHERD, W. O. *Studies in Chaucer's Hous of Fame.* Chaucer Society, 2nd series, XXXIX, London, 1908.

BENNETT, J. A. W. *The Parlement of Foules: An Interpretation.* Oxford, 1957.

CLEMEN, W. *Chaucer's Early Poetry,* tr. C. A. M. Sym. London, 1963. (Partly based on Professor Clemen's *Der Junge Chaucer,* 1938.)

HUPPÉ, B. F. and ROBERTSON, D. W., Jr. *Fruyt and Chaf: Studies in Chaucer's Allegories.* Princeton, 1963. (Allegorical interpretation of the *Book of the Duchess* and *Parlement of Foules.*)

KOONCE, B. G. *Chaucer and the Tradition of Fame: Symbolism in the House of Fame.* Princeton, 1966.

BENNETT, J. A. W. *Chaucer's Book of Fame: An Exposition of "The House of Fame".* Oxford, 1968.

XVI. PROSE

SCHLAUCH, M. "Chaucer's Prose Rhythms", *P.M.L.A.,* LXV (1950), pp. 568-89.

———"The Art of Chaucer's Prose", *Chaucer and Chaucerians,* ed. D. S. Brewer. London and Edinburgh, 1966, pp. 140-63.

XVII. Chaucer apocrypha

Pearsall, D. A. *The Floure and the Leafe and The Assembly of Ladies.* London, 1962.

XVIII. Comment and allusion

Spurgeon, Caroline F. E. *Five Hundred Years of Chaucer Criticism and Allusion, 1357-1900.* 3 vols., Cambridge, 1925.

XIX. Modernisation and translation

Tatlock, J. S. P. and Mackaye, P. *Complete Poetical Works of Geoffrey Chaucer.* New York, 1912.

Krapp, G. P. *Geoffrey Chaucer, Troilus and Criseyde.* New York, 1932.

Lumiansky, R. M. *The Canterbury Tales of Geoffrey Chaucer: A New Modern English Prose Translation, published together with the Original Middle English Text of the General Prologue and the Nun's Priest's Tale.* Preface by Mark van Doren. New York, 1948.

Coghill, N. *Geoffrey Chaucer: The Canterbury Tales.* Translated into Modern English. London, 1951.

Lumiansky, R. M. *Geoffrey Chaucer's Troilus and Criseyde.* Rendered into Modern English Prose. Columbia, S.C., 1952.

Stanley-wrench, M. *Geoffrey Chaucer: Troilus and Criseyde.* Translated into Modern English. London, 1965.

XX. Recordings

Ayers, Harry Morgan. "Prologue" to *Canterbury Tales* and "The Nun's Priest's Tale" (extracts). National Council of Teachers of English 22.

Bessinger, J. B., Jr. The *Canterbury Tales* in Middle English ("General Prologue", "Prologue to Parson's Tale", and "Retraction"). Caedmon TC 1151.

Coghill, Nevill. Extracts from the "Prologue". Columbia DX 1572/73.

——Norman Davis, and John Burrow. "Prologue" to *Canterbury Tales.* Argo Record Co. RG 401.

—— —— Lena Davis, and John Burrow. "The Nun's Priest's Tale" (and other pieces). Argo Record Co. RG 466.

—— —— Selections from the *Canterbury Tales.* Spoken Arts SA 919.

Dunn, Charles W. Early English Poetry: Middle English (including extract from "The Wife of Bath's Tale"). Folkways Records FL 9851.

Kaplan, Victor L. "General Prologue", "The Pardoner's Tale," "The Nun's Priest's Tale", *Complaint of Chaucer to his Purse, Lak of Stedfastnesse.* Folkways Records FL 9859.

KÖKERITZ, HELGE. Chaucer Readings (extracts from "General Prologue", "The Wife of Bath's Prologue", "The Prioress's Tale", and *Troilus and Criseyde*). EAV Lexington LE 5505 B.

————A Thousand Years of English Pronunciation (including extracts from "General Prologue" and *Troilus and Criseyde*). EAV Lexington LE 7650 B.

MALONE, KEMP. "The Nun's Priest's Tale". English Classics XTV 17216.

MILLER, RALPH, and JOHN McNALLY. Excerpts from "General Prologue" and "The Pardoner's Tale". Western Michigan University WMU 1000.

ROSS, ROBERT. "The Pardoner's Prologue and Tale" and "The Nun's Priest's Tale". Caedmon TC 1008.

WYLD, H. C. Pronunciation of Middle English (extracts from "General Prologue" and "The Prioress's Tale"). Linguaphone EWW 44.

SELECT SPECIALISED
BIBLIOGRAPHIES

In the following bibliographies, which relate to the essays, the items are chronologically arranged. These items are limited mainly to periodical articles; the titles of relevant books will be found in the Select General Bibliography.

I. CHAUCER THE MAN

SPITZER, L. "Note on the Poetic and the Empirical 'I' in Medieval Authors", *Traditio*, IV (1946), pp. 414-22.

DONALDSON, E. T. "Chaucer the Pilgrim", *P.M.L.A.*, LXIX (1954), pp. 928-36.

JORDAN, R. M. "The Narrator in Chaucer's *Troilus*", *E.L.H.*, XXV (1958), pp. 237-57.

BETHURUM, DOROTHY. "Chaucer's Point of View as Narrator in the Love Poems", *P.M.L.A.*, LXXIV (1959), pp. 511-20.

BEVINGTON, D. M. "The Obtuse Narrator in Chaucer's *House of Fame*", *Speculum*, XXXVI (1961), pp. 288-98.

NEVO, RUTH. "Chaucer: Motive and Mask in the 'General Prologue' ", *Modern Language Review*, LVIII (1963), pp. 1-9.

II. CHAUCER'S READING

LOUNSBURY, T. R. *Studies in Chaucer*. London, 1892. (Especially Chap. V, "The Learning of Chaucer".)

SKEAT, W. W. *The Works of Geoffrey Chaucer*. Oxford, 1894. (Especially Vol. VI, pp. 381-9.)

LOWES, J. L. *Geoffrey Chaucer*. London, 1934. (Especially Chap. III, "The World of Books".)

BREWER, D. S. "The Relationship of Chaucer to the English and European Traditions", *Chaucer and Chaucerians*. London and Edinburgh, 1966, pp. 1-38.

III. CHAUCER AND PATRISTIC EXEGESIS

BEICHNER, P. E. "Absolon's Hair", *Mediaeval Studies*, XII (1950), pp. 22-33.

KELLOGG, A. L. "An Augustinian Interpretation of Chaucer's Pardoner", *Speculum*, XXVI (1951), pp. 465-81.

DONOVAN, M. J. "The *Moralite* of the Nun's Priest's Sermon", *Journal of English and Germanic Philology*, LII (1953), pp. 498-508.

MAKAREWICZ, SISTER MARY R. *The Patristic Influence on Chaucer.* Washington, 1953.

MILLER, R. P. "Chaucer's Pardoner, the Scriptural Eunuch, and the 'Pardoner's Tale' ", *Speculum*, XXX (1955), pp. 180-99.

OLSEN, P. A. "Chaucer's Merchant and January's 'Hevene in Erthe Heere' ", *E.L.H.*, XXVIII (1961), pp. 203-14.

KASKE, R. E. "The *Canticum Canticorum* in the 'Miller's Tale' ", *Studies in Philology*, LIX (1962), pp. 479-500.

QUINN, BETTY N. "Venus, Chaucer, and Peter Bersuire", *Speculum*, XXXVIII (1963), pp. 479-80.

HOWARD, D. R. *The Three Temptations: Medieval Man in Search of the World.* Princeton, 1966.

IV. CHAUCER'S PROSODY

TEN BRINK, B. *The Language and Metre of Chaucer.* 2nd edn., rev. F. Kluge, tr. M. Bentinck Smith. London, 1901.

McJIMSEY, RUTH B. *Chaucer's Irregular -e.* New York, 1942.

EVERETT, DOROTHY. "Chaucer's 'Good Ear' ", *Review of English Studies*, XXIII (1947), pp. 201-8.

SOUTHWORTH, J. G. "Chaucer's Final -e in Rhyme", *P.M.L.A.*, LXII (1947), pp. 910-35.

DONALDSON, E. T. "Chaucer's Final -e", *P.M.L.A.*, LXIII (1948), pp. 1101-24.

SOUTHWORTH, J. G. "Chaucer's Final -e continued", *P.M.L.A.*, LXIV (1949), pp. 601-10.

MORGAN, MARGERY. "A Treatise on Cadence", *Modern Language Review*, XLVII (1952), pp. 156-64.

V. CHAUCER AND RHETORIC

MANLY, J. M. "Chaucer and the Rhetoricians", *Proceedings of the British Academy*, XII (1926), pp. 95-113.

BALDWIN, C. S. *Medieval Rhetoric and Poetic.* New York, 1928.

HAMILTON, MARIE P. "Notes on Chaucer and the Rhetoricians", *P.M.L.A.*, XLVII (1932), pp. 403-9.

McKEON, R. "Rhetoric in the Middle Ages", *Speculum*, XVII (1942), pp. 1-32.

ATKINS, J. W. H. *English Literary Criticism: The Medieval Phase*. Cambridge, 1943.

MURPHY, J. J. "The Medieval Arts of Discourse: An Introductory Bibliography", *Speech Monographs*, XXIX (1962), pp. 71-8.

———"A New Look at Chaucer and the Rhetoricians", *Review of English Studies*, XV (1964), pp. 1-20.

———"Literary Implications of Instruction in the Verbal Arts in Fourteenth-century England", *Leeds Studies in English*, new series, I (1967), pp. 119-35.

ALSTON, R. C. and ROSIER, J. L. "Rhetoric and Style: A Bibliographical Guide", *Leeds Studies in English*, new series, I (1967), pp. 137-59.

VI. *PARLEMENT OF FOULES*

BRONSON, B. H. "In Appreciation of Chaucer's *Parlement of Foules*", *University of California Publications in English*, III (1935), pp. 193-224.

GOFFIN, R. C. "Heaven and Earth in the *Parlement of Foules*", *Modern Language Review*, XXXI (1936), pp. 493-9.

BRONSON, B. H. "The *Parlement of Foules* Revisited", *E.L.H.*, XV (1948), pp. 247-60.

LUMIANSKY, R. M. "Chaucer's *Parlement of Foules*: A Philosophical Interpretation", *Review of English Studies*, XXIV (1948), pp. 81-9.

STILLWELL, G. "Unity and Comedy in Chaucer's *Parlement of Foules*", *J.E.G.P.*, XLIX (1950), pp. 470-95.

OWEN, C. A., Jr. "The Role of the Narrator in the *Parlement of Foules*", *College English*, XIV (1953), pp. 264-9.

BETHURUM, DOROTHY. "The Center of the *Parlement of Foules*", *Essays in Honor of Walter Clyde Curry*, Nashville, Tenn., 1955, pp. 39-50.

EMSLIE, M. "Codes of Love and Class Distinctions", *Essays in Criticism*, V (1955), pp. 1-17.

McDONALD, C. O. "An Interpretation of Chaucer's *Parlement of Foules*", *Speculum*, XXX (1955), pp. 444-57.

FRANK, R. W. "Structure and Meaning in the *Parlement of Foules*", *P.M.L.A.*, LXXI (1956), pp. 530-9.

BREWER, D. S. "The Genre of the *Parlement of Foules*", *Modern Language Review*, LIII (1958), pp. 321-6.

SPEARING, A. C. "Chaucer the Writer", *An Introduction to Chaucer*, by M. Hussey, A. C. Spearing, and J. Winny. Cambridge, 1965, pp. 115-52.

LAWLOR, J. "The Earlier Poems", *Chaucer and Chaucerians*, ed. D. S. Brewer. London and Edinburgh, 1966, pp. 50-7.

VII. *TROILUS AND CRISEYDE*

LEWIS, C. S. "What Chaucer really did to *Il Filostrato*", *Essays and Studies*, XVII (1932), pp. 56-75.

ROBERTSON, D. W., Jr. "Chaucerian Tragedy", *E.L.H.*, XIX (1952), pp. 1-37.

BREWER, D. S. "Love and Marriage in Chaucer's Poetry", *Modern Language Review*, XLIX (1954), pp. 461-4.

JOSEPH, B. "Troilus and Criseyde", *Essays and Studies*, VII (1954), pp. 42-61.

BLOOMFIELD, M. W. "Distance and Predestination in *Troilus and Criseyde*", *P.M.L.A.*, LXXII (1957), pp. 14-26.

OWEN, C. A., Jr. "The Significance of Chaucer's Revisions of *Troilus and Criseyde*", *Modern Philology*, LV (1957), pp. 1-5.

DUNNING, T. P. "God and Man in *Troilus and Criseyde*", *English and Medieval Studies Presented to J. R. R. Tolkien*, ed. N. Davis and C. L. Wrenn. London, 1962, pp. 164-82.

DONALDSON, E. T. "The Ending of Chaucer's *Troilus*", *Early English and Norse Studies Presented to Hugh Smith*, ed. A. Brown and P. Foote. London, 1963, pp. 26-45.

SALTER, ELIZABETH. "*Troilus and Criseyde*: a Reconsideration", *Pattern. of Love and Courtesy, Essays in Memory of C. S. Lewis*, ed. John Lawlor London, 1966, pp. 86-106.

SHEPHERD, G. T. "*Troilus and Criseyde*", *Chaucer and Chaucerians*, ed. D. S. Brewer. London and Edinburgh, 1966, pp. 65-87.

VIII. "THE FRIAR'S TALE"

TAYLOR, A. "The Devil and the Advocate", *P.M.L.A.*, XXXVI (1921), pp. 35-59.

WILLIAMS, A. "Chaucer and the Friars", *Speculum*, XXVIII (1953), pp. 499-513.

CAWLEY, A. C. "Chaucer's Summoner, the Friar's Summoner and the Friar's Tale", *Proceedings of the Leeds Philosophical and Literary Society*, VIII (1957), pp. 173-80.

BIRNEY, E. " 'After His Ymage': the Central Ironies of the 'Friar's Tale' ", *Mediaeval Studies*, XXI (1959), pp. 17-35.

BONJOUR, A. "Aspects of Chaucer's Irony in 'The Friar's Tale' ", *Essays in Criticism*, XI (1961), pp. 121-7.

MROCZKOWSKI, P. " 'The Friar's Tale' and its Pulpit Background", *English Studies Today*, 2nd series (1961), pp. 107-20.

IX. CHAUCER AND SHAKESPEARE

BELLMANN, O. "Chaucers Einfluss auf das englische Drama", *Anglia*, xxv (1902), pp. 1-85.

HILLEBRAND, H. N. *A New Variorum Edition of Shakespeare: Troilus and Cressida.* Philadelphia and London, 1953.

BULLOUGH, G. *Narrative and Dramatic Sources of Shakespeare*, Vol. I. London and New York, 1957.

MUIR, K. *Shakespeare's Sources: Comedies and Tragedies.* London, 1957.

BRADBROOK, MURIEL C. "What Shakespeare did to Chaucer's *Troilus and Criseyde*", *Shakespeare Quarterly*, ix (1958), pp. 311-19.

COGHILL, N. "Shakespeare's Reading in Chaucer", *Elizabethan and Jacobean Studies Presented to F. P. Wilson.* Oxford, 1959, pp. 86-99.

BERTRAM, P. *Shakespeare and The Two Noble Kinsmen.* New Brunswick, N.J., 1965.

INDEX

204

Roman de la Rose, 20, 49, 52, 54, 57, 58, 62, 67, 73, 82, 136, 150, 151, 171.
Romaunt of the Rose, 23, 52.
Romeo and Juliet, 58, 93, 167, 168, 188.
Root, R. K., 23, 52, 94, 95.
Ruggiers, P. G., 24.
Ruskin, 7.
Rymer, Thomas, 77.

Saintsbury, G., 88, 90.
Santayana, George, 173.
Schaar, C., 20, 21.
Schlauch, Margaret, 26, 90-1.
Schoeck, R. J., 25.
Schönberg, 88.
Scogan, Henry, 170.
Scott, Sir Walter, 143.
Scripture. See Bible.
Seaton, Ethel, 23.
Seznec, J. J., 17.
Shakespeare, 5, 18, 25, 58, 93, 152, 167-90. (See plays listed separately.)
Shannon, E. F., 20.
Shelly, P. V. D., 8.
"Shipman's Tale, The", 188.
Sidney, Sir Philip, 33, 166.
Sir Gawain and the Green Knight. See *Gawain*-poet.
"Sir Thopas", 42, 44, 63, 68, 81, 184.
Skeat, W. W., 23, 24.
Slaughter, E. E., 17.
Smalley, Beryl, 17.
Somnium Scipionis. See Cicero.
Sources and Analogues of Chaucer's Canterbury Tales. See Bryan and Dempster.
Southampton, Earl of, 169.
Southworth, J. G., 22.
Speght, Thomas, 167.
Speirs, John, 9, 14, 141.
Spender, Stephen, 88.
Spenser, 82, 83, 93, 130, 166.
Spicq, C., 17.

Spurgeon, Caroline, 27, 166.
Stanley-Wrench, Margaret, 27.
Statius, 49.
Stevens, Wallace, 45.
Strindberg, 148.
Strode, Ralph, 170.
Suite de Merlin, 102.
"Summoner's Tale, The", 6, 8.
Surrey, Henry Howard, Earl of, 91.
Sutherland, R., 23.
Sypherd, W. O., 26.

Tatlock, J. S. P., 21, 23, 27.
Taylor, J., 25.
Tempest, The, 175.
Ten Brink, B., 20, 88.
Teseida. See Boccaccio.
Testament of Cresseid, 178.
Text of the Canterbury Tales, The. See Manly and Rickert.
Thomas of Wales, 84.
Thrupp. Sylvia, 19.
Thynne, Francis, 167.
Tottel's Miscellany, 91.
Trithemius, Johannis, 38.
Troilus and Cressida, 144, 167, 176-9, 180, 183, 186.
Troilus and Criseyde, 3, 6, 10, 11, 12, 16, 20, 23, 25, 26, 27, 34, 35, 39-42, 44, 49, 52-3, 61-2, 65, 77-9, 80, 81, 87, 93-4, 95-6, 105, 113, 142-54, 167, 168, 170, 176-9, 184.
Truth, 53.
Twelfth Night, 184.
Two Gentlemen of Verona, The, 189.
Two Noble Kinsmen, The, 167, 176, 179-83.
Tyrwhitt, Thomas, 87.

Unity of the Canterbury Tales, The. See Baldwin.
Urry, John, 89.
Usk, Thomas, 170.